NEW VENTURES IN GEOGRAPHY

(IV) THE NORTH ATLANTIC NATIONS

NEW VENTURES IN GEOGRAPHY

(IV) THE NORTH ATLANTIC NATIONS

R. P. BRADY, M.A., B.Sc.

AND

H. M. SPINK, M.C., M.A., B.Sc.

Illustrations by
G. A. W. BRANDRETH
and
T. H. STUBLEY

SCHOFIELD & SIMS LTD.
HUDDERSFIELD

©

SCHOFIELD & SIMS LTD.

1961

First Edition 1961
Reprinted June 1962
Reprinted December 1962
Reprinted January 1964
Reprinted January 1966
Revised and Reprinted October 1966

Printed in England by
Netherwood Dalton & Co. Ltd., Huddersfield

Bound in Scotland

FOREWORD

This series is planned in five books together with a **Map-Reading Book**. **The Foundations** is a general survey of all the basic principles of geography, with special emphasis on the relation between men's activities and the physical environment. In general, the book concentrates on the simplest relationships, *e.g.* on the primitive life, or simple farming communities.

The remaining books are regional in treatment, and all the principles studied in **The Foundations** are applied to countries throughout the world. The other titles are:—

The Southern Lands.

The Asiatic World and U.S.S.R.

The North Atlantic Nations.

Great Britain and Ireland.

The Map-Reading Book issued with the series deals with :

(i) elementary map reading;

(ii) Ordnance Survey map reading.

So much depends on the efficient use of maps in all books of the series that the use of the Map Reading Book is recommended at all stages appropriate to the needs of the pupil.

Throughout the series, one philosophical idea is maintained and presented in various ways. All world phenomena leave their mark on the peoples of the world. Sometimes they influence them directly, as in the type of house they build, the clothes they wear, or the food they eat; sometimes the influence is indirect as in the choice of occupation, or in the siting of towns. Whatever they are, the people never escape entirely from their consequences. As science or invention lessen the influence of certain phenomena, they increase others, *e.g.* by causing a vast shrinkage of space in the world, the once long range consequences become near ones, as in the case of the closure of the Suez Canal in 1956 which resulted in the rationing of petrol in Britain in 1957.

The method of presentation is a text as brief as possible, backed up by maps, pictures, and diagrams. Almost every page has exercises and topics for discussion, designed to ensure that every possible use and understanding is made of the illustrations. Project work is suggested, and everything is done to make the pupil realise that the text is only the beginning of the subject, that he can do a great deal to amplify the information himself, either as an individual, or as a member of a team. It is hoped that the teacher will be able to secure the books, pictures, film strips, pamphlets, etc., that are recommended, as much of the success of the series will depend upon the use of these in the pupil's own studies.

CONTENTS

THE NORTH ATLANTIC NATIONS

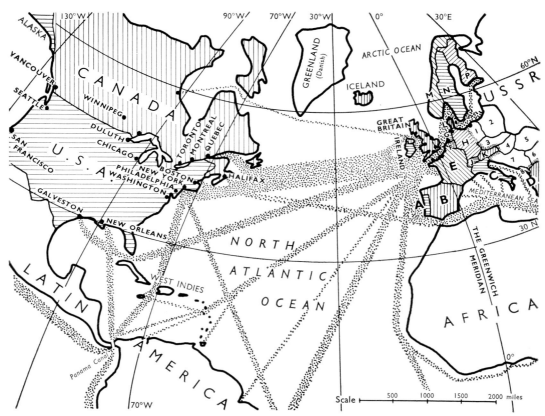

Main sea routes—thickness is a rough indication of their importance

COUNTRIES OF WESTERN EUROPE

A	Portugal	**E**	France	**J**	Switzerland	**N**	Sweden
B	Spain	**F**	Belgium	**K**	Austria	**P**	Finland
C	Italy	**G**	Holland	**L**	Denmark		
D	Greece	**H**	West Germany	**M**	Norway		

COUNTRIES OF COMMUNIST EUROPE

1	East Germany	**5**	Rumania
2	Poland	**6**	Bulgaria
3	Czechoslovakia	**7**	Yugoslavia
4	Hungary	**8**	Albania

Fig. 1.

CHAPTER 1

THE BACKGROUND

In this book we come to a study of those lands which border the North Atlantic Ocean. You will see them all in Fig. 1. Because they all lie north of 30°N., they are in that part of the world which we call *Temperate*, but they extend northwards into the very cold *Polar* regions, and very cold winters are a normal feature of life in most parts. As we study them we shall recall many features noted in *The Asiatic World*, when we studied Russian lands. On both sides of the Atlantic Ocean, the countries form powerful groups. On the American side are the United States of America and Canada, and on the European side, all Europe except the U.S.S.R. There are so many important nations to be studied, that one book is not sufficient, so we are leaving our study of the British Isles to another book.

Finding our way about

We had better begin by studying Fig. 1 at some length. The huge land mass of North America with only two large countries occupying it, is very different from the smaller land mass of Europe in which lie many countries very small indeed by comparison with those in North America. Yet the importance of the European countries is much greater than their size. I wonder how many of their names you know already. They split up into a number of groups which help us to remember them.

The countries of North-West Europe:

France, Holland and Belgium. Along with Great Britain they total about one hundred and twenty million people.

The countries of Northern Europe:

Norway, Sweden, Denmark, Finland. These countries are in a very northerly latitude, so populations are small, about twenty million.

The countries of Central Europe:

West Germany, Switzerland, Austria. They total about eighty million people.

The countries of Southern Europe:

Portugal, Spain, Italy and Greece. They number about eighty-five million people.

The Communist States of Eastern Europe:

They total about one hundred and fourteen million people. There is a *northern group:* East Germany, Poland, Czechoslovakia and Hungary, and a *southern group: The Balkans*, Rumania, Yugoslavia, Bulgaria and Albania.

Task 1. What is the total population of the countries of Europe as given above? Compare, by diagrams, this population total with those for:

The United States of America   189 millions.
China (approx.)   657 millions.
The U.S.S.R.   209 millions

Task 2. Compare the following areas (in 1,000's of square miles):

The United States of America   3,554
Canada   3,560
France   213
The British Isles   120

How many times would France fit into the United States of America?

How many times would the British Isles fit into Canada?

Spanish woman,
Bulgarian peasant,
Dutch girl

Task 3. What is the greatest distance you can measure on Fig. 1:

(*a*) across Great Britain;

(*b*) across Sweden;

(*c*) across Spain?

Compare these distances with the following in North America:

(*a*) from San Francisco to New York;

(*b*) from Winnipeg to New Orleans.

Task 4. How could one fly from the United States of America to Britain without flying for one thousand miles at a time over sea? Is this route used?

The World's Greatest Traders

One thing which is a feature of all these lands is the enormous amount of trade and commerce carried on between them and the rest of the world, and the enormous amount of industry carried on by so many of them. In Fig. 1 you can see the trade routes followed by shipping between these lands and the rest of the world, and in Fig. 2 you can see the great concentration of air routes on them. All the world's most important trade routes are on Fig. 1. The route between the eastern coasts of North America and Western Europe takes nearly half of all the world's trade, and the route through the Mediterranean takes about one quarter.

Task 5. Examine both Figs. 1 and 2 and notice sea and air routes.

The World's Workshop

This title, once used for Britain, can be said to be true of all the Atlantic countries together. Their output of manufactures is enormous. To begin with, the main sources of cheap power for industry are coal and oil.

In 1960 these Atlantic Nations produced 45% of all coal mined in the world, and it was shared fairly equally between each side of the ocean.

United States of America and Canada   21%

Europe and Britain   24%

A Transatlantic plane flying above a great liner

no international air routes

Iceland

Bermuda

Azores

Cape Verde Is.

This map does not show routes inside countries— only those which connect one country to another.

Fig. 2. The main International Air Routes

In 1960 they produced 37% of the world's oil, but this was almost all from the United States of America and Canada. Europe relies on the Middle East for its oil.

One test of the industrial capacity of a nation is the amount of steel it produces. The Atlantic countries produced 60% of all steel in the world, in 1960.

The production of motor cars is even more striking. In 1960 the Atlantic Nations produced 93% of all motor vehicles made in the world.

It has something to do with the climate

We have seen that the lands round the North Atlantic contain highly civilised and industrious people who lead the world in commerce and manufacturing as well as in scientific farming. One reason advanced for these facts is that in the latitudes north of 30°N., occur climates which encourage vigorous activity of mind and body amongst peoples, climates which produce many different kinds of weather, both bad and good, but which avoid great extremes of heat and cold. To understand something of these climates we will study Fig. 3.

At first sight this looks a little complicated but, with a little help, you will soon see that it is quite simple to understand. First of all notice 30°N. and 60°N. which divide the whole region roughly into three belts.

Task 6. In each of these three belts there is a prevailing wind (or "air stream"). Describe these winds by reference to the map. Two of these air streams appear to mix in with one another. Which are they?

Belt 1

South of 30°N., is the region of the Trade Winds. These are steady and strong and give reliable weather. These are the winds of the Hot Lands, as we have seen in studying Latin America and Africa in *The Southern Lands*. They do not directly affect the North Atlantic Lands which we are studying.

Belt 2

Between 30°N. and 60°N., is the region of the Westerly Air Streams. They move up from warm regions and pick up great amounts of water vapour over the Gulf of Mexico and the Atlantic. On the Pacific coasts of Canada and the United States of America you will see similar air streams moving in from the Pacific. Because they contain so much vapour, they produce rain very quickly when cooled, and in winter their warmth prevents "freeze-ups" wherever they blow. Whenever you hear in the Weather Forecasts such descriptions as "cloudy, with rain at times", or "low clouds and continuous rain" or, if it is winter, "temperatures will be above average for the time of the year", you will know this air stream is blowing over the country.

Belt 3

North of 60°N., experiences the cold, dry air stream moving from the pole. Over land this stream is very dry, very cool in summer, and icy in winter. (We saw it operating over China, Korea and Japan in *The Asiatic World*). Over the sea it picks up vapour and is cold and cloudy. It usually reaches us from over the Atlantic. One kind of weather it brings is that referred to as "showers and bright intervals, cool".

The majority of the weather in these lands, however, comes not from these two air streams separately, but from the mixing of the two. The edge of the cold, dry polar air is known as *The Polar Front* and wherever the warm moist westerlies meet this front, the two air streams set up what are called *Cold Fronts* and *Warm Fronts*, at which much rain occurs. Great masses of cold and warm air whirl slowly round one another to create *Depressions* which travel slowly eastwards like whirlpools in a river. All these names must be very well known to you if you listen to radio or television weather forecasts. There is a good deal of Warm and Cold Front rain in a depression and, indeed, the rain which falls over Britain, Europe and much of North America is chiefly rain from either warm or cold fronts.

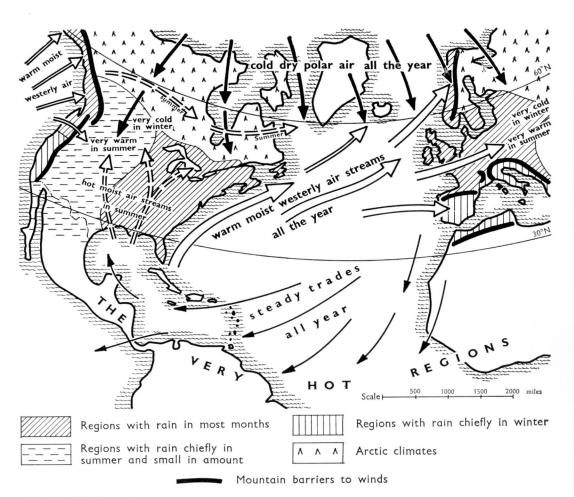

Fig. 3. *Winds and rainfall in the Atlantic Countries*

Regions with rain in most months

Regions with rain chiefly in winter

Regions with rain chiefly in summer and small in amount

Arctic climates

Mountain barriers to winds

cold
Polar air   **COLD**   warm   **WARM**   cold
                   FRONT Westerly air   **FRONT**   Polar air

Rainy areas

*Fig. 4. A section
across a depression*

What happens at a "Front"

Look at Fig. 4. It shows cold, heavy polar air
pushing its way under warmer, lighter westerly air.
As the westerly air is forced upwards it cools and gives
rain. The movement is not steady and continuous,
but occurs at intervals. The winds are gusty, with
many squalls and showers of rain. In between, the
clouds break and blue sky appears. Where the cold
air meets the warm air is the *Cold Front.*

Fig. 4 also shows a *Warm Front.* Here the warm,
light westerly air rises steadily over the mass of colder
polar air. This produces steady cooling of the westerly
air and steady rain is the result. Where the warm air
meets the cold air is the *Warm Front.*

"A Depression is situated West of Ireland"

How often have you heard something like that on
the radio? Fig. 5 shows what is happening in a
depression. The cold air is revolving round the warm
air, which occupies only a small section of the depression.
There is a warm front in the early part of the depression,
and a cold front in the rear of it. Thus depressions
mean plenty of rain, as a rule.

Notice that there are fixed symbols for the fronts:
Warm Fronts are shown by
Cold Fronts are shown by

Temperatures in the Atlantic Lands

If you studied Russia, in *The Asiatic World*, you
read about the dreadful coldness of Siberia in winter,
followed by a very warm summer. Here, in the

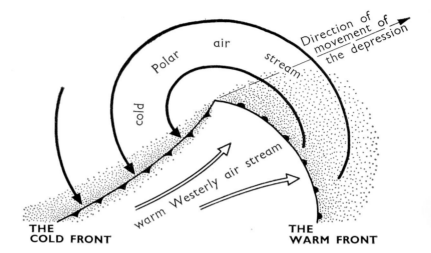

Fig. 5. *A depression*

THE
COLD FRONT

THE
WARM FRONT

Atlantic Lands, we see this same feature once more. Look at Fig. 6. (If you can compare it with Fig. 6 in *The Asiatic World* you will see many things that are similar). It shows the areas frozen in mid-winter. In the middle of both North America and Europe, they extend southwards to below 40°N. (The great bulges in the west of North America are caused by the high mountains there.) Chicago is frozen for three months, Winnipeg for five months, and New York for two months. In Europe, Warsaw is frozen for three months, Vienna for two months, and Berlin for one month. Stockholm has four months of freeze-up. Not much of the Atlantic countries is unfrozen in mid-winter.

Yet, it is very interesting to notice just which parts are unfrozen. Because the westerly air streams pile up warm oceanic air on west coasts, we can see that they remain unfrozen almost up to 60°N. In Canada and the United States of America this western strip would be wider if high mountains near the coast did not stop warm air from moving further inland. Then below 40°N. the angle of the sun is high enough, even in winter, to prevent the lands freezing. Thus southern United States of America and the Mediterranean Sea countries are unfrozen, and have quite mild winters.

Task 7. Name the principal countries of Europe which remain unfrozen in winter, and try to find names of parts of the United States of America which are similarly unfrozen.

Summers are warm everywhere

In summer, when the sun's angle is high over these regions, the lands are warm everywhere. They are very hot indeed up to 40°N., where temperatures are tropical in mid-summer. In the latitude of Britain all the places frozen in winter have summers much hotter than those in Britain. It is only on the west sides of North America and Europe that summers are in any way cool. This is due to the amount of cloud and cool air brought in by westerlies.

Here are some figures to illustrate these facts:

North America

West Coast	Centre	East Coast
Victoria	Winnipeg	Halifax
Jan. 40°F.	Jan. —3°F.	Jan. 24°F.
July 61°F.	July 67°F.	July 65°F.

All these places are approximately 50°N. The town in the centre has a difference of 64° between its January and July temperatures, with extremely low January temperatures. Victoria, on the west coast, has January and July temperatures like those in Britain; warmed by westerlies in winter and cooled by them in summer. Halifax, on the east coast, lies between these two.

Europe

West	West Central	East Central
Cambridge	Berlin	Warsaw
Jan. 39°F.	Jan. 31°F.	Jan. 26°F.
July 62°F.	July 67°F.	July 66°F.

Here there is no true centre, or east, of the great land mass. We saw those in the Soviet Union. What we do see, is that as one goes eastwards from Britain the mild winters of Britain grow less and less mild and the summers grow warmer. As we saw in *The Asiatic World*, by the time Moscow is reached January temper-

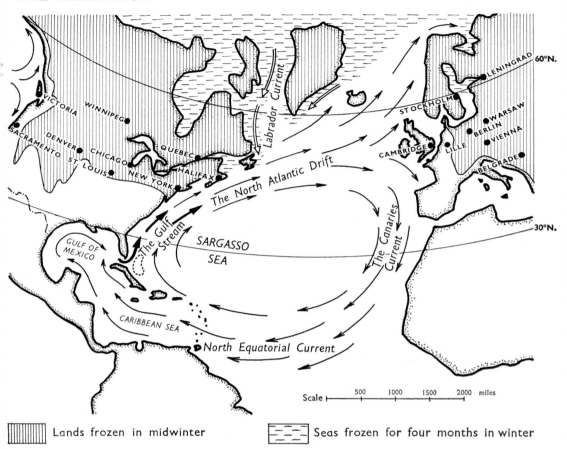

Lands frozen in midwinter   Seas frozen for four months in winter

*Fig. 6. Frozen seas
and lands of the
North Atlantic region*

atures are down to 12°F., and at Omsk, in Siberia, they
are down to 0°F. This makes it very clear how much
the west owes to the warm air brought in by westerly
air streams in winter.

The Atlantic itself takes a hand

So far we have only considered the behaviour of
the air itself over the Atlantic and in the countries round
it. The waters of the Atlantic themselves also play a
big part in influencing men's lives on the land.

The waters of the ocean are never still. Movements,
called *currents*, take place in them. The main reason

for these currents is the wind system which prevails over
the ocean. South of 30°N. currents move westwards,
blown by the trade winds; between 30°N. and 60°N.,
they move eastwards, blown by the westerlies.

The pattern in the North Atlantic is shown in Fig. 6.
The westward movement, caused by the *trades*, is called
the North Equatorial Current, and the eastward movement, caused by *westerlies*, is called the North Atlantic
Drift. On each side, the currents move round to
create a complete circulation of water. The same
circulation is found in the Pacific, and other oceans.

*In the waters of the
Gulf Stream*

The Atlantic Ocean has one special feature of its
own called *The Gulf Stream*. If you look at Fig. 6 you
will see that the *trades* pile the surface currents into the
Caribbean Sea and the Gulf of Mexico, through the
channels between the islands. There is no escape for this
water except between Florida, in the United States of
America, and the island of Cuba. This Florida channel
is narrow, and the waters held up in the Gulf, pour out
through this channel as a very fast current called a
Stream, because, for quite a long way, it keeps itself
separate from the ocean through which it is flowing.
The great bank of small islands, called The Bahamas,
turns the stream northwards and it flows along off the
coast of the U.S.A., from 4-6 miles an hour. By the
time it is half way along the coast of the U.S.A., it
merges into the ocean and becomes the North Atlantic
Drift.

What it has done, is to bring out into the North
Atlantic, great masses of warm tropical water, which
raise the temperature of the Drift, and keep the coasts
of Europe ice-free right up into the Arctic Circle beyond
the north of Norway. Look again at Fig. 6 and see
how the frozen seas are forced back by the Drift. Notice
also how the North Pacific Drift keeps the shores of
Alaska and Western Canada ice-free in a similar way.

There is another series of currents, formed by the
melting ice of the Arctic, and moved southwards by
the Polar air stream. This water is cold, but fresh, *i.e.*
without much salt, and so it is lighter than the warmer,

saltier water over which it flows. Thus it remains on the surface for a great distance.

On Fig. 6 this movement is shown forming the Labrador Current which is such a nuisance to the eastern coast of Canada. Not only does it bring down icebergs and ice-floes from Greenland and the islands, but it freezes the coasts down to the mouth of the St. Lawrence for over four months each year. You should compare it with the Okhotsk Current which does similar things to the Pacific Coasts of the U.S.S.R.

Where the Labrador Current meets the North Atlantic Drift off Newfoundland the warm moist air over the North Atlantic Drift is chilled and much fog results.

Why is it only the east side of the land that is troubled by these currents? The answer is given in *The Asiatic World*. The westerlies blow the warm surface waters to the west coasts and so the cold currents are forced to move down only on the east coasts.

Task 8. Look up, in an atlas, a world map showing ocean currents, and compare those in the Pacific with those in the Atlantic, as shown in Fig. 6. Why do the warm westerly drifts not go so far north in the Pacific as in the Atlantic? Is there anything in the Pacific to correspond with the Gulf Stream?

Task 9. On Fig. 6 there is a part of the Atlantic Ocean called The Sargasso Sea. Look up reference books and see what you can find out about this "sea".

Task 10. This will have to be organised with your teacher. Set up a rain gauge in a suitable place. (see *The Foundations*, Chapter 6) and read the rainfall at a fixed time each day, for about two weeks or more. Note also the direction of the wind at intervals during the day, and the kind of weather that goes with it. Then obtain a weather map of each day from a newspaper and see what weather formations are over Britain. Try to relate your own recordings to these, and make a daily report of your own.

Icebergs in the Labrador Current

CHAPTER 2

FRANCE AND THE LOW COUNTRIES
—EMPIRE BUILDERS

We will begin our survey of the Atlantic Countries by studying the countries of Europe, and in Europe we start by concentrating on three countries on the Atlantic Seaboard. They are three prosperous and densely peopled countries, with much trade and industry. Look at the following figures:

	Population	Area	People per sq. mile
United Kingdom	54 millions	93,000 sq. miles	577
France	48 millions	213,000 sq. miles	226
Holland	12 millions	13,500 sq. miles	896
Belgium	12 millions	11,800 sq. miles	784

These are very high densities. France, which has a density much lower than the others, is still densely peopled. One has only to think of Canada with five per square mile. The densities in Holland and Belgium are enormous. With Great Britain, they are the highest densities in the world! Only Japan and Germany, with 538 and 603 per square mile, respectively, are in the same category. Thus, in studying these countries we have to seek for explanations as to how such large numbers of people are able to live in such comfortable circumstances.

Position is important

The position of these countries, in the world, has had some important effects on their prosperity. In Fig. 2 you can see the "Land Hemisphere", that is,

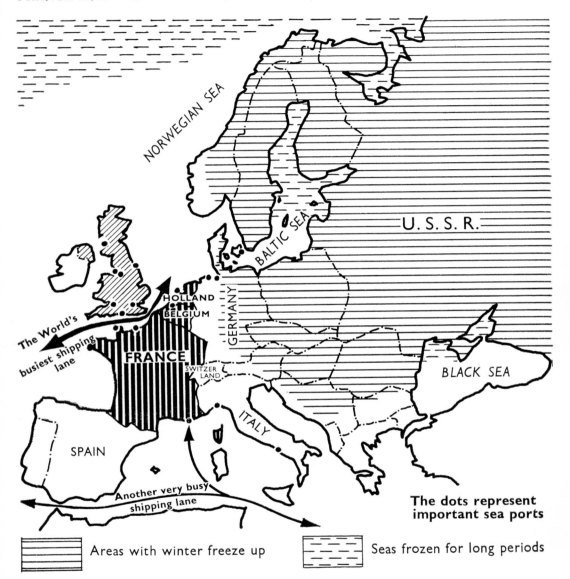

NORWEGIAN SEA

U.S.S.R.

BALTIC SEA

The World's busiest shipping lane

HOLLAND
BELGIUM

GERMANY

FRANCE

SWITZER-
LAND

BLACK SEA

SPAIN

ITALY

Another very busy shipping lane

The dots represent important sea ports

Areas with winter freeze up

Seas frozen for long periods

Fig. 7. The position of France, Holland and Belgium in Europe

the half of the world which contains the bulk of the land masses. The striking thing is that *Britain and the countries opposite to it lie in the exact centre of the world's land masses*. The circle, which includes the land hemisphere, is drawn with its centre on London. To be in such a position means great advantages for trade and discovery. From this central position these countries have established themselves in all parts of the world. Their natural vigour created great empires and trading corporations. Practically all Africa, some of North America and most of Australia, and South-East Asia were linked with these four small lands. The trade and commerce, from so great an area of the world, provided work for large numbers of people in many large and small towns.

Fig. 7 illustrates the favoured position of the Atlantic countries in the continent of Europe. On this map are shown two of the world's busiest shipping lanes, and you can see how close they are to France, Holland and Belgium, as well as to Britain. All the great seaports of Europe are shown by dots, and it is very clear how many more are around the English Channel and North Sea, than in any other part of Europe. Then the areas of frozen lands and frozen seas are shown. France, Holland and Belgium, escape both. Their ports are always open and their trade and commerce is not affected by the winters.

Task 11. Look at Fig. 7. Can you suggest any reason why the Baltic Sea is troubled by ice for long periods in the north, yet the Norwegian Sea is ice-free?

A Region of Great Plains

Now we will look at the countries on the Atlantic seaboard in a little more detail. In Fig. 8 we can see highlands and lowlands, and the main rivers. The first thing that strikes us is that there is an enormous area of plains in all three countries. Holland has no hills; Belgium has only one corner occupied by the Ardennes; whilst in France there is no high land from the Belgian frontier to the Pyrenees: a distance of 500 miles. In general, these lowlands are very fertile

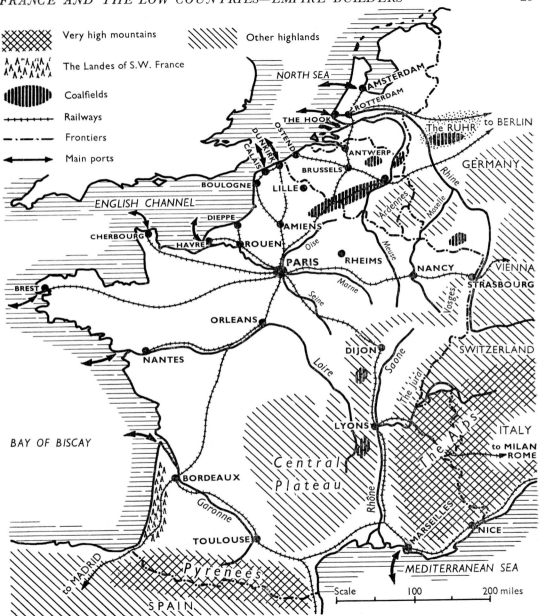

Very high mountains

Other highlands

The Landes of S.W. France

Coalfields

Railways

Frontiers

Main ports

NORTH SEA

AMSTERDAM

ROTTERDAM

THE HOOK

The RUHR   to BERLIN

OSTEND

DUNKIRK

ANTWERP

GERMANY

CALAIS

BRUSSELS

BOULOGNE

LILLE

Rhine

ENGLISH CHANNEL

Ardennes

Moselle

DIEPPE

AMIENS

CHERBOURG

HAVRE

ROUEN

Oise

Meuse

PARIS

RHEIMS

NANCY

VIENNA

Marne

STRASBOURG

BREST

Seine

Vosges

ORLEANS

DIJON

SWITZERLAND

NANTES

Loire

Saone

The Jura

BAY OF BISCAY

LYONS

ITALY

The ALPS

to MILAN

Central

ROME

Plateau

BORDEAUX

Rhône

Garonne

MARSEILLES

NICE

TOULOUSE

to MADRID

Pyrénées

MEDITERRANEAN SEA

SPAIN

Scale   100   200 miles

Fig. 8. France
Holland and Belgium

and extremely well farmed. There is warmth in summer and moisture all the year. Most of the land is owned by the farmers who work it, and the production of crops and animal products is very great. The plains are crossed by very large rivers which have spread fertile mud over their valleys.

Task 12. Examine Fig. 8.

(a) Name the three great rivers which flow across the western lowlands of France.

(b) Name the rivers which flow into the Mediterranean.

(c) In which part of France do the rivers flow **out** of France? Describe the courses they take.

The mountains of France are highest on the south and south-east. Here are two high ranges, the Pyrenees and the Alps. Their highest peaks are over 10,000 feet. Great snowfields spread over the upper slopes and glaciers, or rivers of ice, move very slowly down the upper valleys till they finally melt at some point in the higher part of the valley. From the melting ice come many streams and rivers which flow out of both Pyrenees and Alps, in deep, wide valleys. The Rhône and Garonne are examples.

The ways across these ranges are few, and the passes are difficult. Nobody lives in such uncomfortable wastes of rock and snow, and so the frontiers of France, against Spain and Italy, follow the tops of the ranges.

Task 13. Examine an atlas map of France. Look at the Alps and Pyrenees and count the number of railways which cross the ranges, from France. Do not count the ones along the coasts.

The lower highlands of France and Belgium are old, hard rocks worn down from great ranges, millions of years ago. They have been so reduced in size that the highest parts are only 5,000-6,000 feet high and most of the highland is under 3,000 feet high. Deep valleys bite into these highlands and provide routes across them, and places where people live. Notice on Fig. 8 how they form a wall, inside the Alps and Pyrenees, from the Central Plateau to the Ardennes. Most of the rivers rise on these old plateaus.

Fig. 9. Le Puy, in the Loire Valley

J. ALLAN CASH

Task 14. Name the five rivers which flow to the west from these plateaus and say where they enter the sea. Which river flows southwards from them?

Farming of Rich Variety

The products of the farms of France, Belgium and Holland are enormous in quantity and very varied in kind. Let us take France first. Her forty-four million people are supplied with almost all the necessary foodstuffs for living from her own farms. We will make a survey of the different parts and see for ourselves what France produces.

The Central Plateau

Look at Fig. 9 which is a view of the valley of the Loire in its upper limits. The town is Le Puy. The first thing that strikes us is the richness of the fields, full of crops, chiefly hay, barley, oats and potatoes. These are for human and animal foods. Secondly, one notices the high ridges in the background, often bare rock but, in general, covered with grass on which many sheep and cattle feed. Thirdly, one notices the peculiar steep-sided hills crowned with a church and a statue, which are seen in Le Puy itself.

These three features are closely connected. The steep bare hills are chiefly of granite, a very old and very hard rock which forms much of the Central Plateau. The richness of the landscape around Le Puy is due to its volcanic soils, formed from old volcanoes, of which the small steep hills are the last surviving remnants. Other, larger old volcanoes can be seen in the knob-like hills rising above the general level in the background ridges. Forests cover the lower granite slopes, and timber is floated down the rivers out to the lowlands.

Task 15.
(*a*) Why is it that all the fields in the picture are surrounded by stone walls, not by hedges?
(*b*) At what season of the year was the picture taken? Give your reasons for your choice.
(*c*) Is there any evidence that fruit is grown?

Brittany
This part of France is a peninsula jutting out into the Atlantic, like Cornwall and Devon to the north. It shows many resemblances to those English counties. The heavy rains from the west winds are found in both, so there is much woodland and rich meadow-land in the valleys. Brittany is the only part of France where one finds the small fields surrounded by hedges and trees which are such a feature of British lowlands.

The coast is a rocky one, with hundreds of small creeks and harbours from which fishing boats set out daily. Like the Cornishman, the Breton is a great fisherman. In Fig. 10 you see a view of Concarneau on the south coast of Brittany. It shows striking resemblances to Cornish ports. Sardines are an important catch, and small factories tin them. On the north coast, mackerel, pilchards and herring are caught. Boats from Brittany cross the Atlantic to catch cod off Newfoundland. The extremely mild winters allow vegetables to grow. So early potatoes and greens, as well as flowers, are produced for the markets in Paris and other big towns.

*Fig. 10. Concarneau,
Brittany*

AEROFILMS

Task 16. In Fig. 10.
1. Find one or more small factories, probably sardine-canning factories.
2. Say why the countryside in the rear reminds one so much of a British one.
3. The Breton coast has strong tides in and out of its estuaries. Connect this with the fact that the fishing boats all lie anchored in mid-harbour, and are not tied up along the jetty.

The Paris Basin

We now come to the first of the great lowlands of France, and the most famous. We can see why it is named after Paris, for that city is in the middle of it: but why *basin?*

The answer is to be seen in Fig. 11, which we hope you can follow. The rocks composing the Paris Basin are young ones and they were laid down on a sea-bed of older rocks. Earth movements raised the whole sea-bed on to the land, in the form of a *basin*, with the older rocks raised all round the outer edge, and the younger rocks lying in layers on top of one another inside. Can you follow this from the map and section in Fig. 11?

One interesting thing is that on the east side of Paris the rocks are raised up into steep edges, or scarps, facing outwards towards Germany. This is not so on the west side. The rivers which rise on the older rocks of the Central Plateau and its extensions, flow through these scarps in deep valleys, and give routeways along their floors. Notice how most of them seem to come together near Paris. All the natural routes of the Basin meet near Paris, which is one reason for the city being there.

Task 17. How many scarps are there east of Paris? What river flows along the foot of the most easterly one? Which are the two big rivers found in the Paris Basin? Through what kind of rocks does the Somme flow? What is the chief river of Champagne?

Crops of all kinds

There is a wonderful variety of crops in the basin. Wheat, oats, barley, fruits, sugar-beet and all types of root and green crops grow. There are many cattle bred for both milk and meat. On the dry limestone and chalk ridges are many sheep. Chalk is a form of limestone, and both have dry surfaces producing good, crisp grass. The most important crop, however, is the grape from which wine is produced. Vineyards occupy south-facing slopes where the sun gives extra heat. Two areas very famous for vineyards are Champagne and the Loire Valley.

In Normandy are many thousands of acres of apple orchards. Cider is a popular drink. The combination of apples, cider and rich meadows full of dairy cows, makes Normandy very like Devonshire in Britain.

Fig. 12 is a view in the Ile de France. The richness and prosperity of the countryside is clear. There are few trees, for there is no room for trees and hedges.

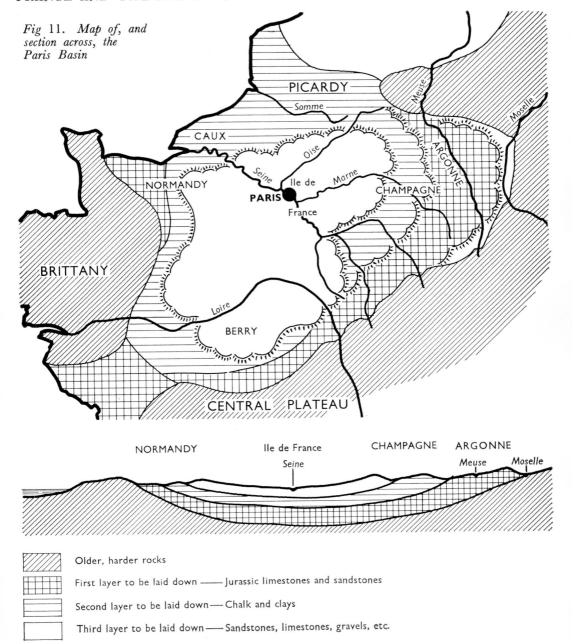

Fig 11. Map of, and section across, the Paris Basin

Older, harder rocks

First layer to be laid down ———— Jurassic limestones and sandstones

Second layer to be laid down —— Chalk and clays

Third layer to be laid down —— Sandstones, limestones, gravels, etc.

Fig 12. *The Ile de France, with the River Seine*

ROGER SCHALL

Every square yard is cultivated. What trees there are, are usually in orchards, as in the foreground, or have been planted for shade.

Task 18.

(*a*) The river in Fig. 12 is the Seine. Do you think it will be a useful river for commerce? Why?

(*b*) Do the houses differ much in appearance from houses you know?

Basin of Aquitaine

This is another basin of rocks similar to those of the Paris Basin and equally fertile. Because it is farther south, its summers are very hot and, in addition to wheat, maize is grown extensively.

Fig. 13 is a picture taken to the east of Bordeaux. It shows a landscape covered with vineyards. The grape vines are grown on poles and wires. The fruit is collected in August, each bunch being snipped from the vine by hand. The baskets of grapes then go to the presses. The juice is pressed out of them and runs into the vats under the presses. Wine varies enormously in taste and quality from one district to another and from one vineyard to another.

Task 19. Compare Fig. 13 with Fig. 12. In what ways are they similar? In what ways do they differ?

The Rhône Corridor

This region lies in a trough between the Alps and the Central Plateau, and gives a route right through Europe from the North Sea to the Mediterranean. In the northern part, which is Burgundy, life is like that in the Paris Basin. There is another great wine region on the lower slopes of the Central Hills. In the southern part the climate changes. Rains are very scarce in

Fig. 13. *Vineyards of Aquitaine*

FRENCH GOVERNMENT
TOURIST OFFICE

summer. So in Provençe, east of the Rhône, and
in Languedoc, west of the Rhône, one finds, in addition
to wine, wheat, apples etc., fruits like oranges and
olives. In Fig. 14 one sees that the countryside looks
barer than Aquitaine or the Paris Basin, because of the
summer drought. Nevertheless, fruit orchards or

Fig 14.   *A Provençal
Landscape*

PAUL POPPER LTD.

cultivated fields occupy all the foreground. The hill-sides look very bare, but the lower slopes contain many vineyards. Many fields, and the buildings, are surrounded by lines of tall trees, generally poplars. These are a protection against a very cold and deadly wind, called *the mistral*, which blows fiercely down from the Alps into the valleys from Autumn to Spring.

East of the Rhône, the coast is steep and rocky as the Alps come near the sea. Here is the *Riviera*, a great holiday resort for the world. Its beauty is well shown in Fig. 15. Lovely bays and peninsulas, towns and villages nestle on the bays at the foot of the hills, and a *Mediterranean* vegetation of shrubs and trees resists the summer drought.

Task 20. In both Figs. 14 and 15, the buildings seem to be in light colours. Why is this? The *Riviera* is famous for producing flowers and perfumes. Every year there is a "Carnival of Flowers" at Nice. Why should these industries be here?

Fig 15. Beaulieu, on the French Riviera

R. CHAZOULE

North-Eastern France

This is the only region in France where the rivers flow out of the country. As a result there has been conflict in the past to decide which parts of the valley were French, and which were German. Even to-day, many people in this region speak German, though they are French in allegiance. Two famous provinces of France lie here. Alsace, along the Rhine, and Lorraine around the Meuse and Moselle. They were taken into Germany after the war of 1870-71, and recovered by France in the First World War in 1918.

The farming is typically French. Lorraine has great areas of wheat; Alsace has many vineyards along the lower slopes of the Vosges Mountains. It is, however, a region more important for industry than for farming, and we will deal with it again under that heading.

Dutch and Belgian Farmers

We have now seen how great a farming country is France. The small countries of Holland and Belgium are not far behind, though they cannot hope to feed all their closely packed populations. Unlike France, these lands import food in large amounts, but also produce it at home in large amounts. Look at Fig 16. You can see that the amount of fertile plain in Holland and Belgium is limited, although the countries are so low-lying. In the great plains of Brabant and the valleys of the Rhine and Meuse, (*Maas* in Holland), the farming is like that of the Paris Basin, but with smaller fields and more intensive cultivation. Enormous crops are produced per acre including wheat, sugar-beet and fruits. There are no vineyards. The summers are hardly warm enough, being like those of southern England.

There are, unfortunately, large areas, in the east, of infertile sands, almost impossible to farm. Great ice sheets lay over the region during the Great Ice Age, and these spread sheets of sand and gravel when they melted. Poor heath covers most of it, with thin pine-woods in many places. Both Belgium and Holland have developed industry in this region. Animal rearing is

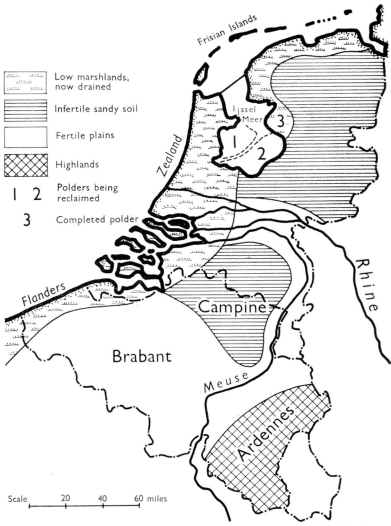

Fig 16. Regions of Holland and Belgium

Scale 20 40 60 miles

carried on, and *fen colonies* are being established to grow potatoes, sugar-beet, rye and oats, making use of fertilisers and scientific farming. The pressure of people on the land is so great, that some use must be made of these infertile regions. Nevertheless, they are still thinly peopled.

The remainder of the region, in Flanders and

Zealand (*Sea Land*), now attracts our attention. Even if it is marshy, it must hold tremendous numbers of people to make up for the empty east. How has this been done?

"God made the sea, we made the land"

This is a saying in Holland where most of the low marshlands are below the level of the sea and have been seized from the sea only by the enormous efforts of men. The land so seized is known as *polders* in Holland. Since life in Flanders and in the Dutch polders is similar, we will concentrate on the polders.

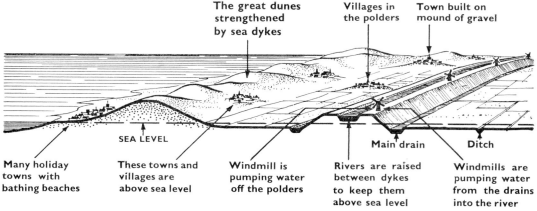

The great dunes strengthened by sea dykes

Villages in the polders

Town built on mound of gravel

SEA LEVEL

Main drain   Ditch

Many holiday towns with bathing beaches

These towns and villages are above sea level

Windmill is pumping water off the polders

Rivers are raised between dykes to keep them above sea level

Windmills are pumping water from the drains into the river

Fig. 17. Section across Polder Country

Fig. 17 is an attempt to show how the country is organized. Winds have blown huge sand dunes up along the coasts, as in the Landes of France. The shallow seas and marshes behind these dunes are now the polder country, except in north Holland where the dunes form a line of islands, (see Fig. 16). The shallow seas between these Frisian Islands and the mainland are so valuable for fishing that the Dutch do not reclaim them.

Since the land lies below sea level when reclaimed it will not allow water to drain into the sea. Further, the rivers must remain above sea level or they will not flow into the sea. Hence rivers are dyked above the polders, as seen in Fig. 17. Then a new problem arises. How is the water from the polders to drain into the

Fig 18. *Dutch bulb-fields on a Polder*

J. ALLAN CASH

rivers? First, every field is surrounded by ditches into which the water drains from the fields. These ditches empty into a main drain along the river dyke. Wind pumps driven by windmills, and electric pumps, raise water from the drain into the river. That is the reason for so many windmills in Holland and Flanders. They are pumping water off the polders.

Fig. 18 is a view on a polder near Haarlem. This district is just behind the dunes and has very sandy soils. Here has grown up the great trade in Dutch bulbs which supplies all the world. The flowers are cut and piled into heaps for manure. It is the bulbs which are sold, not the flowers. Notice the flower heaps in the picture. You can also see the drainage ditches.

The village is on slightly higher ground near the dyke.

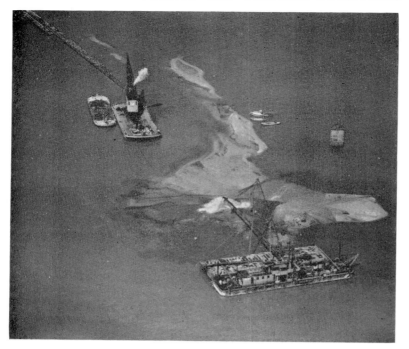

Fig. 19. *A dyke*
being built-up in
the sea

AEROFILMS

Task 21. Why are hedges and fences not needed as farm boundaries in the polders? Is any land not used? Will much labour be required in the bulb industry?

The Dutch people are still creating polders from the sea. In Fig. 19 the operation is in full swing. The dyke is being built up in the sea. When completed the sea water is pumped out and a polder is begun. The boats are laying the material down in the water. A completed dyke is shown in Fig. 20. This is the Great Dyke across the mouth of the Zuyder Zee, (*South Sea*) which has created several new polders out of the sea, and left a large fresh water lake, the Ijssel Meer (Fig. 16). It is the great increase in population in Holland which caused these Zuyder Zee polders to be made. More and more land is required for food production.

Task 22. What is the barge doing in Fig. 19?

Fig. 20. *A completed dyke*

PAUL POPPER LTD.

In the foreground is a dredger which is depositing sand. Why is it doing this? How can you tell the water is very shallow? In Fig. 20, which side would you say was the North Sea and which the Ijssel Meer? Why do you think so?

The polders in both Holland and Flanders are great producers of crops. In Flanders they grow many crops for use in industry: sugar-beet for the sugar factories, flax for the linen mills, and chicory for the coffee industry. Wheat and barley are grown for food. Many cattle feed on the rich meadows, to supply milk to the numerous towns of Belgium. In Holland, the same crops are grown, but there is much more dairying, for milk for the towns and for cheese for export.

Industry in France, Holland and Belgium

In these three countries there is a great deal of mining and manufacturing. If we look at Fig. 21, we see that most of the industry lies in a belt between the rivers Seine and Rhine. It lies on each side of the hill country which we call the Ardennes, in Belgium, and there is some, also, on the edge of the Vosges Mountains and Central Plateau.

In this belt are a number of important coal-fields. Pick out the following:

1. The Franco-Belgian, along the Meuse. This is continued into Germany as far as the Ruhr.
2. The Campine Fields, north of the Franco-Belgian. They are new fields developed since 1900, and contain very good coal. One small field is in Holland.
3. The Saar, in Germany. This is vital to French industries in Lorraine.
4. Small fields at Le Creusot and St. Etienne on the edge of the Central Plateau.

Coal still counts

Industry, as we know it to-day, is concentrated into big factories and mills, with enormous machines turning out vast numbers of articles. It is a product of the nineteenth century and has depended very largely on the power of *steam*. Coal was the chief means of producing the steam. Thus it is not surprising that in the nineteenth century big industries grew up near to coal-fields.

Task 23. The following table shows the production of coal in the three countries and the Saar. Make a diagram to compare them.

France	50 million tons	Holland	12 million tons
Belgium	21 million tons	Saar	16 million tons

British production is about 200 million tons

The Nord

Two industrial areas stand out in France. The first is the district round Lille and Arras, a district

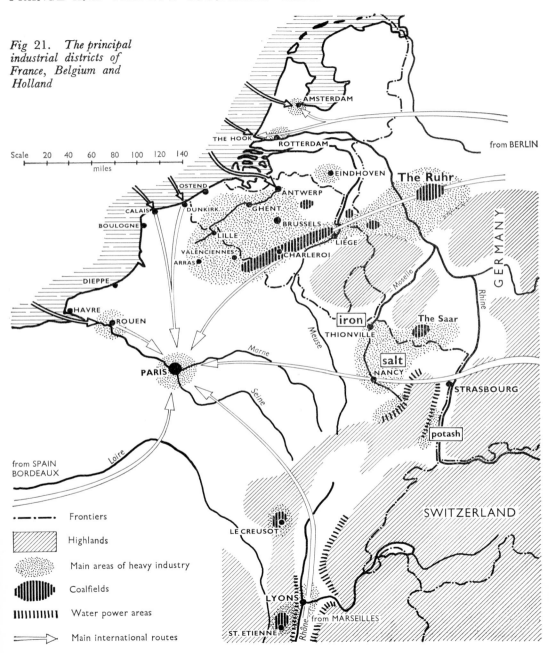

Fig 21. *The principal industrial districts of France, Belgium and Holland*

closely connected with Belgian industries, where workers from each country cross the border daily in going to their work. This is the Nord. *Engineering and metal goods are important*, using iron from Lorraine. *Linens* are made from locally grown flax, and from imported Baltic flax. The town of Cambrai gave its name to *Cambrics*, a fine linen cloth. *Woollens* are made partly from local wool from sheep on the chalk pastures of the Paris Basin, but mostly, now, from wool from Australia and Argentine. Arras gave its name to the woollen hangings which decorated the walls of mediaeval castles. *Cottons* are made from cotton from the United States and Egypt. Most of this comes in via Rouen, which has also developed cotton industries, *e.g. velvets* and *corduroys*. Valenciennes has always been connected with *lace-making*. Dunkirk and Calais are the ports through which raw materials are imported.

Lorraine

This is the second big industrial region. Because there is good coal in the Saar, and good iron in plenty in Lorraine, great *steelworks* are found here around Thionville and Nancy. The saltfield near Nancy has been the basis of a large *chemical* industry in that city. The swift-running streams of the Vosges Mountains provide hydro-electric power for small *cotton* mills and for the production of *fertilisers* on the potash field in Alsace.

The largest city in this area is Strasbourg. It is a great river port on the Rhine where two *very important canals* join it. This makes it a very busy business centre. It also has iron industries.

The centre of the city is seen in Fig. 22. Behind the cathedral you can see the warehouses and factories along the river. In the square the buildings contain many offices. You can see the German type of buildings in the city.

Task 24.

(*a*) Why should Strasbourg contain many German types of buildings?

Fig. 22. Strasbourg
FRENCH GOVERNMENT
TOURIST OFFICE

Fig. 23.   Autoroute du Nord

LUCIEN VIGUIER

(*b*) From which port will the Algerian wheat and Middle East oil come to Strasbourg?

(*c*) Fig. 23 is a scene in the Nord.   How can you tell it is a coalfield district?   What is there to show it is not a British coalfield scene?

The Lyons Area

Fig. 21 shows the position of the great city of Lyons, which makes more silk goods than any other city in the world.   The industry began when silkworms were reared locally on mulberry leaves.   To-day none are reared locally and silk comes from Japan or China.

There was always ample water-power around Lyons, and in the nineteenth century the St. Etienne coalfield was useful.   In the twentieth century the looms are driven by electricity, generated by water-power.   Silk ribbons are made at St. Etienne.

Le Creusot is the centre of French armament and locomotive-making.

Fig. 24.   A hydro-electric plant under construction in the Rhône valley

PAUL POPPER LTD.

The Rhône valley and the Alpine valleys to the east, are used in several places for hydro-electric power stations. In Fig. 24, you can see a new plant being constructed in the Rhône valley. A great amount of power is now obtained from this station. The French Alps contain good quantities of bauxite from which *aluminium* is obtained. This metal has to be smelted in electric furnaces. Hence the industry flourishes here.

Fig. 25. *Steel works near Liège.*

OFFICE BELGE DU COMMERCE EXTERIEUR

Belgian Industry

This small country has a very large amount of industry. In the plain of Flanders is the great textile district similar to that in the Nord. *Linens*, *woollens* and *cottons* are made in ancient cities like Ghent, Bruges, Mechlen and Brussels. Belgian lace is very famous. Brussels has given its name to a type of carpet. Along the Meuse valley, is a belt of heavy industries, steel and iron, cutlery, chemicals and glass. Liège is the chief centre and has big engineering works. The new Campine coalfield is a great help to the Meuse Valley region where coal is very difficult to mine. Industry is developing on the Campine field, *e.g.* very large stainless steel plants.

Task 25. Fig. 25 shows steel works near Liège. Note the pit heaps in the rear. Where is the nearest iron ore to these works?

Industry in Holland

Since Holland has very little coal, and no water-power, we would not expect to find much heavy industry. Nevertheless, there are textile and electrical industries around Eindhoven. Tilburg and Twente in south-eastern Holland, developed on land too poor for farming. Dutch electrical products are sold all over the world, and are well known in Britain.

In 25 years, the chemical industry has grown enormously. In 1961 it was fifth largest in Europe, and tenth largest in the world.

There has recently been found at Groningen, in North Holland, the largest gas field in Europe. The gas is used in the manufacture of ammonia and aluminium. Some of the gas will be exported to Britain, Belgium and France.

The Motor Industry

One of the largest industries in the world to-day is the making of motor-cars. Not many countries actually make them on a large scale. France is one of the countries which does. The industry is concentrated in and around Paris. Motor-cars mean many engineering industries, metal-works, rubber-works and electrical works. All these are found in and around Paris.

Task 26. Have a competition to see who can identify the greatest number of makes of French cars.

A Region of many Seaports

Fig. 8, shows the chief ports. The Hook of Holland, Ostend in Belgium, Calais, Boulogne and Dieppe in France, are cross-channel ports (see Fig. 21).

Task 27. To what ports in Britian do steamers sail from: The Hook, Ostend, Calais, Boulogne and Dieppe? What distances are travelled in each case?

The Large Seaports

Cross-channel ports are generally small, taking ships up to about 5,000 tons. A few big ports take liners of 40,000 tons or more, and large cargo ships.

There are five really large ports in this region. In Holland are Amsterdam and Rotterdam, in Belgium is

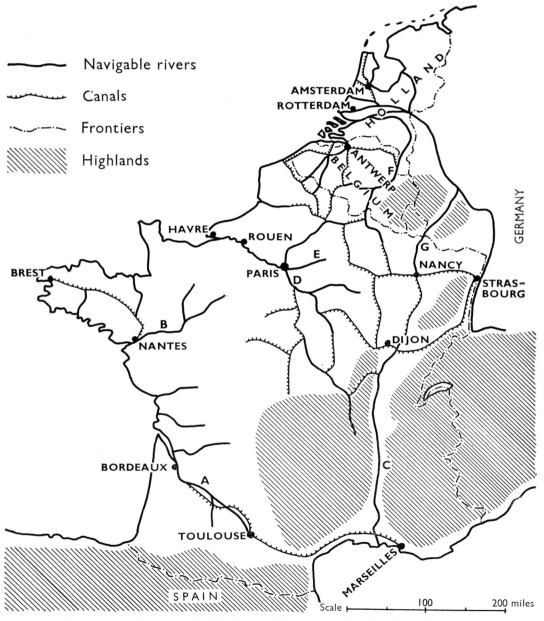

Navigable rivers

Canals

Frontiers

Highlands

AMSTERDAM
ROTTERDAM

HOLLAND

GERMANY

ANTWERP
BELGIUM

F

HAVRE ROUEN

BREST

PARIS D E

NANCY G

STRASBOURG

B

NANTES

DIJON

C

BORDEAUX

A

TOULOUSE

MARSEILLES

SPAIN

Scale 100 200 miles

Fig 26. The main canals and navigable rivers of France and the Low Countries

Antwerp, in France are le Havre and Marseilles. These are five of the biggest ports in the world, comparing with London, Liverpool, Manchester, Hull, Southampton and Glasgow in Britain. Less, but still important, are Dunkirk, Cherbourg, Brest, Nantes-St. Nazaire, and Bordeaux. Find them all on Fig. 8.

Because ports are gateways, they must have good harbours in which ships can lay up. A river mouth, with a deepened channel, is one of the commonest.

Task 28. Which ports in Fig 8 are on the mouths of rivers? Name the rivers in each case.

Inland Waterways

Ports have also to be places with good routes leading inland, because goods must be able to move easily in and out of them. All big ports have a network of roads and railways meeting there. There are other methods of moving goods, that is, by rivers and canals. There are many navigable rivers, and a dense network of canals in constant use. Notice how dense is the network of canals in the industrial areas. From the seaports, goods can move by water to almost any part of the region.

Task 29. Using Fig. 26, describe routes by which goods could travel:

(*a*) from Rotterdam to Marseilles;

(*b*) from le Havre to Strasbourg.

A Survey of the Chief Ports

1. Amsterdam, Rotterdam and Antwerp

Amsterdam was built on the Zuyder Zee (*South Sea*) when it could be used by ships. To-day the ships come from Ijmuiden by a ship-canal. Amsterdam has enormous trade with South-east Asia, where so much land was under Dutch control. Rice, rubber, coffee, oils, petrol, tin, sugar, etc., come in to be made up into articles for sale in shops all over Northern Europe. Large barges bring exports from the Ruhr. Amsterdam is the world's chief centre for diamonds and other precious stones. It is a very large city, with over eight hundred and fifty thousand people.

*Fig. 27. The port of
Rotterdam*

J. ALLAN CASH

Rotterdam is on the Rhine, and does a great trade, by barges, with the Ruhr. Fig. 27 shows the port with numerous barges and ships in it. It builds and repairs ships and barges. In Fig. 28 you see the new business centre which has been built in the 1950's to replace that destroyed by bombing during the Second World War. Building still goes on in the foreground. The population is nearly seven hundred and thirty thousand.

*Fig. 28. The business
centre of Rotterdam*

AEROFILMS

Antwerp is on the Scheldt estuary with a difficult, but deep, channel to the sea. It is connected by rail and water to every corner of Belgium and northern France. It has much trade from both these areas, and until recently with the Congo, in Africa. Many exports from the Ruhr go to Antwerp, for it has always been a cheap port.

2. Le Havre and the Seine Ports

Le Havre handles liners and big cargo vessels with cargoes to and from America and Africa. Rouen handles smaller steamers. Large barges sail from both to Paris, which is an important barge port. Cherbourg is a port where liners, calling in France, disembark French passengers, mail and cargo.

Fig. 29. *The old harbour at Marseilles*

J. ALAN CASH

3. Marseilles

This great city is the second in France, with a population of six hundred and sixty thousand. It is the only great port in France on the Mediterranean Sea. It is not built on the mouth of the River Rhône because it is too shallow and silted. Instead a small natural harbour was chosen to the east. This forms the Old Harbour, seen in Fig. 29. There has been a port here since early times, but ships to-day are so large that a big new harbour has been made outside the old harbour. Marseilles handles the trade with the Far East, the Middle East, North Africa, the Mediterranean lands, and West Africa. Such cargoes as Japanese silk, Malayan rubber, Vietnam rice, Arabian coffee, Egyptian cotton, North African wheat and iron ore, Italian fruits, oil from the Middle East and the Sahara, cocoa and palm oils etc. from West Africa, all come to Marseilles. Hence industries in food preparations, soap, margarine and vegetable oils have been developed.

Toulon, like Brest, is a large naval base.

Task 30. In Fig. 27, the cargoes of the ships in the river are being unloaded on to barges. Study carefully how this is being done, and then describe the method either in words or by drawings.

Task 31. Compare the views of Rotterdam and Marseilles, Figs. 27 and 29. There is a great difference in the brightness of the two pictures. Can you explain this?

Paris

We conclude our survey of France, Belgium and Holland with a glance at the capital of France, a city far larger than any other city in these three countries. Greater Paris has a population of 8,500,000. We have already seen that it grew up on the Seine where so many river routes came together. All valleys led to this point, and the city first arose on an island in the Seine, where bridges could be put across. To-day the city extends for miles from this island. Fig. 30, shows a section of it as viewed from the Eiffel Tower, looking towards Montmartre where the Sacré Coeur church crowns the hill. What magnificent buildings of all ages are to be seen, what wide stately avenues along the river. This part of Paris includes offices, hotels, theatres, museums and shops. Away to the west, to the left of this picture, are the industrial districts and warehouses of the barge port.

Every railway and most main roads diverge from Paris to all parts of France.

Fig. 30. Paris, seen from the Eiffel Tower
J. ALLAN CASH

It has many light industries, especially luxury goods, and many clothing, food and furniture factories. (See also page 48).

Task 32. Find out, from any source, the answers to the following questions:
1. What are the capitals of Holland and Belgium?
2. Have the Belgians a national language? If not, what languages do they speak?

3. Strasbourg is the meeting place of the Council of Europe. What is this Council? Is Britain represented on it?
4. Where, and what are the following:
   the Louvre, the Boulevards, the Arc de Triomphe, Versailles?

Task 33. To test your knowledge of facts in this chapter.

1. Which French port will export claret?
2. Which part of France produces the most sailors?
3. Which part of France has rich soils formed from volcanic dust?
4. Where are (*a*) brandy and (*b*) olive oil obtained?
5. What and where are polders?
6. Which French port imports cotton and makes cotton goods?
7. What are the industries in the Nord?
8. To which port do ships go by ship-canal?
9. Which Belgian town is famous for engineering?
10. What are the five big ports of France, Belgium and Holland?

CHAPTER 3

THE GERMAN LANDS
—A PEOPLE DIVIDED

From France the great ranges of the Alps swing away in an eastward direction across the middle of Europe. They form a great wall separating the cool and cloudy northern plains from the sunnier lands round the Mediterranean. From the crests of these ranges right to the shores of the North Sea and the Baltic Sea lie the lands of the German peoples. They occupy the valleys of the rivers Rhine, Weser, Elbe and Upper Danube; a solid block of people in the middle of the Continent.

Task 34. Look at Fig. 31.

(*a*) What countries lie to the east amongst the Slavs?

(*b*) Which country separates the Baltic Sea from the North Sea?

(*c*) Of all German rivers, only one flows entirely through German-speaking territory, and only three rise in German-speaking territory. Name these rivers.

A Nation of Changing Frontiers

The German peoples are not all in the country we call Germany. Two thirds of the Swiss and all the Austrians, as well as some of the people of Alsace-Lorraine in France, speak German and are German in their way of living. All through history, the Germans have moved out of their homeland, especially

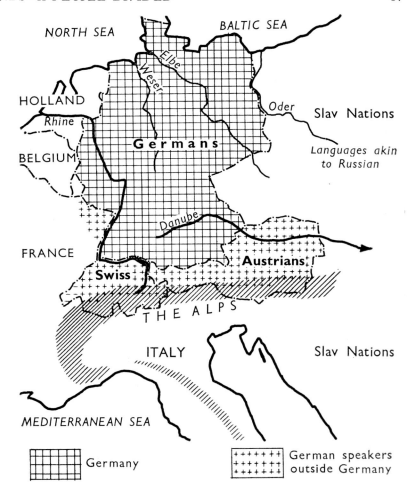

Fig. 31. The position in Europe of modern Germany

to the east. Before 1945 there were Germans in Poland, Czechoslovakia, Hungary and even Russia, men skilled in crafts and industry, good businessmen and farmers. They were especially numerous along the Baltic coastland and in 1914 the frontier of Germany stretched a long way along that sea.

Look at Fig. 32. It shows all the changes in the frontiers of Germany since 1914. In that year, the German Empire extended from Konigsberg to the

Fig. 32. *Changes in the frontiers of Germany since 1914*

Boundary 1914

In Germany 1918-45

Boundary 1945

Boundary between East and West Germany

Vosges Mountains. After 1918, Poland was re-created and Germany lost territory to that country. As well, Germany lost Alsace-Lorraine, which she had taken from France in 1871. Under Hitler and in the Second World War, Germany absorbed Austria, Czechoslovakia, and most of Poland but, following her crushing defeat in 1945, she found herself confined within the present frontiers west of the Oder, the rich province of Silesia and her ancient territory of East Prussia entirely lost. An even more crushing burden was added to these. The country was divided into two separate republics. West Germany is in the Atlantic World, working closely with the Western Nations. 58 million Germans live here. East Germany is a Communist republic in the Russian sphere of control. 17 million Germans live there. The city of Berlin itself is divided. One part is the capital of East Germany. The other part is under the protection of the U.S.A., Britain and France and is linked to West Germany.

Task 35. On Fig. 32.

(a) What is the width of the East and West German republics on a line east-west through Cologne?

(b) What is the distance from Szczecin eastwards to the 1914 German frontier? All this has been lost since 1918.

(c) What countries have gained territory from Germany since 1918?

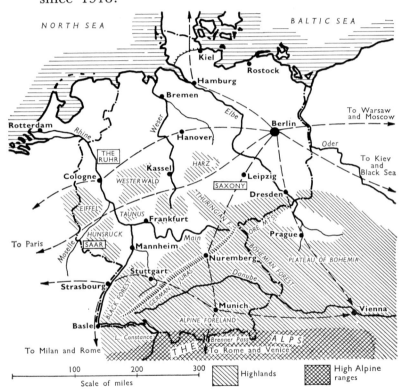

Fig. 33. *Germany*

The Regions of Germany

Fig. 33 is a general map of modern Germany. The first thing one notices is that the north is chiefly low land, and the south is chiefly high land. The centre seems to be a mixed region of highlands much cut up by river valleys. The main rivers on the northern plains are the Weser, Elbe and Oder, but Germany only reaches the Oder along a short stretch of frontier.

The main river of the south is the Danube.

The chief rivers breaking up the central highlands are the Rhine and its tributaries, especially the Moselle, Main and Neckar. Their valleys are sunny and sheltered and of great fertility. They are one of the most favoured farming regions in Germany.

Task 36.

(*a*) In what highlands does the Danube rise? Into what country does it flow from Germany?

(*b*) In what country does the Elbe rise?

(*c*) What is the line of hills which separates the Danube from the Rhine and its tributaries?

(*d*) Which rivers help to form the frontiers of Germany and what countries do they separate?

(*e*) What are the seas on to which Germany faces?

The German Climate

It is in Germany that a British visitor would notice the great change from the mild, rainy winters of his own land, to the cold and snow of an Eastern European winter. On the Rhine, winters are colder than those in Britain. The river has ice forming on it in mid-winter, though it seldom stops barges using it. However, they do have many raw wet days and cold windy days rather like those in Britain. On the Oder, on the other hand, winters are severe, the river freezes for some weeks, and there is much ice and snow on land. In January and February, especially, snow lies most of the time. The warm air from the Atlantic does not affect the region very much, but cold Russian air does. Summers are warm all over Germany, and everywhere they are warmer than in Britain.

The Rhine Basin

The Rhine is one of the most famous European rivers. It rises in the Alps and makes a broad corridor right through the tangle of highlands in which the Germans live. From earliest times, it has been a great highway of commerce and trade. Ancient castles crown its slopes and great cities lie on its banks. Germans have always lived along both its banks and it is, in a

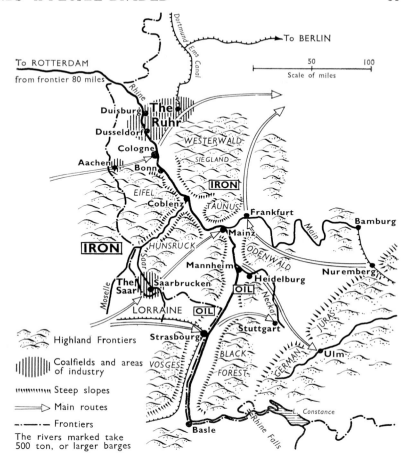

Fig. 34. The Rhine Basin

special sense, their river. Few other rivers have gathered round them so many legends, songs and poems. To-day it is probably the best organised riverway in the world. Ships sail up it to Cologne.

Huge 2,000-ton barges sail up to Mannheim and 1,000-ton barges to Strasbourg. Find these towns on Fig. 34. Large barges also use the Neckar and Main and in 1965, the Moselle was canalised to Thionville in France.

Task 37. Look at Figs. 33 and 34.

(*a*) How far is it from Rotterdam to Cologne, Mannheim and Strasbourg? Compare these distances with those from London to Liverpool, 200 miles, and London to Edinburgh, 370 miles.

(*b*) Name the two rivers flowing into the Rhine on the east bank. At what towns do they join the Rhine? Both rivers take 500-ton barges for long distances.

Task 38.

(*a*) Name two cities where main routes from Paris to Berlin cross the Rhine. Each route passes through a region of heavy industry. Name them.

(*b*) Name a city where: (*i*) the Paris-Vienna route crosses a river flowing to the Rhine; (*ii*) the Rhine to the Danube canal crosses the German Juras.

The Middle Valley

The first part of the Rhine valley lies in Switzerland. This part ends at the great Rhine Falls at Schaffhausen (Fig. 34). From there the Rhine is more manageable. At Basle it turns suddenly north and enters a great valley. It flows along this valley for 200 miles, up to Mainz. The valley is blessed with good soils and hot, moist summers. It is Germany's finest farming region. Wheat, vegetables and tobacco are the chief crops. On the lower slopes of the valley sides are extensive vineyards, as in Alsace. The main cities are river ports, notably Mannheim. Here most of the goods destined for South Germany and Austria are taken off the river, *e.g.* coal from the Ruhr and oil from the Middle East. Great chemical works lie across the river in Ludwigshafen.

Oil in the Valley

Since the Second World War ended, oil has been discovered on both sides of the valley. One discovery is at Pechelbronn, just inside the French frontier, but the others are on the east side, in Germany, to the south of the Neckar (Fig. 34). The German fields were supplying one-quarter of West Germany's needs in oil by 1957, and production was still increasing.

The Black Forest

This received its name from the dark shade of the masses of conifer woods that clothe its slopes. These are well shown in Fig. 35, which is a valley in the

Fig. 35. A Black Forest Valley
PAUL POPPER LTD.

Black Forest. The hills slope fairly steeply up to heights of over 3,000 feet, and the highest point, the Feldberg, is just over 5,000 feet. The valleys are wide and fertile with rich meadows that produce crops of hay every few weeks in summer. Many cattle are kept. The house shown in Fig. 35 is typical. It is built into the hillside so that the lowest level is for animals, and opens to the valley. The family occupy the upper floors and enter from the hillside. Everything is of wood. Fruit trees surround the house.

Task 39. Looking at Fig. 35.

(a) How can you tell that heavy snowfalls are expected in winter?

(b) What is the difference between the trees in the background and the trees nearer to the house?

(c) What kind of summits do the hills have?

South German Crafts

Timber is an important product of the Black Forest and other areas in South Germany. The region is most scientifically forested, trees are always being cut, yet the forest never seems to miss them. Pit props for the Ruhr mines form a stream of exports. Much timber is grown for furniture-making in the valleys, and for the crafts for which this part of Germany is famous. All over South Germany the farmers have long winter evenings to spend on some kind of hobbies, and from early times they became very clever in working in wood and metal. In Fig. 36 you can see a shop in the Black Forest, which shows how these skills are organised to-day. Clocks are one of the main things made, but toys of all descriptions and pottery and glassware have become famous. On a larger scale, these industries are found in many South German towns. Stuttgart has become famous for pianos, violins, etc. Nuremberg is a great toy and pencil making centre. Pforzheim makes jewellery and scientific instruments. The electrical industry is very important in Nuremberg. Motorcars are made in Stuttgart, Frankfurt, Cologne and Nuremberg.

Task 40. Paper is made in the Main valley and at Stuttgart. Why should this industry be there?

Task 41. Study the shop scene in Fig. 36. Apart from the articles exhibited for sale, what else is there to suggest that wood is plentiful in the district?

Task 42. The Black Forest does a great trade in catering for tourists. From what you have read and seen in this section, name some attractions.

Task 43. Using Fig. 34, describe the positions of Frankfurt, Mainz and Nuremberg as places where routes meet.

The Saar

Just to the west of the rift valley, on the frontier of France, is the river Saar, flowing to the Moselle. In the Saar valley is a valuable coalfield, and an important industrial region has arisen. Close by are the great ironfields in Lorraine, so the Saar has many

Fig. 36. A gift-shop in the Black Forest
RENNER, FRANKFURT

Fig. 37. The Rhine Gorge at Bacharach
E.N.A.

blast furnaces where steel is made. Much coal goes to Lorraine for the French steel industry.

The Rhine Gorge

Once past Mainz, the Rhine passes through the Middle Rhine Highlands, into which it has cut a deep and narrow valley of great beauty. The Moselle has a similar valley as it flows to join the Rhine at Coblenz. A typical scene is shown in Fig. 37. The steep sides of the gorge are seen on both sides of the Rhine, and the small amount of level land which occurs here, has been used for the small town of Bacharach. On the far bank, there is just room for a railway and a road, the usual case in the Rhine Gorge. A train of barges moves downstream, and a pleasure steamer is tied up at Bacharach pier.

Task 44. If the barge train is moving downstream, on which bank of the river is Bacharach?

On the near bank magnificent vineyards spread down the slope to the town's edge. There are many on the far bank, too, and cultivated fields stretch far up the steep slopes as do the woodlands.

The Moselle valley also has slopes covered with vineyards. *Hock* and *Moselle* are well known wines which come from these vineyards.

Task 45. By using Fig. 34 and Fig. 37:

(*a*) Name the hills across the river in Fig. 37.

(*b*) To what city is the railway moving as it leaves the picture to the right?

(*c*) On which side of the picture will the Moselle join the Rhine?

Cologne

Fig. 38. Cologne from the Rhine

CAMERA PRESS

After nearly 70 miles of gorge, one reaches the pleasant town of Bonn, a small holiday town until it became the capital of West Germany after World

War II. Here the gorge opens out and the river enters the great plain of Northern Europe. Almost at once we come to the great city of Cologne (*Köln* in German). This great city is built where the road and railway between Paris and Berlin cross the important Rhine waterway. It has always been a great centre of routes and an important commercial city.

Fig. 38 shows the great cathedral and river steamers moored at the quays. You can see many new buildings which have replaced those destroyed in World War Two.

Task 46.

(*a*) The Allied bombers made many attacks on Cologne during the War. Why was Cologne so important a target?

(*b*) How does one go on board the steamers?

(*c*) How do the old and the new buildings differ in appearance?

Fig. 39 is a large scale map of the Ruhr. There is a

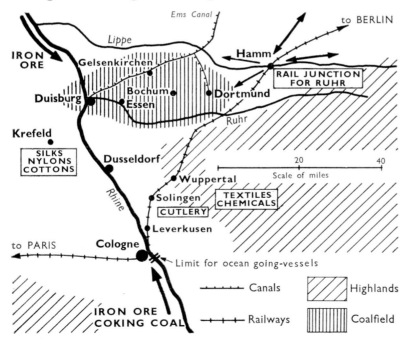

Fig. 39. *The Industrial Ruhr*

large and valuable coalfield. Iron from Siegland comes down the Rhine (Fig. 34), and from Lorraine, but not as much as is needed. Much also comes from Sweden. These two minerals have given rise to a tremendous steel industry. Almost every type of steel object is made in the Ruhr. Essen is a well known centre but each of the towns on the coalfield in Fig. 39 has over a quarter of a million people. They are steel centres. Textile industries have also settled in Wuppertal and on the west of the Rhine.

Task 47.

(*a*) Look at Fig. 39. From where does the iron and the coking coal come?

(*b*) What rivers does the coalfield lie between?

(*c*) Which town is famous for cutlery?

Duisburg and Dusseldorf are the main Ruhr ports on the river and are themselves big industrial towns. Hamm collects all the railway goods for distribution to the east. The Dortmund-Ems canal connects the Ruhr to Emden and German North Sea ports, but most of the traffic goes on the Rhine, through Holland.

Fig. 40 is a view in Duisburg. The steelworks are easy to see, as is the packed mass of factories and houses which covers the background. There are the usual

Fig. 40. *Duisburg*
ROTGANS

Rhine barges on the river, but also one ocean steamer. What a contrast from the beautiful scenes in the Gorge and Black Forest!

Task 48. Notice the shadow of the bridge on the water.

Are we looking at the east or west bank of the river?

Task 49

(*a*) Why should the Ford Motor Corporation establish their German works near Cologne?

(*b*) Why should it be cheaper to send a shipload of Swedish iron ore to the Ruhr via the Rhine rather than via Emden and the Dortmund-Ems Canal?

The Danube Basin

The valley of the Danube, in Germany, is of much less importance than that of the Rhine. The river rises in the Black Forest and flows south of the German Juras to enter Austria at Passau. The ridge of the Juras separates rivers flowing to the Danube from those flowing to the Rhine, *i.e.* it is the *watershed* between the two rivers.

Fig. 41. *Munich*

OERTER

There is one big city in the basin, however, Munich (or *Munchen*, in German). (Fig. 41). This city was the capital of the old kingdom of Bavaria, and is a big centre of routes to-day. On Fig. 33 you can see how the route from Paris to Vienna crosses the route from Berlin to Rome at Munich. The swift-flowing Isar provides water-power for electricity and salts are found locally, and so chemicals are manufactured. Surgical and other scientific instruments are also made here. Its population has grown to over one million.

The Weser Highlands

In the heart of Germany occurs a tangled mass of highlands of old, hard rocks, well worn into deep, wide valleys by the Weser and its tributaries. In Fig. 42 is a typical scene. The Weser flows through a very wide fertile valley, its floor covered with farms, cultivated fields and orchards. Its sides are densely wooded, and the tops of the ridges are either wooded or cleared for farms. Steamers and barges use the river, and roads and railways follow the valley. The hills rise to about 3,000 feet, the highest area being the Harz Mountains where the Brocken reaches 3,700 feet.

Fig. 42. On the banks of the Weser
HANS WAGNER

Task 50. In the background of Fig. 42 is a small town on the banks of the Weser. What can you see in the picture, which might explain why a town is there?

*Fig. 43. On
Luneburg Heath*
DEUTSCHE ZENTRALE

The Northern Plain

It is a large plain which grows larger as one moves eastwards into the East German Republic. Yet many areas are quite thinly peopled.

The reason is that a great deal of the region is like the view shown in Fig. 43, taken on the Luneburg Heath.

Task 51. Find the Luneburg Heath on Fig. 44. Between which towns does it lie? Examine Fig. 43 and note that there are **four** different features to be seen in this landscape. Make a list of them.

How Ice made the Landscape

During the Great Ice Age, sheets of ice moved slowly out of Scandinavia, across the Baltic and North Seas, and over these Northern Plains of Germany. They brought with them great quantities of earth, stones, boulders, sand and other things which they tore off the surface of the ground. Some of the boulders travelled in the ice from Scandinavia. When the ice sheets reached warmer latitudes, they melted, leaving extensive dumps of all the materials they carried in the form of ridges of hills, sandy plains, and large areas covered with *boulder clay*, a stiff soil, full of boulders and stones, formed under the ice-sheets as they moved

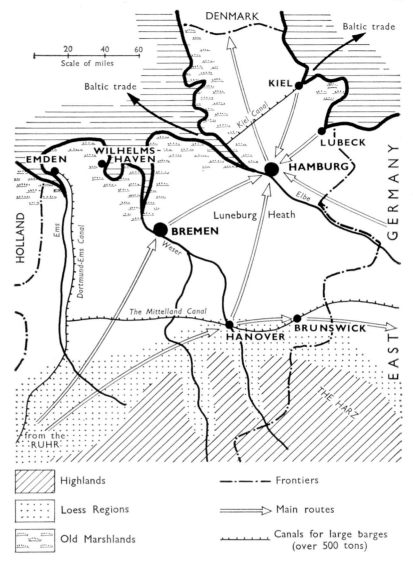

Fig. 44. German Seaports

along. The North German Plain is covered with these deposits.

Now we can see what happened to the landscape in Fig. 43. Great sheets of infertile sands mixed with huge boulders lie there. Great ridges of hills were formed, as in the background; sometimes fairly level plains were left behind, as in the foreground. Poor grass, heather, broom, and coniferous trees like pines and firs are all that will grow.

Scenes like that in Fig. 43 are typical of great areas of both East and West Germany, along the central portions of their plains.

To the south, round the hills, the soils are very fertile. They are called "loess", and were deposited by winds blowing fine particles from the ice-sheet deposits in the north, against the highlands of the south. Here large numbers of people live. Many towns are to be found, amongst them Hanover and Brunswick, with industries based on farming. Sugar-beet is a very important crop. Dairy cattle are fed on the crushed beet after the factories have finished with it.

Task 52. Look at Fig. 44, which shows six German seaports. Which of these:

(*a*) are on estuaries of large rivers;
(*b*) are in the marshland belt;
(*c*) are not on estuaries of any kind;
(*d*) are over 50 miles from the open sea?

Hamburg and Bremen are 60 miles from the open sea. Emden has some Ruhr trade. Kiel and Lubeck handle imported Danish dairy produce for the German cities. Bremen is a cotton and oil port, where American cotton and oil come into Germany. Wilhelmshaven is a naval base. Hamburg, with a population of nearly two millions, is a great world port. If you look at Fig. 33, you will see that, for all trade with America and the outside world, it is the natural port for Czechoslovakia and Eastern Germany. It is also a great route centre, as can be seen in Fig. 44. It has a great shipbuilding industry. In Fig. 45 you can see the docks. Notice what a great area they occupy. Cranes and warehouses stretch as far as the eye can see. This view, taken about twelve years after the end of World War II, shows the extraordinary amount of work that has gone into rebuilding the port, which was severely damaged in that War.

Fig. 45. *Hamburg Harbour*
CAMERA PRESS

Task 53. In Fig. 45:
(*a*) Can you see any evidence of rebuilding of damaged areas?
(*b*) What are the structures for, which stand out of the water in the middle of the docks?
(*c*) What is the structure in the extreme left fore-ground?

Waterways on the Plain

On Fig. 44 you will see three canals marked:
1. The Dortmund-Ems Canal, which we have already described.
2. The Kiel Canal, which takes ships up to 30,000 tons, was built for the convenience of the German navy so that it could move from the North Sea to the Baltic Sea without having to sail round Denmark. It has proved a tremendous boon to Baltic traffic and much of this now passes through the Canal. All the iron ore from Sweden to the Ruhr goes this way.
3. The Mittelland Canal (*Middle land*). This was opened in the 1930's and goes right through Germany to Berlin. It crosses rivers by aqueducts but for most of its length it follows a huge valley running from east to west across the plain.

Task 54.

(a) What effect do you think the creation of the East German Republic has had on the trade of Hamburg?

(b) Why should a portion of the dock there be reserved for Czechoslovakia?

THE EAST GERMAN REPUBLIC

This republic was separated from the rest of Germany in 1945 and is in the Russian sphere of influence.

Fig. 46 shows its main features. Nearly all of East Germany is in the northern plain with its infertile soils in the centre and north, and its fertile loess in the south. Most of its people live in the South, the old kingdom of Saxony, and here farms are rich and towns numerous. The large area of poor soils in the republic results in its small population of 17 millions, compared with the 58 millions in West Germany.

The Rich South

Saxony is not only a rich farming region, it is also a great manufacturing district. There is a small coal-field of good coal, and very extensive deposits of "brown coal", an inferior kind of heating material, often containing woody bands. The Germans have perfected methods of using brown coal in furnaces. The chemical industry is important. This is based on common salt and potash found at Stassfurt, and is located round Halle and Leipsig. Out of this chemical industry has grown a world-famous dyestuff industry, and another making photographic materials.

A large iron and steel industry has established itself around Chemnitz (Karlmarxstaat). This industry needs the good coking coal found here. Saxony also has a very large cotton industry around Chemnitz and woollens are manufactured at Gorlitz.

Task 55.

(a) How would iron ore from Spain and Sweden reach Chemnitz?

(b) Look at Fig. 46. Why should there be large new steel-works at Furstenburg in the north of the republic?

(c) Textiles use up large quantities of soft water. Where will Chemnitz and Gorlitz obtain this water?

Fig. 46. *The East German Republic*

Fig. 47. *Dresden*
E.N.A.

Leipsig is the largest city of the region. It is a great route centre in the middle of a rich plain and has developed printing and publishing industries as well as chemicals. Dresden was a very beautiful city, as you can see in Fig. 47, but it suffered severe damage during the Second World War. It was the residence of the kings of Saxony, and is built where the Elbe comes out of the Bohemian Highlands. The famous Dresden china is made some miles away. In the picture are the large 1,000-ton barges on the Elbe. These come right up to Dresden.

Berlin

Another concentration of people is found across the middle of East Germany in the great east-to-west valleys described in the pages on West Germany. In this corridor, full of important routes, stands Berlin, a city of $3\frac{1}{2}$ million people. It was the capital of all Germany before 1945, and the centre of all roads and railways. It is a great inland port and has a wide variety of light industries connected with food, clothing, furniture and

Fig. 48. *The Wall dividing East and West Berlin.*

EMBASSY OF THE FEDERAL
REPUBLIC OF GERMANY

luxury goods. To-day it is a curious political unit. East Berlin is the capital of the East German Republic, but West Berlin is in the control of American, British and French troops and forms a separate city, under a German mayor and corporation. This island of western life can only be approached through East German territory, and control is exercised over all traffic. In Fig. 48 you see, in the distance, East Berlin, in the foreground the Western sector. The wall and other obstacles were erected in 1961 by the East Germans to separate the two sectors.

Task 56.

(*a*) Examine Fig. 46 and say from what cities the arrows shown moving into Berlin on the west, south, and east, are coming.

(*b*) Why should over 80% of the trade of East Germany be with Russia and not with West Germany?

(*c*) From Fig. 46 suggest an area very suitable for open-air holidays in East Germany.

(*d*) Why has the trade of Rostock and Stralsund increased since 1945? Which great ports will have lost this trade? Why?

Task 57. Examine Fig. 48. What is the line of 'crosses' running along behind the wall?

CHAPTER 4

SCANDINAVIA

—HOW TO MAKE DO WITH VERY LITTLE

Britain and Scandinavia

The Scandinavian World of this chapter comprises the countries of Norway, Sweden, Finland and Denmark. It is a region of special interest to British people, partly because there is such a large element of Norwegian and Danish blood in British people; partly because of the close ties of World War II and, more recently, because Norway, Sweden and Denmark became members of the community known as "The Outer Seven" (*see Chapter* 10). The ties of blood come from past history. The Norwegians had a kingdom in the Shetlands and Hebrides in the Middle Ages, and the Norwegian to-day can make himself understood to the Shetlanders. The Danes settled all over the eastern half of England in the 10th and 11th Centuries, and Danish kings ruled over England in the 11th Century. The Danes settled even in Ireland, and Dublin is a Danish name.

Task 58. Look at a map of Europe, and answer the following questions:

(*a*) In what latitude do Stockholm, Helsinki and Oslo lie? These are the capital cities of Sweden, Finland and Norway.

(*b*) What part of Britain lies in this latitude?

(*c*) What British city lies due west of Copenhagen, the capital of Denmark?

(*d*) Which British cities lie west of the extreme south of Denmark?

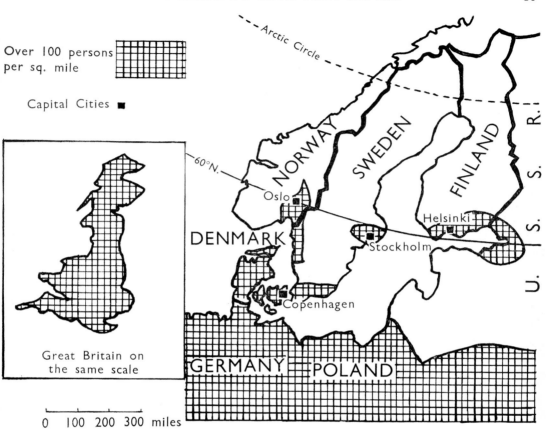

Over 100 persons per sq. mile

Capital Cities ■

Great Britain on the same scale

0   100 200 300 miles

Fig. 49. *Scandinavia*

Lands of Few People

If you look at Fig. 49 you can easily identify the four countries which make up Scandinavia, each with its capital city. On this map are shown those regions which have over 100 people per square mile of land, assuming the people to be spread evenly over the land. One hundred per square mile is not a great density. In ordinary terms it means that every person would have enough ground round him to make four full sized football fields. As you can see in Fig. 49, all of Germany and Poland, and much of Russia have more than 100 per square mile, and so has the British Isles. But notice how few districts in Scandinavia have such a density. All Denmark has, certainly, but only an odd patch here and there in the other countries. Scandinavian peoples are, in most cases, few and scattered.

Task 59. The following are the populations of these countries.

	Population in millions	Area in sq. miles
Denmark	$4\frac{1}{2}$	16,000
Norway	$3\frac{1}{2}$	120,000
Sweden	$7\frac{1}{2}$	170,000
Finland	$4\frac{1}{2}$	130,000

Work out the number of people per square mile in each country. Compare them with the following:

Great Britain   577 per square mile.
Germany (West and East) 603 per square mile.

From *Task* 59 you should have found that whilst the density of people in Denmark is only one-half of that in Britain or Germany, yet it is more than ten times greater than that in Norway, and over seven times greater than that in Sweden or Finland.

Naturally, we ask ourselves, why are Norway, Sweden and Finland so thinly peopled, and why should Denmark have so much greater a density? There are a number of reasons for this, and we will take them one by one.

Lands of the Midnight Sun

First, the position of Scandinavia, without Denmark, is very far north. It lies from 56°N. to beyond 70°N. This means that the northern ports are within the line of latitude called The Arctic Circle, $66\frac{1}{2}$°N. This was dealt with in *Map Reading Book*, Chapter 17. So, at Hammerfest, the sun shines for six weeks without setting (June and half July), and then never rises for six weeks in winter (December and half January). For the rest of the year it rises and sets, but days in winter are very short and nights long, whilst days in summer are very long and nights short.

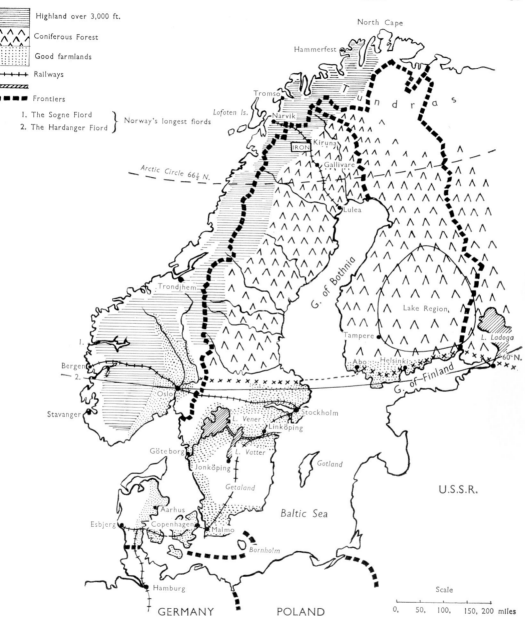

Highland over 3,000 ft.

Coniferous Forest

Good farmlands

Railways

Frontiers

1. The Sogne Fiord
2. The Hardanger Fiord
} Norway's longest fiords

Fig. 50. The Scandinavian Lands

The effect of this on the climate of Scandinavia is most marked. The winters are of great length. The heat received from the sun is very small. Summers are warm but very short. The angle of the sun is very low most of the year, and the land freezes for long periods. The Baltic Sea freezes for three months in its northern parts. Scandinavia is not a region likely to attract large numbers of people.

Denmark, however, in the latitude of northern England, has better conditions, similar to those in northern England, though colder in winter.

Task 60. If the sun moves round the sky at Hammerfest for six weeks without setting, try to work out its daily path, *e.g.* where is it at noon; at midnight?

Mountains and Fiords

The second reason for the small number of people in Scandinavia lies in its surface features. On Fig. 50 you can see that down the middle runs *The Kiolen* (Keel), a mass of high mountains and moorlands which are often over 5,000 feet high. The great bulk of Norway consists of these mountains and Sweden has a large share, too. They are made of very old, tough rocks, with poor, thin soils, and because they are so far north, they are generally useless to man. The area shaded on Fig. 50 is almost unusable land.

Fig. 51. Part of the coast of Norway

On the Atlantic coast these mountains descend steeply by short valleys which end at the sea in long, deep, steep-sided inlets called *fiords*. Norway consists of one fiord after another, with steep rises to the hills behind. Look at Fig. 51 which shows a section of the coast. You may amuse yourselves by

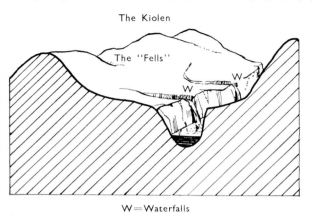

Fig. 52. Section of a fiord

trying to count how many fiords there are.

Fig. 52 shows a drawing of a fiord. The upper slopes are useless. The lower slopes are too bleak, except in the short summer, and too exposed for any villages or farms. The fiord sides are too steep and there is little lowland to build on or cultivate. No wonder so few people live in Norway.

In Fig. 53 is a view of a fiord to illustrate this. You can see the Kiolen in the background, the poor nature of the lower slopes, and the steep sides of the fiord. One waterfall is seen. The few houses and the road hug the sides of the fiord.

Sweden and Finland are lower than Norway, but they have the same hard, tough rocks in most parts, so farming is just as difficult as in Norway.

Fig 53. The Sognefjord

J. ALLAN CASH

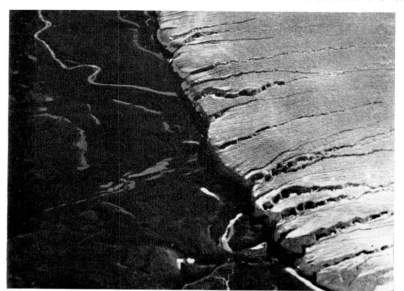

Fig. 54. *An ice-sheet*
in Greenland
THE TIMES

Ice has been at work

Another great drawback to the use of the land in Scandinavia is the effect of ice-sheets in the Great Ice Age. Thousands of years ago, for reasons not entirely clear to us, enormous ice-sheets slowly spread out from Scandinavia into large areas of Russia, Poland, Germany and Britain. They were hundreds of feet thick. Under pressure from more and more ice forming in Scandinavia, they moved slowly outwards until they reached lands where the sun melted them as fast as they moved forward. In Fig. 54 you see a Greenland ice-sheet of to-day. Its edge is breaking up under the action of the sun, and many streams run from it. Notice how it seems to break up along long gashes. This is because, as the sheet nears its end, friction with the ground melts the ice underneath and rivers begin to flow in tunnels under the ice. These *gashes* mark ice tunnels which have collapsed.

The ice-sheets ground their way over the land surfaces, removing soils and pulverising them, along with rocks and vegetation, into very stony clays called *boulder clays*. These were formed under the ice as it moved steadily forward. When the ice-sheets melted, the boulders, sand, gravel and clay carried under and in the ice were dropped in great untidy mounds and ridges called *moraines*. In Fig. 54 there are many, but they are not very clearly seen. You can tell they are there by the behaviour of the streams running from the ice. None of them flow straight, but all wind among the moraines. Notice, also, the sheets of water left amongst the moraines.

This is yet another reason why Scandinavia has so few people.

Task 61. From what you have learned so far, write down two reasons why there are so few people in: (*a*) Norway; (*b*) Sweden; (*c*) Finland.

Look at Fig. 55, which shows the main facts about the climate of Scandinavia. In Chapter 1 you read of the kind of weather brought by the Atlantic streams of air between 30°N. and 60°N. Frontal rain is heavy in most months. Here, in Scandinavia, this weather extends to 70°N. Also, as winds rise against the Kiolen, very heavy relief rains occur. Thus, for most months of the year, Norway has extremely heavy rains and dense clouds. Look at the picture of Tromso (Fig. 58), and notice how the rain clouds are piling up against the hills. This is quite normal in Norway. Bergen has 73 inches of rain in a year, the usual rainfall on the Atlantic coasts.

Fig. 55. The climate of Scandinavia

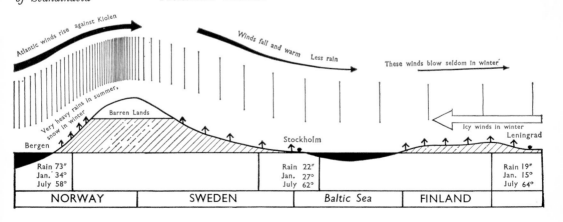

Denmark, too, has this Atlantic air but, because it is very low-lying, the rainfall is much less and its climate rather like that of the English or Scottish lowlands.

Across the Kiolen things change rapidly. The westerly streams begin their descent of the slopes and become drier. Rainfall diminishes to totals of 22 inches at Stockholm and 19 inches at Leningrad, just east of Finland. There is less cloud and summers are sunnier. However, winters are most severe, for Atlantic air cannot penetrate as far east as this. The very cold air over the Russian region moves in and makes the Baltic region very cold indeed. Norway and Denmark, under the influence of warmer Atlantic air, are not so cold in winter as is the rest of the Baltic region.

Task 62. From what you have just read you should easily find the answers to the following:

(*a*) Why are the January temperatures at Bergen, Stockholm and Leningrad progressively lower as one goes east? (*N.B.* 32°F. is the freezing point of water.)

(*b*) Why are the July temperatures of these three towns progressively higher as one goes east?

The Atlantic Drift

One other feature of the climate has yet to be mentioned. Blown by the westerlies, the surface waters of the Atlantic move up from the warm regions, as the North Atlantic Drift (Fig. 3), and flow right round the North of Norway. The effect of this is to keep the coasts of that country, even in the far north, free from serious ice trouble all through the year. On Fig. 56, a view in the Lofoten Islands, you can see the wintry, snow-covered land. Yet the waters are free of ice. This is at 68°N., well inside the Arctic Circle.

Hydro-Electric Power

Another drawback to life in Scandinavia is that none of the countries has any coal, but they do have enormous supplies of *white coal*, *i.e.* electricity which they obtain cheaply from their swift-flowing rivers and waterfalls.

Fig. 56. Henningsvar, in the Lofoten Islands

E.N.A.

In Finland, the rivers, breaking through the great end-moraine, provide rapids and falls for hydro-electric power, and much is used in the towns and farms along the south coasts. Only Denmark is without both coal and hydro-electric power. The other three countries require very little coal from abroad, but Denmark requires a great deal.

Task 63. Of what use will cheap hydro-electric power be to:

(*a*) a farmer;

(*b*) a lumberer;

(*c*) those who work near and within the Arctic Circle?

Task 64. Make a list, from what you have read so far in this chapter, of the ways in which Denmark differs from Norway and Sweden.

*Fig. 57. Norway:
a saeter on the high
pastures*

E.N.A.

The Countries of Scandinavia
1. NORWAY

Norwegians live in scattered communities in the fiords wherever a little flat land is available. A few fields of hay, oats, potatoes, and vegetables are found but there is no room for animal pastures. Hence, the cows and goats are driven to pastures high up in the mountains, when the snows of winter and spring have melted. Here, women and boys live all summer in huts called *Saeters*, where they tend the animals. In autumn the men come up and take the animals down to winter stalls where they are fed on crops grown on the valley floors by the men during the summer. During autumn and winter many of the men go to the fishing fleets.

Fig. 57 is a typical *saeter*. The women make butter and cheese from cows' and goats' milk. Boys tend the animals on the hills. The buildings to the right of the picture are those where cheese and butter are made and stored. Notice the rough condition of the buildings and the poor nature of the plant life. As usual, winds are piling clouds against the mountain tops.

Task 65. After looking at Figs. 53, 56 and 57, write a brief description of a typical Norwegian house.

A Nation of Fishermen

Because the Norwegians can obtain so little from the land, they look to the sea instead. They make use of the sea in two ways. First, they own a very great number of ships which they use, on all the world's trade routes, to fetch and carry for other nations. Mostly, they are all modern ships and although there are so few Norwegians they have more ships than any other country, except the U.S.A., Britain, and Japan. Shipping brings much wealth to Norway.

Second, they have very large fishing fleets of three types. There are big inshore fisheries which catch brisling, or sardines as we call them, and take them to Bergen and Stavanger for tinning. They also have trawler fleets in the northern seas, and small boats offshore, which catch cod and herring. In Fig. 56 is a scene in the Lofoten Islands where the fleets bring in cod to be made into cod liver oil.

Finally, they have a large whaling fleet in Antarctica every year.

Task 66. Look at the boats in Fig. 56. Make a drawing of one of these boats. Would you expect these boats to venture far out into the Atlantic? Give your reasons.

Fig. 58. Tromsö, a fishing port
PAUL POPPER LTD.

Many of the towns of Norway are small fishing ports, where catches are landed, then frozen or tinned, and where extracts like paste, glue and fertilisers are made. These towns are not up fiords, but on the open coast between fiords, usually on islands. Fig. 58 shows Tromso, a typical fishing port. Hammerfest, further north, is also on an island. Bergen (114,000) is a large port and headquarters of the fishing industries. Stavanger (52,800) is also very important.

Task 67.
(*a*) On Fig. 58, from which side would a steamer from Oslo come into Tromso?
(*b*) In what direction are you looking on Fig. 58?

Oslo

The capital of Norway is not a large city, as capital cities go. It is the size of Edinburgh or Dublin (460,000). It has a wonderful situation for a capital of a country where land routes are so difficult. Fig. 50 shows this.

Task 68. Study carefully Fig. 50, then write down three advantages that Oslo possesses as Norway's capital.

Task 69. One railway to Oslo on this map was most difficult to build and was opened as recently as 1916. Which railway do you think it is?

2. SWEDEN

Sweden has the largest population of the Scandinavian countries. This is because it has more farmland than any of them. The Swedish slope, generally eastwards, is cut into by swift rivers which contain many lakes and waterfalls. These are a valuable source of hydro-electric power but, even more useful, they provide transport for logs in the great lumbering industry.

In the Northern Forests

Half the country is covered by great coniferous forests, the type which we saw occupied so much of Russia (*The Asiatic World*). Because Sweden has so many usable rivers leading to the Baltic, timber and made-up timber products can be readily sent abroad. All these forests are lumbered but especially the southern part, which has better trees.

Fig. 59. Collecting timber for the saw-mill

AEROFILMS

Logs are cut in the winter, taken to the rivers, and in spring, when these thaw, the logs float down to the great saw-mills run by electric power, near the mouths of the rivers.

Fig. 59 is a scene typical of both Swedish and Finnish forests. The forests stretch endlessly away from the camera, and in the foreground a lake is being used to collect the timber together as it moves down with the current. Notice the booms which are used to control the movement of the logs. Nearby there is a saw-mill which will cut up the timber.

Task 70. In Fig. 59 there is a saw-mill in the far rear (centre). Examine the booms, then work out how the logs nearest the camera could be moved down to the mill.

Swedish Farmers

The farmland of Sweden is in the south, mainly in the *Lake Depression*. Most of the farms are fully electrified, because hydro-electric power is so cheap in Sweden. Dairying flourishes and butter, cheese, eggs, bacon, and meat are plentiful. These food products are actually exported to the less favoured lands of Norway and Finland.

High Grade Manufactures

The Swedes have a great reputation for the making of high grade articles, in both metal and wood. The metal used is chiefly iron, of which large amounts are mined around Kiruna inside the Arctic Circle. During the winter, when there is very little daylight, arc lights are used to help the miners. This iron ore is extremely valuable and is in great demand in Germany and Britain. In summer, when the Baltic Sea is open, the iron ore is brought by train to Lulea for export. But, in winter, when the Baltic is frozen, the iron ore is sent by another railway crossing the Kiolen to Narvik, in Norway. Yet Narvik is 500 miles further north than Lulea.

Fig. 60. *Lulea*
SWEDISH TOURIST
TRAFFIC ORGANISATION

Fig. 60 is a scene in Lulea during the busy summer season. In the foreground a train of ore is being loaded into a steamer. In the harbour are ships waiting their turn to be loaded.

Task 71.

(*a*) Why are all buildings in Lulea made of timber?

(*b*) What kind of waggons carry the ore?

(*c*) What latitude is Narvik? One other railway in the world reaches this latitude. Can you find it? It was dealt with in *The Asiatic World*.

The steel industries are found chiefly around Kiruna and Gallivare, in the north. The timber industries are in the coast towns north of Stockholm.

The towns of Jönköping, Linköping, and Norrköping, all in the Lake Depression, produce a great variety of goods; textiles, chemicals, farm machinery, telephones, etc., all in small quantities, chiefly for the home market.

In this Lake Depression there is a canal for small ships which connects Göteborg with Stockholm. It runs through Lakes Vener and Vatter, and although 240 miles long, has only 56 miles of made canal. The rest is rivers and lakes. It is a very useful means of moving raw materials to the industrial towns.

In Fig. 61 you can see a lock on the canal.

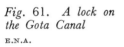

Fig. 61. A lock on the Gota Canal

E.N.A.

Fig. 62.   *Stockholm*
FOX PHOTOS

Swedish Towns

The capital, Stockholm, has well over one million people living in and near it. It is a beautiful city, built on many islands in the channel between Lake Malar and the sea. From this it receives its name *The Venice of the North*. It has a commanding position in the Baltic. On Fig. 62 one sees the business centre, with its impressive buildings and modern arrangements of flyover roads.

Task 72. Look at Fig. 62.

(*a*) On which side of the road does traffic move in Sweden?

(*b*) Find: (1) an open air market;

(2) a park for cars;

(3) the Royal Palace.

Fig. 63. Göteborg, the Atlantic port of Sweden

FOX PHOTOS

Göteborg (pronounced yu-te-bor) has over 400,000 people. It is the chief Atlantic port of Sweden, and so has all the American trade. It makes matches for export. It is the place where the Gota canal begins. Fig. 63 shows the port front. If you look carefully, you may see a line of cars waiting to be loaded into trains. They are one of Sweden's chief imports.

Another large town in south Sweden is Malmo. It connects by train ferry with Copenhagen. There are ironworks, textile factories and breweries. It exports dairy produce, matches and timber.

The Swedish people are modern and very progressive in their outlook, whereas the Norwegians are much more conservative.

The country of Sweden is prosperous, for it avoided taking part in both World Wars, which took a heavy toll of all the other Scandinavian countries.

Task 73. The following are the chief exports of Sweden, in order of importance: timber, wood-pulp, paper, machinery, iron ore, steel, ball-bearings, matches, food products.

(*a*) How many of these come from the coniferous forests?

(*b*) How many depend on the Kiruna iron ore?

(*c*) What food products are exported, and from where?

*Fig. 64. Helsinki,
the Market Square
and Harbour Front*
PAUL POPPER LTD.

3. FINLAND

Finland, though linked with Sweden, is a republic dependent largely upon Russia. It has a harsh, cold climate, like that of its neighbour, Russia.

Glaciers have scraped away most of the soil, and left the countryside covered with hundreds of lakes. It is primarily a country of rocks and lakes, with here and there small patches of soil.

There are no high mountains but there are two very high moraines. They are called the Salpausselka and follow the coastline. South of the Salpausselka lies the only good farmland in Finland.

The language is Finnish, though Swedish is spoken in the coastal districts. Finnish is not like Swedish, but is more like Bulgarian.

The country is poor, and there are few minerals. The greatest asset is the numerous waterfalls from which electricity is obtained. There are hydro-electric stations everywhere. Railways are mostly electric. Indeed, it is difficult to see how Finland could survive were it not for her waterfalls.

Finland has extensive forests which are cut and then the logs are floated down the rivers and lakes in summer.

Industries connected with timber are numerous and important.

The principal town is Helsinki, the capital, a town of nearly 500,000 people. It is a city of fine buildings of which the railway station is a striking example.

In Fig. 64 one sees the harbour front at Helsinki. When compared with Stockholm (Fig. 62), its buildings are not so imposing. There is not the same air of prosperity as in Sweden.

Task 74. Fig. 65 is a Finnish paper mill near Helsinki. Paper is a big export from the country. There are workers' houses in the background and a very modern mill in the foreground.

(*a*) What kind of trees are they in the picture, deciduous or coniferous?

(*b*) From this, say why the picture must have been taken in the extreme south of Finland.

(*c*) Find evidence that (*i*) rail transport is used by the mill; (*ii*) market gardening is being carried on near the mill.

(*d*) What does the absence of smoky chimneys suggest to you about how the mill is run?

Fig. 65. A Finnish paper mill, near Helsinki

AEROFILMS

*Fig 66. A typical
Danish village*

AEROFILMS

4. DENMARK

Denmark is a small land without any hills higher than 500 feet, in the entrance to the Baltic Sea. Nature has been kinder to Denmark than to the other Scandinavian countries. Her basic soils are good and her climate not unlike that of Britain. Parts of Jutland have been spoiled by morainic dumping but the boulder clays over the rest are quite good soils. With fairly warm summers, winters cold but not long, rainfalls light but in all months, it is a very fine country for grass and animal farming and on that all its prosperity is based.

When Britain and Germany developed so many large industrial towns in the nineteenth century, and enormous numbers of people went to live in them, a huge demand arose for foods of all kinds to feed these populations. So, Denmark made herself into a great dairy farm, with enormous success. Butter, bacon and eggs are exported to Britain and Germany. Wheat and other human foods, as well as some animal foods, are imported. Danes eat scarcely any butter; margarine is more in demand there.

A Danish Village

Look at Fig. 66. It is a village of a type which can be seen all over Denmark, the same kind of pleasant houses and farms, the same type of church, the same neat roads. Every house is gaily painted and has a red tile roof. Much of the village is made up of smallholders, who own their farms, and who farm perhaps 5 acres, or 15 acres or even 50 acres. Their small strips of cultivation can be seen around the village, in contrast to the bigger fields of the large farmers. Often the smallholders own strips in the larger fields.

All farmers grow grass in rotation with oats, rye, green crops, and lucerne, a large clover-type of plant. Meadows, of the British fashion, are seldom seen. All these crops are used to feed cattle, sleek, fat, dark red animals, which are found all over Denmark (*The Danish Reds*). Their milk goes to creameries, where the fat is taken out to make butter and cheese, and the skimmed-milk returned to the farmer to feed pigs. Co-operative societies, amongst the farmers, own dairies, creameries, egg stations, machinery to lend out to small farmers, experimental farms, and even banks. Government inspectors grade produce for export. The small towns are centres for collecting and despatching produce, and for buying and selling from and to the farmers.

In Fig. 67 you can see the routes by which Danish produce reaches Britain and Germany. There is a very good system of train ferries connecting the islands and mainland, and express trains and long goods trains take only a few minutes to run on board. In Fig. 68 are two small ferries, at Elsinore, plying across the Sound.

Task 75. In Fig. 66.

(*a*) (*i*) Find the village school; (*ii*) Find the home of a large farmer.

(*b*) Find a large barn stocked with fodder.
Who do you think will own it?

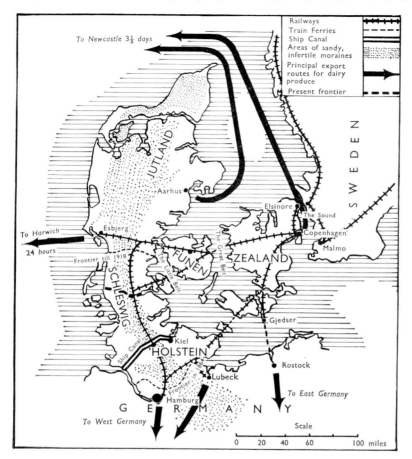

Fig. 67.   Denmark

Task 76. Look at Fig. 67.
(*a*) Name the two chief islands of Denmark.
(*b*) Describe the journey of a cargo of butter from Zealand to Britain by two different routes.
(*c*) From which ports does Jutland butter go out?
(*d*) Note the frontier changes since 1864. In that year Germany attacked Denmark. What happened after that?

Copenhagen

The capital of Denmark has a wonderful position on the Sound, commanding the entrance to the Baltic

Sea. (The other entrances, the Little and Great Belts, are too shallow for larger ships). The Sound begins at Elsinore (Fig. 68), where an ancient castle barred

Fig. 68. Elsinore. A railway ferry-boat at the landing-stage

E.N.A.

the way to all ships. It is seen in Fig. 68 in the background. It is famous to British people as *Hamlet's Castle*, for Shakespeare laid the scene of that great play in this castle at Elsinore. To-day the town is famous for its small, but very efficient ship-building yards, seen in the picture. In Fig. 69 a ship is seen leaving for Stockholm. Once again, notice the ship-building yards in the rear. Denmark makes all its own ships, chiefly along the Sound.

Fig. 69. Leaving Copenhagen for Stockholm

E.N.A.

Because it has such a good position, Copenhagen has become a great market and business centre for Baltic trade. It is the largest city in Scandinavia, with a population of about 1 million. This is one-quarter of all the Danish people. Its business streets are very dignified as is seen in Fig. 70.

Fig. 70. *Copenhagen*
E.N.A.

Task 77

(*a*) Which side of the road does traffic drive on in Denmark?

(*b*) Where will Denmark obtain iron and steel for her ship-building?

(*c*) Look at the crowd in Fig. 69. Does it differ much from a British crowd? Are the Danes a blonde people, like the Swedes?

CHAPTER 5

SWITZERLAND AND AUSTRIA
—LIFE IN THE MOUNTAINS

In chapter 3 we studied the German peoples lying from the Alps to the northern seas. There are, however, two small nations in the Alps themselves, and they are also of German culture and civilisation. They are Austria, which is entirely German-speaking and has seven million people, and Switzerland of which two-thirds is German-speaking, and numbers five million people.

Different Kinds of Mountains

Look at Figs. 71 and 72. Fig. 71 is a highland region like the Vosges Mountains or the Central Plateau of France, or the Rhine Highlands, but Fig. 72 is like the Alps. In the Alps, the ranges run in lines, with wide valleys between. The rocks of which they have

Skyline of rounded hills—of more or less similar height

5,000 ft.

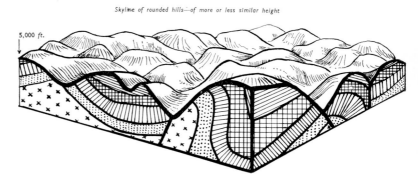

Fig. 71. Old, worn-down highlands

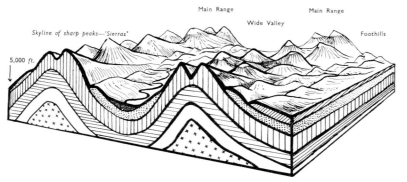

Fig. 72. A region of young folded mountains

been composed have been folded up by gigantic earth movements (see *The Foundations*, Chapter 1). The upfolds have formed the ranges, and the downfolds the valleys. Frost has shattered the high parts and formed sharp peaks; running water and ice have worn away the slopes and added soils to the valleys.

These foldings took place in what is regarded as recent times in the long history of the earth, that is, a matter of 50-million years ago. There has not been time for frost, ice and water to wear them down to lower hills and ridges, or for movements of the outer crust to break them up into blocks. The highlands were probably once high folded ranges, but are now worn down to low rounded hills and deep valleys. This is shown in Fig. 71. The highlands of Britain are in this condition.

Now look at Fig. 73 which shows the two kinds of mountains in Central Europe. It is obvious that the great earth movement which folded the younger, softer rocks, did not fold the old, tough, highland blocks. The folds seem to have *wrapped themselves round* the old resistant blocks and formed into loops. You may get a similar effect by covering a table with a heavy cloth. Place books here and there on the cloth, and then push the tablecloth up into folds against the books.

Inside the loops of the mountains, extensive sinking took place, and great hollows formed. These often filled up with fertile sediments brought down by rivers from the mountains. On Fig. 73 you see the plains

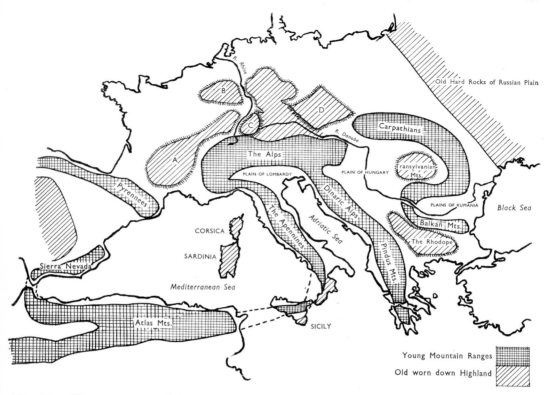

Fig. 73. The mountains of Central Europe

of Lombardy, Hungary and Rumania, which were formed in this way. Such plains are the best farmlands in southern Europe.

Task 78. On Fig. 73:

(*a*) Name highlands A-D. What rivers are shown?

(*b*) Why are the Alps curved into an arc?

(*c*) Why are the Carpathians and Balkan Mountains shaped like a question mark?

(*d*) How was the Adriatic Sea formed?

Life in an Alpine Valley

Life in Switzerland and Austria is largely life in the valleys, both great and small, between the mountain ranges. A typical valley is shown in Fig. 74. There is a lower square-shaped portion, where the ice was at work during the Ice Age, and an upper, less steep portion not so much affected by the ice, which collected mainly in the lower parts. The ice still exists in the higher ranges, for they lie above the *snow line*, *i.e.* snow never melts there. So snowfields occur, and these are slowly pressed into ice, which moves down the slope as *glaciers*, or rivers of ice. In the Alps these glaciers are small, but they occur in many upper valleys. From them issue the rivers of the Alps, like the Rhine and the Rhône.

In some ways these valleys are like those of Norway except that in Norway the sea has invaded the valley floors and converted the lower parts into fiords.

Fig. 74. *Andermatt, a Swiss valley*
PAUL POPPER LTD.

There are the same steep sides of the ice-shaped lower part, the same waterfalls on the sides which provide electric power, the same forests on the lower slopes, the same summer pastures above the forests. In Switzerland these summer pastures are called *Alps*, and they have given their name to the mountains.

Task 79.

(*a*) In what ways do the mountains of Norway differ from the Alps?

(*b*) Why should Alpine valleys contain many more people than Norwegian valleys?

Fig. 74 is a view of Andermatt and shows a great valley in the heart of Switzerland. You can see the

Fig. 75. Milking-time, 6,000 feet up. The Eggishorn, Switzerland

FOX PHOTOS

snowfields in the rear, the forest belt, and the *Alps* still partially under snow, for the view was taken in early summer. Dotted all over the valley and lower slopes are small buildings, called *chalets*. These correspond to the *saeters* of Norway. In Fig. 75 you can see a chalet, the *dairy shed* near it, and boys milking the cows. You can also see the deep valley behind, the forest belt and the snowfields of the high ranges. Down in the valley the farmer is cultivating wheat, oats, rye, root-crops, fruits and even vines on the sunny lower slopes, for Switzerland is only 46° from the equator.

Task 80. Compare the chalets in Fig. 75 with the saeter in Fig. 57 and say what you notice.

In Fig. 76 you see a herd coming down to the valley in September. Notice the big cowbells hung round their necks. All cattle carry bells of different tones. When they are wandering on the alp they can always be found by the sound of the bells.

Fig. 76. Cattle returning to the valley in September
SWISS NATIONAL TOURIST OFFICE

When the cattle have left the alp, the men stay to collect all grass left there, to be taken down for winter fodder.

Winter Sports

With the coming of holiday-makers to the Alps a

Fig. 77. Winter sports at Arosa
J. ALLAN CASH

use has been found for the upper summer pastures even in mid-winter. They become winter sports centres. In Fig. 77 is one such centre, Arosa near St. Moritz, at a height of about 6,000 feet. Together with summer tourism, this winter sports activity has become a major industry in Switzerland and Austria.

Task 81.

(*a*) Contrast conditions on the mountain tops with those on the skating rink in Fig. 77.

(*b*) Estimate the depth of snow on the hotel roof in the centre.

Fig. 78. Switzerland and Austria

A Survey of Switzerland

If you look at Fig. 78 you will see that there are three regions in Switzerland.

1. The Juras, on the French frontier.
2. The great Alpine ranges covering half the country.
3. The plateau between these regions.

The Juras

These are perfectly formed folded ranges, not very high, with ridge and valley formation in parallel lines.

Fig. 79. Cattle in a Jura valley
SWISS NATIONAL TOURIST OFFICE

The ridges are densely wooded except on the tops where summer pastures occur. These are used as in the Alps. The valleys are fertile and well farmed. Fig. 79 shows typical meadows with sleek dairy cows. The milk is made into butter and cheese, but also into condensed milk, cream cheese and chocolate, for export to other countries. Small factories do this in the towns.

The great industry is watch-making. There is plenty of hydro-electric power in the Juras and, indeed, all over Switzerland, so factories are all-electric. Fig. 80 is a scene in a factory where watches are assembled.

The people of this part of Switzerland all speak French as a glance at names in an atlas will show.

Task 82. Look carefully at Fig. 80. Write down

Fig. 80. The Longines Watch Factory, St. Imier, Switzerland
PAUL POPPER LTD.

anything that shows Swiss industry to be very modern, well organised, and pleasant for the worker.

Alpine Switzerland

Much has been said about this already. If you look at Fig. 78 you will see that the ranges run in two great masses with a great valley between. This valley is really two valleys, running in opposite directions from the St. Gotthard mass of mountains. In one valley runs the Rhône and in the other the Rhine. In the ranges to the south are the two great passes, the Simplon and the St. Gotthard.

Task 83.

(*a*) Into what lakes do the Rhône and Rhine flow as they leave the Alps?

(*b*) What other river valley flows in a similar direction out of Switzerland into Austria? In Switzerland this valley is called the Engadine. It is a popular tourist district.

The same industries are found, based on cattle products, as in the Juras. The milk from the *alps* is now being transferred to the valleys by plastic pipe-lines. This has overcome the difficulty which farmers had to face of moving the milk to the valleys whilst it was still fresh. Unable to do so, butter and cheese had to be made on the *alp*. Now the pipe-lines convey it quickly to the factories producing cream-cheese, choco-late, and condensed milk.

Fig. 81. A train which has just travelled south through the St. Gotthard tunnel

SWISS NATIONAL TOURIST OFFICE

There is a great amount of hydro-electric power in the Alps, enough for all Switzerland. All railways are electrified. In Fig. 81 you see a train which has just emerged from the south end of the St. Gotthard tunnel. Much hydro-electric power is obtained from the water running down the hillsides in the rear of the picture.

Task 84.

(*a*) What are the small buildings on the rear slopes?

(*b*) This view is facing towards Italy. Why should there be so little snow on the mountains?

(*c*) What is the shield with a cross on the front of the train?

In Fig. 81 the train has passed through the St. Gotthard tunnel and is moving down the Italian slope of the Alps called Ticino. This is much sunnier and warmer than the rest of Switzerland. The people speak Italian. The station name, Airolo, is Italian. In Fig. 82 is the town of Lugano, in Ticino, on the shores of Lake Lugano. It is one of the most beautiful towns in the world. You will see how *Mediterranean*

Fig. 82. *Lugano*
FOX PHOTOS

are its buildings. The forests extend high up the hillsides, too.

Task 85. Compare the buildings in Lugano with those in Fig. 77. What do you notice?

The Plateau

Here the mountains die away, leaving a rough surface crossed by many low ridges. Rivers from the Alps make deep valleys across the plateau to enter the Rhine and Aar. At the mouths of the Alpine valleys, where they come out on to the plateau, is a line of lakes, formed behind moraines from the Ice Age. The rivers flow strongly and many big hydro-electric power stations are sited on them. This is one of the densely peopled parts of Europe, and helps to give Switzerland a very high density of 361 people per square mile.

Industry

Swiss industry has to depend on imported raw materials for, except for some iron, the country contains none. Since the country is difficult to reach from the ocean ports of Europe, it does not pay to import big quantities of materials. So the industries are those using small amounts of material, but requiring great skill. In the towns are found light engineering, some heavy engineering like steam engines and turbines, textile machinery, cotton goods, silk goods, embroidery, knitted goods and, of course, watches and clocks. Recently, chemical industries have been set up in Basle, and manures and aluminium in the Rhône valley, in the Alps.

Towns

The main town is Zurich (444,000), by far the largest town in Switzerland. It has become a great route centre, for all plateau routes north-eastwards into Germany, and eastwards to Austria, meet there, together with a route from Milan via the St. Gotthard. It has many industries and is a great centre for technical education. Fig. 83 is a view of the town and lake. This makes clear that in addition to being a rail and industrial centre, it also attracts tourists.

Fig. 83. *Zurich*
SWISS NATIONAL TOURIST
OFFICE

Task 86.

(*a*) To import and export, Switzerland can use one of her towns which is a barge port on a big river. Name the port and river.

(*b*) Which is the nearest port to Switzerland on the Mediterranean? Which railways will she use to connect with this port?

(*c*) Describe (*i*) the route of a box of watches from Switzerland to London; (*ii*) the route of a consignment of cotton from Egypt to Zurich.

Lucerne is another town at the end of a lake. The beauty of the surroundings makes its biggest industry catering for tourists, but there are also metal industries.

Basle (214,000) is the great river port and railway centre, and it has many industries. Berne (170,000) is the capital in the centre of the plateau, and on the Simplon route. Geneva (178,000) is a beautiful city at the end of Lake Geneva.

Task 87. The number of people per square mile in Norway is 29, but in Switzerland it is 361. Both are mountainous countries. Try to suggest some reasons why there should be so many more people per square mile in Switzerland.

A Survey of Austria

Austria is much larger than Switzerland, and its population is 7 millions. This works out at about 224 per square mile, lower than that of Switzerland, but a great density for a mountainous land.

The Austrian Alps

These are similar to those of Switzerland, but are wider and not so high. Life is much the same. There is a great deal of lumbering from the forests, which cover over one-third of Austria, and much timber is supplied to the treeless plains of Hungary and Yugoslavia, to the east.

The crops on the valley floors include much fruit, and excellent wines are produced.

Innsbruck, where the main east-to-west line is crossed by the north-south line over the Brenner Pass, is a great tourist centre.

The Brenner Pass is the lowest of the Alpine passes, being only 4,500 feet high. It carries the traffic from

Fig. 84. The Frontier post on the Brenner Pass

ITALIAN STATE TOURIST OFFICE

Central Europe into Italy. In Fig. 84 you see a view of this pass, showing how much motor traffic uses it.

Task 88.

(*a*) The Brenner pass is on the frontier between Austria and Italy. What is there in the picture which shows it to be a frontier? (Middle distance, on left.)

(*b*) What time of the year was the picture taken? Give reasons.

(*c*) The view is looking north. To which country are the cars in the front of the picture going?

Salzburg, on the Salz, is another great tourist centre noted for its festivals of music.

Industry in the Alps

The valleys of the Mur and Drava run eastwards from the Alps into Yugoslavia, and there is quite a concentration of industry in this region. Valuable deposits of mercury are found and extracted at Klagenfurt. Copper, lead and brown coal are mined, too. There is a useful oilfield as well. Graz is another industrial town. Both Klagenfurt and Graz are on the main railway from Vienna to Trieste, a seaport on the Adriatic.

The Danube Valley

Here lies a broad and fertile valley, well farmed and with numerous villages and small towns, which is also one of Europe's great highways of movement.

Thus it is not surprising to find the capital, Vienna, and a good deal of industry there. In the valley, too, lives the bulk of the Austrian people.

Industry centres in Linz and Steyr, in Upper Austria, and Vienna and Wiener-Neustadt (Vienna New Town) in Lower Austria. The iron ore from the Ems valley comes down to Steyr and Linz where there are important steel industries. As well, it can go by rail to the Vienna area where cars, cycles and lorries are now being made.

Task 89. Compare the kinds of industry in Switzerland with those found in Austria.

(*a*) How are they alike?

(*b*) How do they differ?

Fig. 85. Wachau, in the Danube Valley

AUSTRIAN STATE TOURIST DEPARTMENT

Task 90. When coal is needed in these metal industries, it will have to come from Germany. Which coalfield could supply it? Trace out a route for the coal, bearing in mind that water transport is cheaper than land transport.

Task 91. Look at Fig. 85 which shows the Danube in Austria.

(*a*) The fields on the far side of the river are chiefly for hay and corn. There are no fruit orchards or vineyards as on the near side. Why is this?

(*b*) The town shown is Wachau. Why do you think it was built in this position?

Vienna

This great city, of over $1\frac{1}{2}$ millions, contains nearly one-quarter of the Austrian people.

Fig. 78 shows it to have a wonderful position on the Danube, where the last spurs of the Alps approach the river, and where routes meet from all south-eastern and eastern Europe on the way into western Europe. It is here that the reason for Vienna's size is to be found. The city was the capital, till 1918, of a great

Fig. 86.   *Vienna*
PAUL POPPER LTD.

empire round the middle Danube, with a population of 45-millions.

Much distress was caused after 1918 when the city had to adjust itself to a small country of (at that time) 6 millions. Many people had to leave Vienna, and its population dropped from $2\frac{1}{2}$ millions to just over $1\frac{1}{2}$ millions.

It is a very beautiful city, full of historic buildings and memories of greatness. In Fig. 86 you get some idea of its magnificence. The hills in the background are the first signs of the Alps.

Task 92. Compare Vienna in Fig. 86 with Paris in Fig. 30. Make a list of the ways in which the two cities resemble one another.

CHAPTER 6

ITALY—A CROWDED PENINSULA

The next chapters will take us south of the great mountain ranges of Central Europe into the warmer regions bordering the Mediterranean Sea. Here lie four countries occupying three peninsulas which thrust themselves into the Mediterranean.

They are shown in Fig. 87.

Task 93.

Fig. 87. The position of Italy in the Mediterranean

(*a*) Which are the three peninsulas, and the four countries?

(*b*) How many countries in Europe have coastlines on the Mediterranean Sea? Name them.

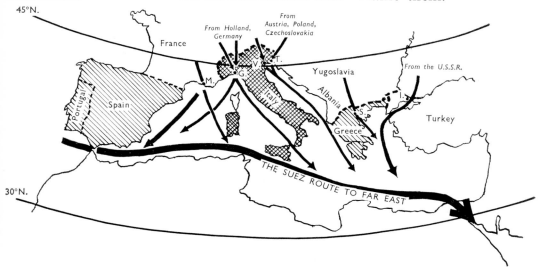

The Most Important Mediterranean Country

Of these Mediterranean nations, Italy is the most important.

It lies in the centre of the Mediterranean, dividing it into two basins, and so controls all Mediterranean shipping routes. This commanding position is shown by the way that the Romans, working from Italy, were able to conquer and hold the whole region round the Mediterranean.

To-day, the shipping route along the Mediterranean is the second most important in the world, and its feeders come from all over Europe. Fig. 87 shows the most important ones.

Task 94.

(*a*) Name the ports shown by initials on Fig. 87. These are the places where land routes reach the Mediterranean.

(*b*) How many are there? How many are in Italy?

(*c*) How many land routes are shown? (*N.B.*—the one from Yugoslavia is much less used than the others).

(*d*) How many go to Italian ports?

In Chapter 1 it was shown that most of western and central Europe was affected by Atlantic winds in which many depressions and fronts occurred, giving much rain. The Mediterranean regions receive these winds only in autumn, winter and spring, when much Atlantic air moves along the Mediterranean. The sea itself remains warm in winter but, near it, in eastern Europe, is an icy cold continent. The warm sea air meets the cold land air, setting up depressions and fronts on the sea itself.

In summer, the Atlantic air streams move north, the cold land mass becomes a warm one and hot dry air from Africa often moves in. Summers are hot, dry, and dusty.

Task 95. Italy, Spain and Greece have a great attraction for holiday makers in all seasons of the year. How far does climate help to create this attraction?

Fig. 88. *Italy*

The Two Regions of Italy

If we now turn to Fig. 88 we shall see that Italy is entirely surrounded by Alpine mountains on all its land frontiers. They cut it off from the rest of Europe, but the passes allow traffic to cross the mountains and enter Italy (Fig. 84). Inside the mountain-ring there are two distinct regions:

(*i*)   the northern plain, called Lombardy;
(*ii*) the peninsula.

Lombardy

Task 96. Examine Fig. 88.

(*a*) How far is it from Turin to Venice?
(*b*) How far is it from Verona to Bologna?
(*c*) What is the name of the main river of Lombardy? Near what pass does it rise?
(*d*) What does this river form on reaching the sea? What other river joins it in forming this feature?

Lombardy is an enormous level plain of fertile soils laid down by the many rivers which rush out of the Alps loaded with silt, laying it on the plain when they flood. Thus, Lombardy has been slowly built up by these rivers, which now flow across it in slow, wide courses to join the Po. There is always great flood danger, and the rivers are embanked above the surrounding lowland. To cross the plain by road or rail, is a constant crossing of rivers and drainage channels by bridge after bridge.

Because so much mud is brought down to the sea by the rivers, the coastline is shallow and full of sandbanks. The rivers build out deltas into the sea. Notice the bulging coastline on Fig. 88 where the Po enters the Adriatic. What is happening is that the rivers are still filling up the hollow between the Alps and the Apennines, and the plain extends further into the Adriatic, slowly but continuously.

Rice is grown in flooded fields. This is very important in Lombardy and especially in the east where the deltas are found. Special varieties of hardy rice are grown, but large flooded fields and much hand-labour in sowing and harvesting are conditions reminding one of Asia. Fig. 89 shows such a ricefield.

Task 97. Read the account of Lombardy again,

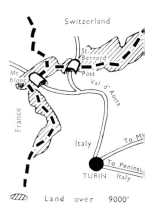

Fig. 88a. The Road Tunnels under the Alps. Opened in the 1960's, they are engineering marvels and will revolutionise road traffic into Italy. The roads shown are all Autostrada, i.e. Motorways.

Fig. 89. A ricefield in Lombardy
CAMERA PRESS

and then examine Fig. 89. Write down anything you notice which was described there.

Away from the rice-growing areas, the farmers grow many crops and also rear cattle and poultry. The region is famous for cheese, like Gorgonzola, the name of a village near Milan. Vines give grapes and wine; flax is grown for linen mills; sugar-beet is well established and, amongst the peasants, maize is a universal bread crop. Unlike the rest of Italy, Lombardy's winters are often very cold due to the icy wind, called the *Bora*, which blows off the mountains of Yugoslavia, straight across the Adriatic into Italy. But it has a good deal of summer rain from depressions.

This is the reason why sugar-beet, flax and maize grow in Lombardy, for they need much summer rain. The olive is absent, a sure indication that the Mediterranean climate does not extend to Lombardy.

Industry in Lombardy

Lombardy is Italy's chief industrial district. It has several advantages for large scale industry:

1. Italy has a large home market of 50 million people. This ensures sales which justify production.

2. Lombardy has enormous amounts of electrical power from the Alps.

3. Her workers, who have a long tradition of skill, have
    made Italy famous in the past for glass, statuary,
    lace, weapons and bridge and road-building.

Industry to-day in Lombardy lies near to the
Alps, and to the seaport of Genoa through which raw
materials come. It is also near the Alpine passes and
tunnels, along which the railways bring German coal.

Since the war, the development of oilfields in Sicily
and many gas wells, has reduced the need for coal in
Italy, and has also cheapened production costs. A pipe-
line from Genoa into Lombardy and Switzerland was
made in 1961.

Woollens made around Turin have a large home
market because the winters of Northern Italy are so
cold. Cottons are made in most towns along the edge
of the Alps. Silks centre on the Milan district where
many local silkworms were produced. These are being
replaced by imported Japanese silk. Venice imports
this silk, as well as much cotton from Egypt.

The iron and steel industries are very large, and

Fig. 90. *The Fiat*
Car Factory

ITALIAN STATE TOURIST
OFFICE

are expanding. The Isle of Elba produces great amounts of iron ore. More is imported via Genoa.

Fig. 90 shows the works of a famous firm which exports cars, buses, tractors, etc. to most countries. It is called F.I.A.T. (Fabricano Italiano Automobile Torino.) The vast scale of the works is obvious. The picture shows a remarkable view of the Alps, more than 30 miles away.

Task 98.

(*a*) Describe the position on this picture of:—(*i*) The main office block. (*ii*) Oil storage tanks. (*iii*) A testing track for cars. (*iv*) The main line of railway.

(*b*) Would you say the plain was densely peopled?

Ship-building is an important industry in Italy, chiefly at Spezia, Genoa and Venice.

In Fig. 91 you see some buildings going up in Milan and some blocks of modern flats near them.

Fig. 91. Modern buildings in Milan

CAMERA PRESS

The engineering and industrial skill of the Italians is well shown by these buildings.

We have already seen that Milan and Turin are very large cities with great industries. Quite a number of valleys and many important routes lead to them. Milan and Turin were important long before industry came to them.

At the eastern end of the plain, on the coast, lies the great city of Venice. Venice is built on sandy islands, so the channels between the islands have been made into canals which are the main thoroughfares of the city. In Fig. 92 you see one of these canals, called The Grand Canal.

Task 99.

(*a*) Name three different kinds of boat in use on the canal.

(*b*) What evidence is there of the fact that the heat is very great in summer?

(*c*) What are the tall poles, painted like barbers' poles, used for?

Fig. 92.   Venice, the Grand Canal

CAMERA PRESS

The Peninsula

The peninsula of Italy is a collection of separate regions. On Fig. 88 you can see how the Apennines run down the centre in a broad belt of young folded mountain ranges which become very wide in Central Italy and reach their highest point in the Gran Sasso, 9,584 feet high. These mountains separate a narrow eastern plain, on the Adriatic, from broader and more fertile plains on the west. In Fig. 88 three of these plains are named. They are very fertile. Much volcanic dust has gone to form their soils. All the volcanoes are now extinct except Vesuvius, near Naples, Etna in Sicily, and Stromboli in the Lipari Islands.

With such large and fertile lowlands as Tuscany, the Tiber Valley and Campania, it is not surprising to find that most of the people live on the west side of the peninsula. The eastern plains are not only narrow and much interrupted by spurs of mountain ranges, but they have bitter weather in winter and spring when the cold Bora wind blows across the Adriatic.

Task 100. Look at Fig. 73 which shows the young folded mountains and the old worn down ones, then look at Fig. 88 and find Vesuvius, Etna and Stromboli.

(*a*) Why do the Apennines curve round into Sicily?

(*b*) Where are they continued after passing through Sicily?

(*c*) What is the relation between the volcanoes, the young folded mountains and the seas?

Farmers of Fruits

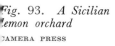

Fig. 93. A Sicilian lemon orchard

CAMERA PRESS

The Mediterranean climate of the Italian peninsula is a fine one for cereals and fruits. They grow well during winter and spring and ripen in the hot, dry summer. (See *The Foundations* Chapter 12).

All over central and southern Italy the valleys and plains, and lower slopes are occupied by farms where grapes, olives, oranges, lemons and peaches are seen on every side, and where fields of wheat and maize extend up the slopes till they reach the chestnut woods of the upper slopes. Even the chestnuts are eatable and form a useful food. Oranges and lemons are grown, chiefly in the west and south, especially in the Genoa area, the Campania, Calabria, and Sicily. In Fig. 93 one sees a lemon orchard in Sicily. This island has a great export of lemons through its chief city and port, Palermo.

Much wine is made from the grapes, and all over Italy wine is the chief drink of the people. Italian wines are not

Fig. 94. *Perugia*
J. ALLAN CASH

so famous as those of France or Spain, but certain wines are famous outside Italy, *e.g.* Marsala (from Sicily), Chianti (from Tuscany), and Asti (from the Turin area).

Because the hot, dry summer spoils grass, animal rearing is not important, but every summer sheep go up into the mountains to feed, and return every winter to the valley farms. Their wool goes to the factories of Lombardy. Goats are used for milk. Olive oil is much used with food, and takes the place of butter. There is a great export of olive oil and bottled olives. Lucca, in Tuscany, is an important centre of this industry.

Fig. 94 is a typical landscape. It is a view of Perugia, north of Rome. The town is on a hill, where all used to dwell for safety from armies and brigands. Part of its old walls can be seen.

Task 101.

(*a*) What evidence is there, in the buildings, that very little snow ever falls here?

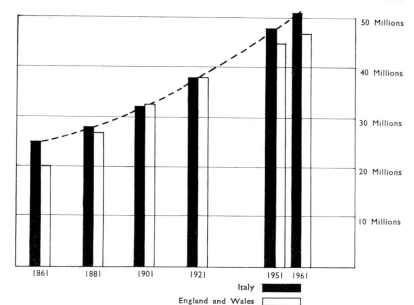

Fig. 95. The populations of Italy and England and Wales compared

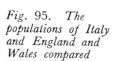

1861   1881   1901   1921   1951 1961

Italy ▮
England and Wales ☐

(*b*) Note the state of the fields on the terraces. In what season was the picture taken?

(*c*) What are the lines of walls on the left of the picture?

Making more use of the land

Italy, with 51 million people, is the most crowded state in the Mediterranean region. A more serious feature is the rapid increase in the population within recent years. Look at Fig. 95 which shows how population has grown in the last hundred years. The population of England and Wales is compared with it. Fig. 95 shows that Italy is not only crowded, but since 1921 its *population has increased much faster than that of England and Wales.*

Task 102. Copy and fill in blanks in the following table, referring to Fig. 95.

	1921	1961	Increase
Population of Italy (in millions)	38		
Population of England and Wales (in millions)	38		

As the population of Italy continues to rise rapidly, the Italians have to turn to their land to increase its production of food. Great efforts have been made by modern governments to reclaim extensive marshlands.

Beware of Malaria

When the Roman Empire existed, Italy was a land of forests. All the slopes of the hills were clothed in forests of chestnut, cork oak, cypress, pine, laurel, etc. After the fall of Rome, chaos reigned in Italy, and there was much disorder right down to the nineteenth century. Forests were destroyed for building ships and for use as firewood; goats roamed half-wild, and destroyed many young trees; slopes were ploughed up, loosening the soils which were washed down on to the plains and valley floors. Great masses of soils were thus moved downhill and large marshes developed.

Fig. 96. *Malarial areas in Italy*

Because the southern parts of Italy are so hot in summer, mosquitoes flourish. They breed in these marshes and spread malaria amongst the people. Many regions were abandoned altogether.

In the 1930's and subsequent to the war of 1940-1945, a campaign was waged to reclaim these marshes and convert them into good farmland. If you look at Fig. 96 you will see how much of Italy's best plains were stricken with malaria. These plains have now been reclaimed and many thousands of farmers settled on them. One large town, Littoria, south of Rome, has been created on an old marsh. Thus, more food is produced than ever before. Much still remains to be done, especially in Sardinia, but malaria is disappearing from Italy.

Task 103.

(*a*) Why should Pisa and Florence not have been troubled by malaria?

(*b*) How would you explain the fact that there was no

malaria in the middle of the peninsula, and in Calabria?

Task 104. Because Italy is so crowded, there has been a large emigration of Italians to the U.S.A. and to South American countries. Can you suggest why more emigrants go through the port of Naples, and many fewer through the port of Genoa?

The Cities of the Peninsula

There are many small towns, some of them of great historic interest. In Tuscany are Pisa, with its leaning tower; Assisi, always associated with Saint Francis; Leghorn the port, and Spezia, the naval base. There is one bigger city, Florence (438,000), the size of Belfast or Edinburgh, which has a most commanding position where the route from Bologna crosses the Apennines and enters the peninsula. It was a very wealthy city in the Middle Ages, and accumulated enormously valuable art treasures. Its beautiful buildings are of great interest to visitors to-day.

Fig. 97. Rome, with the Colosseum in the background

AEROFILMS

From Florence, in the Arno valley, an easy route

leads to the Tiber valley and this is the principal route down the peninsula. It leads to Rome, on the lower Tiber. Rome is the greatest city in the peninsula, the capital of Italy and of the Roman Catholic Church, the Eternal City, the great centre of the Roman Empire, a city full of historical buildings, every street reminding us in some way of its long and interesting history.

To-day it has a population of 2 millions and is the largest city in Italy. It has no particular industries but, as capital of Italy, it has grown quickly since 1870 when modern Italy was created. It has an enormous tourist industry, for pilgrims come regularly to Rome, the seat of the Pope, as well as to Rome, the great city of Ancient Times. In Fig. 88 you can see that it is well placed for routes to all parts of Italy.

Figs. 97 and 98 are two views of the city. Fig. 97 shows the Colosseum, the great theatre of Ancient Rome, where so many spectacles were staged, and so many Christians died. Near it is a triumphal arch, erected to commemorate some great victory of the Roman armies. Fig. 98 is a view from the roof of St. Peter's, looking into the square where crowds assemble to greet the Pope. In the left distance can be seen the Quirinal Palace where lived the kings of Italy until 1946, when Italy became a republic.

In the far distance rise the Alban Hills.

Task 105. The foreground of Fig. 98 is part of

Fig. 98. Rome, from the roof of St. Peter's

MANSELL-ALINARI

Fig. 99. *Naples*
AEROFILMS

"the Vatican City". What is the Vatican City? What do you know about it?

Task 106. What evidence is there in Fig. 98 that Roman summers are very hot?

Task 107. Fig. 97 shows most of the types of building of which there are many in Rome. Apart from the ancient monuments, can you find:
(*a*) a church; (*b*) a monastery or convent; (*c*) an hotel; (*d*) a block of flats?

About 120 miles south of Rome is the second big city of the peninsula. Naples, with a population just over one million, is situated on a beautiful bay with angry old Mount Vesuvius smoking and fuming behind it. You can see what a magnificent view it gives us if you look at Fig. 99.

The city has textile and engineering industries, but

tourists are its main industry. One interesting export is sulphur from the Vesuvius region.

From its quays, as emigrants, go many thousands of southern Italians to seek life in other lands.

Sicily

This is a sunny and fertile island crossed in the north by low ranges which are a continuation of the Apennines. In the east is the great volcanic region of Etna which rises to over 10,000 feet and is still active. One rich and beautiful plain occurs on the north coast, and here is Palermo (587,000), the chief city.

Vines, olives, oranges and lemons are grown in great numbers. Lemons are a big export and Marsala wine is a lesser one. The island has five large towns, although most of the people are farmers. This is typical of all Italy, for the farmers like to live in towns and go out daily to their fields.

Sardinia

This large island is more backward than Sicily. From earliest times it has been famous for copper, lead, zinc and iron. Even before Roman times, the Phoenicians were mining there. It is a mountainous island, whose soils are not very good. Until modern times it was regarded merely as a source of metals. Its malarial regions were very extensive and its population scanty.

To-day, malaria is being tackled, hydro-electric power dams are being constructed, and a bid is being made for the tourist trade. Cagliari, the capital, has increased its population from 100,000 to 180,000 in twenty years.

CHAPTER 7

SPAIN AND PORTUGAL
—THE FIRST OCEAN ADVENTURERS

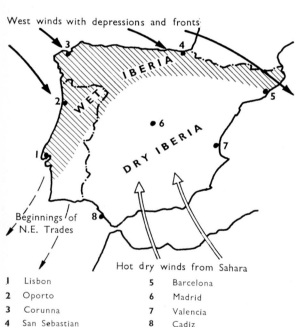

West winds with depressions and fronts

Beginnings of N.E. Trades

Hot dry winds from Sahara

1	Lisbon	5	Barcelona
2	Oporto	6	Madrid
3	Corunna	7	Valencia
4	San Sebastian	8	Cadiz

Fig. 100. The wet and dry regions of Iberia

Iberia is the name for the peninsula south of the Pyrenees. It comprises the two countries, Spain and Portugal.

It is a dry dusty land of heat and low rainfall, as can be seen from Fig. 100. In summer the whole of the interior has less than 1 inch of rain. From Fig. 101 it can be seen that much of the peninsula has a temperature of over 80°F. It is only in the north-west corner, round Corunna, that rainfall is heavy, and that summers are cooler.

It is a compact land. There are no large inlets running into it, continuing the moderating influence of the sea. It stretches, more or less, like a huge square block, from latitude 41°N. to latitude 36°N., and from longitude 3°E. on the east to longitude 9°W. on the west. Thus, there is a large area in the middle which is cut off from the sea, and this is the reason for its hotter summers and colder winters. Except along the northern coast, *i.e.* along the Bay of Biscay, it is nowhere exposed to rain-bearing winds. These blow from the west, along the north coast; but on the south, or Mediterranean coast, they blow from Africa and are hot and dry. On the south-west, or Atlantic coast, the winds blow south and outwards as the beginning of the north-east trades (see Fig. 100). Thus it was that Columbus, sailing from Cadiz, soon came under their influence and was blown across the Atlantic to the Caribbean Sea and the West Indies.

Sunny Spain is therefore a very good name for it, as it is sunny most days of the year, and people, just like those of Italy and Greece, avoid the hottest part of the day by enjoying the *siesta*, a sleepy or restful time, in the afternoons.

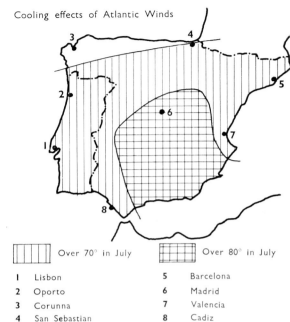

Cooling effects of Atlantic Winds

| | Over 70° in July | | | Over 80° in July |

1	Lisbon	5	Barcelona
2	Oporto	6	Madrid
3	Corunna	7	Valencia
4	San Sebastian	8	Cadiz

Fig 101. *Temperatures in Iberia*

Task 108. Which is the longest straight line which can be drawn:
(*a*) in Spain; (*b*) in Portugal?

Task 109. Where would you choose to live:
(*a*) in Spain; (*b*) in Portugal? Give your reasons.

Task 110. After studying Figs. 100 and 101, say what kind of climate you would expect to find in:
(*a*) Madrid; (*b*) Corunna; (*c*) Cadiz?

Fold Mountains and Blocks

Look at Fig. 102. It shows how Spain was built up into its present shape. First of all there were ancient folded mountains, which were worn down, over vast periods of time, into old *block mountains* and plateaus. Then, in much later times, came more foldings from north and south against these old blocks. From these foldings came the great ranges of the north and south of Spain, the Cantabrians, Pyrenees and Sierra Nevada. Between lies the Meseta (*table*), a remnant of the old

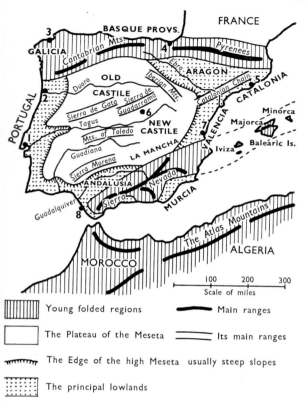

||||| Young folded regions	━━━ Main ranges
☐ The Plateau of the Meseta	═══ Its main ranges
ᚚᚚᚚ The Edge of the high Meseta	usually steep slopes
⠿ The principal lowlands	

I Lisbon	3 Corunna	5 Barcelona	7 Valencia
2 Oporto	4 San Sebastian	6 Madrid	8 Cadiz

Fig. 102. *The relief of Iberia*

blocks caught between the two foldings. This great block forms a plateau, deeply cut into by rivers, of which three are shown on Fig. 102. They flow in deep valleys, and between them the plateau rises into ranges of mountains which lie between 3,000 feet and 7,000 feet high.

In the folded mountains many peaks reach 7,000 feet and a few are over 10,000 feet high.

Round the edge of the Meseta are the lowlands. Notice the three large ones, the Ebro valley, Andalusia and the plains of Portugal.

Several smaller ones are shown, around the coasts.

Task 111. Look at Fig. 102.

(*a*) In what direction do most of the Iberian rivers flow?

(*b*) Which river runs in quite a different direction?

(*c*) Which lowlands are named, apart from the three large ones mentioned in the text?

(*d*) What does the map show you about the build of: (*a*) the Balearic Isles; (*b*) North Africa?

Task 112. Describe the relief, temperatures and rainfall of the following Spanish provinces: Galicia, New Castile, Andalusia.

Great Explorers

On Fig. 103 one sees Iberia in relation to the Atlantic Ocean and bordering lands. Notice its relation to the west winds and trades. It is the best starting

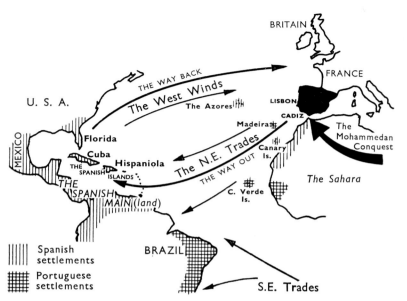

Fig. 103.   *The position of Iberia in the Atlantic*

point in Europe from which to sail outwards on the trades and return on the westerlies, making use of both winds.

One result of this was that Columbus, Vasco de Gama and other Iberian explorers, set out to discover the new world of America, and to round Africa to reach the Far East. They were the first Europeans to do so, and established great empires for both Spain and Portugal.   In the 16th and 17th centuries they were the leaders amongst European nations. Their empires, however, drained them of much man-power, and they declined in the 18th and 19th centuries. Unlike Britain, Holland and France, who followed them into the New World, they had not the dense populations or the industry needed to maintain their colonies.

Task 113.   If you have read *The Southern Lands* and *The Asiatic World* in this series, you will have come across many facts about Spanish and Portuguese activities in Africa, South America and Asia.

Try to see these books again and answer the following:

(*a*) Which countries in South America speak Spanish?

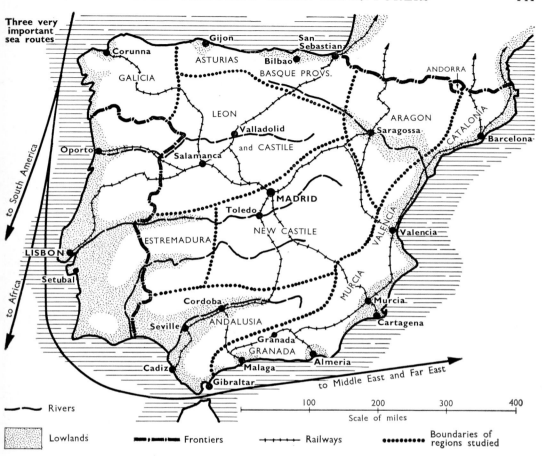

Fig. 104. *Iberia*

(*b*) Where in North America does the Spanish language change to English?

(*c*) Which country in South America speaks Portuguese?

(*d*) Which lands in Asia and Africa were once held, or are still held, by Spain or Portugal?

Task 114. Lisbon and Cadiz were the chief ports from which Iberian ships sailed to the new lands. Look at Figs. 103 and 104 and then say why they should have been chosen.

The Regions of Spain

The main regions are shown in Fig. 104. They

can be divided broadly into four different types of country.

1. The Atlantic Margins in the North: Galicia, Asturias, Basque Provinces.
2. The Atlantic Margins in the South: Andalusia,
3. The Mediterranean fringe: Granada, Murcia, Valencia, Catalonia.
4. The Interior: The Castiles, Estramadura, Aragon.

The high ranges of the Pyrenees form a distinct type in themselves and can be called the fifth region. We will deal with them first.

The Pyrenees

These high ranges make a formidable barrier between Spain and the rest of Europe. The mountains rise, in places, to 11,000 feet, and a typical view is shown in Fig. 105. The view in Fig. 105 is taken on the French slope, which has heavy rains and much forest. The Spanish slope is much drier, almost bare in places, for the mountains are a great barrier to rain from the depressions moving along to the north of the ranges (Fig. 100).

In Fig. 105 one sees a valley 9,000 ft. up, where one of the two railways which cross the high Pyrenees, is making its way. Notice again how the road climbs in hairpin bends. It is easy to see how isolated and difficult are these valleys of the Pyrenees. No railway crossed the ranges, except on the coasts, until 1929.

Andorra, high up in the Pyrenees, is a tiny country of 12,000 people. It is ruled jointly by the French President and the Bishop of Urgel (Spain). One good road enters from France and another from Spain. There is considerable hydro-electric power, and tourism is of increasing importance.

Task 115. From what you can see in Fig. 105, write down some of the difficulties to be met with in building roads in the Pyrenees.

It is only at the Basque end that the Pyrenees become reasonably low, and here roads and railways enter Spain from the rest of Europe.

Fig. 105. *A valley in the Pyrenees,* 9,000 *feet above sea-level* FOX PHOTOS

The Atlantic Margins in the North

Here the land rises quickly from the sea up to mountain ranges, leaving small plains along the shore. In Galicia are many wide openings into the land, where valleys have sunk under the sea. These make excellent harbours.

Rain-clouds pile up frequently against the mountains, and often there are westerly gales. Dense forests clothe the lower and middle slopes. The valleys are warm and apples, cherries, oranges and grapes are grown. However, it is the sea which attracts people. Many are fishermen, some going far afield in trawlers. Sardines are caught and tinned. Boats sail yearly to Newfoundland for cod. This coastal area also contains minerals. Around Bilbao, an excellent port, are rich iron ore deposits, exported from Bilbao chiefly to Britain. Coal is mined around Oviedo, but poor communications across the mountains hinder development.

In recent years the San Sebastian area has become one of Europe's holiday playgrounds. It has very good extensive beaches.

Task 116.

(*a*) Why do you think no large seaports have grown up on the north coast of Spain, despite the many good harbours?

(*b*) Which part of France resembled this region in its coasts, climate and occupations?

The Mediterranean Fringe

From the French frontier down to Gibraltar, the east coast of Spain is a region of very hot summers with drought. During the warm winters there are only moderate rains. Shortage of rainfall is always a problem, and irrigation is frequently used. Thus, the region has oases of cultivation, where water is available, separated by barren spurs and hills which are almost deserted.

The *huertas*, or irrigated terraced slopes, were first introduced by the Moors when they conquered this region. Rivers from the hills are dammed and used to supply water down the slopes. In Catalonia, rains are

Fig. 106. *An orange grove near Alcudia (Valencia)*

PAUL POPPER LTD.

better north of Barcelona. The Catalan Chain makes the plain very narrow here. The Ebro has a delta where rice is grown, as in Lombardy, but all along the coast oranges, olives, grapes and almonds are grown and exported to Britain. There is a great variety of crops in all the *huertas*. Fig. 106 is a view in an orange grove near Valencia. So rich are the soils that two or three crops per year are grown. On the south coast the Nevada mountains are so close to the coast that only a few *oases* are found, *e.g.* Malaga and Almeria.

The richness of the oases can be judged from the size of their towns, Almeria, Alicante, Cartagena, each has over 100,000 people, Murcia and Malaga, each over 200,000 and Valencia has over 500,000.

These oases also produce wheat, maize, barley, and some of the heaviest rice crops in the world.

Barcelona (1,560,000) is the largest city in the area, second only to Madrid in all Spain. It is the only large centre of modern industry in Spain. It imports both

Fig. 107. *Barcelon*
RADIO TIME
HULTON LIBRAR

coal and iron, but uses hydro-electric power from the hills. Like Italy, its materials are all imported, especially cotton, and it makes machinery, glass, chemicals and cotton goods. There is plenty of cheap labour, and the goods sell at home.

The Catalans are the most progressive of the Spaniards and have a strong sense of apartness from the rest. There have been many clashes with Madrid.

Fig. 107 is a scene in the industrial section of Barcelona showing factories and blocks of workers' flats. It is a view not to be found in many Spanish cities.

Task 117. The two most important needs for hydro-electro power (H.E.P.) are:

(*a*) good rainfalls throughout the year;

(*b*) plenty of long slopes for water to fall down into the H.E.P. stations.

Keeping these in mind answer the following:

1. Why has the Barcelona region better conditions for H.E.P. than the rest of the Mediterranean coastlands? (look at Fig. 100).

2. Which part of Spain is likely to produce H.E.P. most easily?

Fig. 108. *The Rock of Gibraltar*

FOX PHOTOS

The site of Gibraltar

3. Why is the country, *as a whole*, not good for H.E.P.?

Gibraltar

In the extreme south of Spain is a famous British fortress and naval dockyard, the Rock of Gibraltar or just simply *The Rock* as it has been known to many generations of soldiers and sailors garrisoned there. You can see the Rock in Fig. 108 as it stands up out of the Mediterranean Sea. It is of limestone which absorbs water very quickly. The illustration shows, on the right, one of the catchment areas on Gibraltar. Rain falls on this flat surface and is trapped into large cisterns underground. Without this the garrison on the Rock would go short of water.

The actual Rock belongs to Britain. It was captured from Spain in 1704 and commands the entrance to the Mediterranean Sea.

Task 118. How do you think the smooth slope in Fig. 108 is used to collect water on the Rock?

Andalusia

Here is a large lowland facing out to the Atlantic. It has only a small rainfall, because the depressions and fronts seldom come so far south. Summers are intensely hot and dry, and the farming is chiefly of plants which require small rainfalls, *e.g.* wheat, barley and olives. In the most favoured places grapes are grown, and one wine, *Sherry*, is exported.

The river Guadalquiver runs through the lowland and on it lie two of the chief towns. Seville (442,000) is at the head of navigation for ocean vessels. Cordoba (160,000) is the centre of roads and railways in Andalusia. Like Granada, in the Nevada, they are both old Moorish cities, with many traces of the Moors in their buildings, and in the dark colouring of their people.

Cadiz (100,000) is the port of Andalusia and the main port of Spain for trade with the Atlantic.

Task 119.

(*a*) In addition to *Sherry*, a certain fruit is exported from Seville and Cadiz. Named after Seville, what is the fruit?

(*b*) A special type of bull is reared in large numbers on the Andalusian steppes. For what are these bulls required?

The Interior of Spain

This central region is cut off from most of the rainy air streams. All over it, dry and dusty conditions prevail. The best rains are in Leon and Castile in the north-west, the part nearest to the Atlantic. The poorest rains are in La Mancha, which in many parts is little better than desert.

The higher ranges are bleak and barren areas, snow-covered in the winter. There used to be forests of oak and pine on them, but few now remain. They are scantily peopled by sheep farmers who move the sheep up and down the valleys from summer to winter.

Out on the plateaus one sees great expanses of open land rising to stony hills, an occasional village of poor stone houses almost lost in the landscape. In Leon and Castile conditions are better, and most of the wheat and barley of Spain is grown here. There are scarcely any trees. Population is scattered, and even the towns are small. Only one, the route centre of Valladolid, has over 100,000 people. Comparet his with the Mediterranean coastland.

New Castile and Estramadura have an even drier and more stony appearance, but there are some trees. Evergreen oaks and heath cover great areas and salty, tufty grass covers others. It is shepherds' country, only sheep and goats can be reared. But in damp districts, or in river valleys where soils are damper, wheat, grapes, and olives will grow.

Towns are even smaller than in Old Castile. None reach 50,000 population.

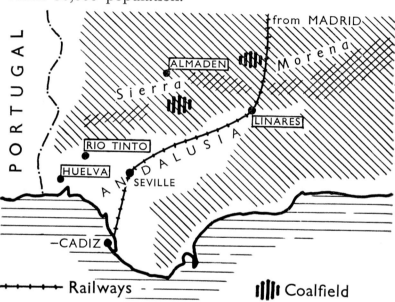

Fig. 109. The Mineral Belt of the Southern Meseta

The Sierra Morena is the last ridge of the Meseta and from it there is a steep slope into Andalusia. Along this Morena range is a belt of important minerals. Copper is mined at Rio Tinto and Huelva; mercury at Almaden, and lead at Linares (see Fig. 109). There are two small coalfields also, but there is no industry. The minerals are exported to Britain and Western Europe.

Task 120. On an outline map of Spain, mark clearly the minerals found in the Sierra Morena, and those in the Cantabrians in the north. Name the towns where they are mined.

Fig. 110. *Madrid*
FOX PHOTOS

Madrid

There is one great city on the Meseta. It is very large indeed. This is Madrid, the capital, whose population is 2,300,000. It was made the capital in 1561, taking the place of Toledo, and all roads were made to centre on it. Similarly all railways centre there. It has become a business centre as well. Fig. 110 is a view in the centre of the city.

Task 121.

(a) Why should it be necessary to advertise the night club on the left as "Refrigerado"?

(b) Would you expect to find the centre of a great city paved in the manner of this one? What would be normal?

(c) These two things apart, would you say there is anything which distinguishes Madrid from any other European city you have had described in this book?

Aragon

Aragon is very different from Andalusia. The Pyrenean streams carry down much water for irrigation, and Aragon is the most irrigated part of the interior. Unlike Lombardy, Aragon is not a level plain, but is criss-crossed by hills. This limits the size of the areas to be irrigated but when any large area is so treated it looks much like Lombardy and has similar crops.

There is one big city, Zaragoza (Saragossa), with 326,000 people. It is on the Ebro and is the main route centre (see Fig. 104).

Task 122. Why should Aragon have more hydro-electric power than Andalusia?

PORTUGAL

The Portuguese have always been great sailors and fishermen. Not many of the Spanish provinces can equal them in this respect, only the northern provinces along the Bay of Biscay. As Fig. 104 shows, the coastline of Portugal lies close to several important world sea routes, and Lisbon has a very fine harbour. If only the position of Portugal on land had not been so poor, being so far away from all the main centres of people and trade in Europe, the Portuguese would have been one of the great trading nations of the world.

Fig. 111. *A Douro Vineyard*
FOX PHOTOS

Task 123. Britain and Portugal have been allies for over 600 years. Portugal is known in Britain as "Our Oldest Ally". What have the two nations always had in common, to keep them allies for so long?

Portugal has very few minerals and no means of building up heavy industry. Her prosperity depends upon her farms and her fishing fleets.

Commencing in the south with dates, Portuguese farms produce great quantities of oranges, olives and grapes. Wine-making is very important in the Douro area where port wine is made. Fig. 111 gives a view of this district. An olive tree is on the extreme right, up the slope.

Task 124. Making use of Fig. 111, describe how the vines are cultivated and harvested.

The main fishing industry is for sardines. These are very numerous off the coasts in the south. There is a canning industry at Setubal, near Lisbon, and sardines are exported. Around here, too, salt is collected by evaporating it from the sea. Fig. 112 shows great mounds of it on the sea shore.

The wetter northern area has many forests of pine, oak and chestnut on the hill slopes. These supply an important lumbering industry.

Task 125. In the canning of sardines, what else is needed besides the fish? Can Portugal supply them? What will they be forced to import?

Fig. 112. Salt from evaporated sea-water

PAUL POPPER LTD.

Fig 113.   The harbour at Oporto

FOX PHOTOS

Oporto

Portugal has only two large towns. In the north is Oporto with a population of nearly 300,000. It is the port from which port wine is exported. Fig. 113 is a view in the port showing ships loading the wine. The mouth of the Douro makes a very good harbour.

Lisbon

The capital city has 1,400,000 people. It has many beautiful buildings and squares, as seen in Fig. 114, but it has also some bad slums, like most Mediterranean cities. Its harbour is one of the finest in the world. Lisbon manufactures gold and silverware,

Fig. 114.   Lisbon

PAUL POPPER LTD.

Fig. 115. *Corpus Christi procession*
PAUL POPPER LTD.

tobacco and textiles. Its world position on important routes makes it a big port.

It exports wine, cork, sardines, almonds and olive oil from the Portuguese farms and fishing fleets. Tourist traffic is becoming very important.

Task 126. Suggest some of the things of interest to a tourist in Portugal.

The Peoples of Iberia

To a foreigner the Iberian peoples seem reserved and the Spanish rather haughty, though courteous. Once one has got to know them, however, both Spanish and Portuguese show themselves to be rather like all Mediterranean peoples, fond of bright colours, music and movement. They love great spectacles, whether it is a bullfight, or a great football match. In the same way, they enjoy celebrating religious festivals. Fig. 115 is a religious procession in Tarragona, near Barcelona.

CHAPTER 8

GREECE, A LAND OF SMALL PLAINS AND ISLANDS

Peninsulas, Inlets and Islands

If we look at Fig. 116 we see modern Greece as created in 1922, after World War I. The merest glance shows it to be a peninsula of mountainous country with many small lowlands, many peninsulas, and an enormous number of islands, some just offshore and others spread over the Aegean Sea. Only the main ones can be shown in Fig. 116. The mountains are folded mountains; the islands are ranges partly submerged beneath the sea.

All the coasts of Asia Minor and Greece have sunk in past times and that explains the inlets and islands.

Task 127. Study Fig. 116.

(a) What are the distances from (i) Corfu to Lemnos; (ii) Salonika to Cape Matapan?
Compare these with the following distances in Britain, taken from an atlas: (i) London to Newcastle-on-Tyne; (ii) Birmingham to Glasgow.

(b) What is the chief mountain range in the Peninsula?

Task 128.

(a) The lowlands of Greece are not extensive. Which is the largest? Which is the largest in the peninsula of Greece?

(b) What four countries border Greece in the north?

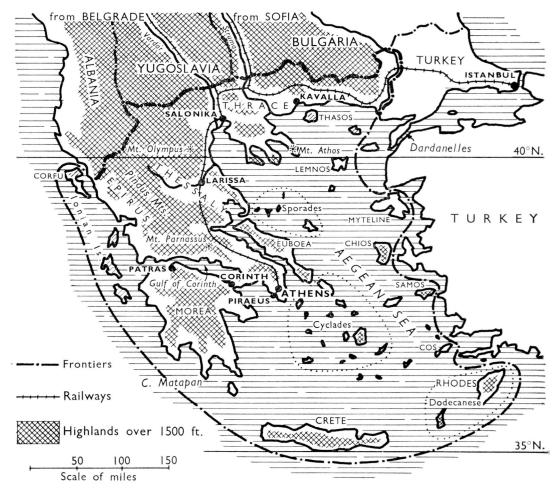

Fig. 116. *Greece*

The mountains of Greece are highest in the Pindus Mountains, where peaks reach over 8,000 feet, except Mount Olympus over 9,000 feet, not in the Pindus range. It is the highest mountain in Greece. Fig. 117 shows a view of Olympus in spring when snow is still thick on it. You can imagine, from this view, how terrible winters are in the Greek mountains, and that few roads cross them. Epirus is cut off from the rest of Greece except by sea. The western shores

Fig 117. *Snow-covered Mt. Olympus*
GREEK GOVERNMENT

of Greece are troubled by earthquakes. The Ionian Islands have had two bad ones in the 1950's. Notice that high folded mountains lie close to deep seas in this region (see *The Asiatic World*, Chapter 9, Task 150).

Task 129. Examine Fig. 116.

What is the latitude of Mount Olympus? In this latitude, the snow line, above which snow never melts, is about 9,000 feet. Will Mt. Olympus have snow all the year? Will any other Greek mountains have snow all the year?

The Regions of Greece

Even this small country has a number of quite different regions. First there is the mountain region with cold, unpleasant winters and much snow, very poor communications, and a scattered population of sheep and goat farmers who move into the upper valleys in summer, and down to the sea in winter.

Not a single railway is found here. Second, there is Epirus, the valleys of the west coast. Because the rain winds from the west rise against the mountains, rains are very heavy here. Olives, wines and barley are grown in the valleys and on lower slopes, whilst woods of beech and chestnut are found higher up. There is a great deal of sheep and goat pasture in the woodland zone. Down on the coasts malaria is a menace, as in Italy. Similar conditions exist in the Ionian Isles. There are no important towns and no railways. Communications are mostly by sea.

The rest of the peninsula and the islands form Classical Greece, the glory of ancient times

Everywhere it has a true Mediterranean climate with fiercely hot, dry summers, for most of it is south of 40°N. Because of the mountains, most of the low-lands are rain shadowed, and rainfalls are small. For example, Athens has only 15 inches per year, against over 40 inches per year in some places in Epirus.

It is in its build that *Classical Greece* is so striking.

Fig. 118. Classical Greece, a typical town

Fig. 119. On the hillsides in Greece

FOX PHOTOS

All down the coast, small plains occur between spurs of highland, a small river flows across the plain, and near its mouth is a small town. This pattern is repeated over and over again. Hills, sea and plain lie close together, and nearby, at sea, islands are usually to be seen. Look at Fig. 118. It shows the sea, a town, and the plain rising to the hills very quickly. The small plain is ploughed for wheat, barley and vegetables, but the area of it is very small. Not one of these little plains ever grew enough corn for its people. Hence Greece always was, and still is, an importer of corn. Above the plain the hillsides are dry and stony (Fig. 119). Here olives flourish and grapes can be grown. Above the olive and grape regions are poor pastures for sheep and goats, with scattered groups of chestnuts, pines and cypresses. Once there were forests here but, just as in Italy, they have been destroyed. The Greek, because he has so little lowland here, has always farmed the slopes.

Task 130. In Fig. 118 there is a harbour. Is it a natural one? Does there seem to be much ground to plough? In Fig. 119 do the slopes look to be rich with crops? Describe what you see there. (The ruins are those of the famous temple at Delphi).

Because the climate is so dry, the Greeks grow special varieties of small black grapes which they make into currants. (Compare with Turkey in *The Asiatic World*). There is a large export of currants, especially from Patras on the Gulf of Corinth. The currants go there chiefly by sea to be loaded on to steamers.

Thessaly is the one large lowland in *Classical Greece*, but it is very dry, and covered with steppe. The Greeks of the peninsula, who are used to tiny plains and much hillside, do not take kindly to the cultivation of large plains. After 1922 a new type of Greek appeared in Thessaly, Greeks who used to live in Asia Minor and whom the Turks expelled in exchange for Turks living in Greece (see *The Asiatic World*, Chapter 3). These Greeks were at home on large plains and have made Thessaly into an important region for tobacco and corn. In Fig. 120 is a scene where the tobacco is being dried.

Fig. 120. Thessaly, drying tobacco

GREEK GOVERNMENT

Task 131. Describe the general appearance of Greeks, as seen in Fig. 120. Remembering how dry and poor Thessaly used to be, would you say these men were hard working and intelligent farmers? Why?

Sailors and Traders

Because the land is so limited in what it can offer, many Greeks have turned to the sea for a living. Here they find a great difficulty. The Mediterranean is not a good sea for fish. Each settlement has its fishermen, who catch such fish as sardine and anchovy, but there are no fishing fleets in any Mediterranean country to compare with those of Britain, France, Norway and other northern lands. So the Greek has become a trader and a mover of goods for other nations. From earliest times he has done this, and to-day, for the size of the country, the Greeks have a very large merchant fleet.

Task 132. Norway and Greece are both lands with small populations but large merchant navies. Compare the conditions in each country which have created this situation.

Task 133. Greeks, along with Italians and Iberians are great eaters of fish on the abstinence days of the Church. From where do they secure their supplies?

Thrace

This part of Greece contains large lowlands, with colder winters than the peninsula, because it is near to the great land mass of Eastern Europe from which cold winds blow in winter. It was never very popular with the Greeks of ancient times, but for centuries, until 1912, it was ruled by the Turks and many Turks lived there. Since 1922 they have been replaced by Greeks from Asia Minor, and now the population is almost all Greek. Great crops of tobacco are grown (called *Turkish tobacco*). The best tobaccos in the Near East are from Greece. Much malarial marsh has been reclaimed. The great amount of wheat being grown here is of tremendous value to a country which used to be so short of that crop.

Fig. 121. *Athens, ar* *the Parthenc* AEROFILM

The Cities of Greece

There are only two large towns in Greece, Salonika and Athens.

Salonika (373,000) is a seaport in a very favourable position. Look at Fig. 116 and notice the Vardar Valley. This is a very good thoroughfare through the mountains and leads from the plains of Hungary and Yugoslavia to Salonika, the nearest sea outlet. The Sturma Valley leads from Bulgaria (see Fig. 116).

Because the hinterland of Salonika is so mountainous and is inside the Iron Curtain, its trade is not so great as its position suggests.

Athens is the capital and with Piraeus, its seaport, forms one large town of 1,850,000 people. It was always well situated in the centre of *Classical Greece*, and is still quite central in modern Greece.

It has become a very modern city during the last 30 years, but the relics of its great past are to be seen everywhere. In Fig. 121 you see the Parthenon, regarded as the most perfect building in the world, an open air theatre, and other buildings of the Classical

Age. All round them is modern Athens. In the background are the hills, always present in any view in *Classical Greece*. Notice how bare they look.

Modern Athens and Piraeus have received many Asia Minor Greeks, who are active in the shipyards, iron foundries, tobacco, silk and soap works. They have also brought their own carpet-weaving and pottery trades.

Task 134. Notice the shadows cast by the Parthenon in Fig. 121 and so find the direction of the sun. This can be assumed to be in the south. Thus determine the direction of Piraeus, from this view (use Fig. 116).

Fig. 122. A Greek villager white-washes his house

CAMERA PRESS

Greece is still backward

This small country has many features of life common to the other lands of Eastern Europe. In general they are poor countries. Their agriculture needs modernising and their farmers need better homes. In Fig. 122 you see a better type of village home, its owner giving it a coat of whitewash. It is obviously a poor home. The man himself is barefooted, as are most rural Greeks, for shoes are so expensive that he only wears them on special occasions, *e.g.* to church on Sunday. Notice the primitive arrangement of telephone wires in the village. How bare and useless the land looks in the background. The donkey is the usual beast of burden.

Task 135. The people whitewash their homes every two or three months. Why this anxiety to keep the walls white? Another feature of the backwardness of Greece, in common with countries in Eastern Europe, is the lack of coal and iron and of any minerals in really useful quantities. This prevents the development of heavy industry. The Pindus and Epirus with their heavy rains and steep slopes could produce much hydro-electric power, but they are so remote from the rest of the country.

Task 136. The entire exports of Greece are specialised farm products. Suggest some export that might be important. Why should grain and textiles be the chief things imported?

Task 137. Greece is a monarchy, *i.e.* it is ruled by a king acting with an elected Parliament. Which other European countries are monarchies?

Task 138. Suppose you were advising a Corporation which wished to invest millions of pounds in Greece. On what would you advise them to spend it in order to create wealth for Greece and so profit for the Corporation?

An evzone, a member of the Greek Royal Guard.

Task 139. Here are some questions for a general knowledge quiz.
(*a*) What and where is the Corinth Canal?
(*b*) What is Mount Athos famous for?
(*c*) In what part of Greece was the story of the Minatour laid?
(*d*) Who was Alexander the Great?

Task 140. Greece relies a great deal on tourist traffic for income. What has it to offer to tourists?

CHAPTER 9

THE COMMUNIST NATIONS OF THE EAST

We now come to the borderlands of Atlantic Europe, to that area between the Baltic and Black Seas where the Europe of peninsulas, islands and seas, changes to the Europe of enormous plains, occupied chiefly by the U.S.S.R. We call it East Central Europe, and it is occupied by seven countries, whose names are shown in Fig. 123. (East Germany is not included in this chapter, since it was surveyed in Chapter 3).

As we look at these countries on Fig. 123 we must remember that they have only been formed, in their present shapes, since 1918. If, now, you look at Fig. 124 as well, and compare it with Fig. 123, you will see how things have changed since 1912. Frontiers have changed frequently and peoples have been mixed up together. There has been extensive interference by outside powers and a great feeling of uncertainty exists. Terrible destruction of lives and property has been caused by wars.

After 1945, along with Eastern Germany, they were all occupied by Russian armies, and Communist governments were established in them. Their farming, industry and trade, were made to fit closely into the pattern of Russian development. Their contacts with non-Communist countries were severely cut down: Yugoslavia has broken away from this Russian domin-

Fig. 123. *The Communist Nations of Eastern Europe and the changes in the Russian frontier since* 1920

ation, but remains a Communist country. The rest are so cut off from the rest of Europe that the peoples of the west talk of *The Iron Curtain* as separating them from these Communist lands.

Task 141. Study the maps, and answer the following questions:

1. Out of what countries (or Empires) was Poland formed in 1918?
2. Which countries were formed entirely out of Austria-Hungary in 1918?
3. Which other countries took parts of Austria-Hungary in 1918?

Fig. 124. Changes in the frontiers of Eastern European countries since 1912.

4. How far, on average, has Poland moved westwards from 1920 to 1945?

5. What countries took slices of the Turkish Empire after the wars of 1912-13?

6. Of what was Yugoslavia formed in 1918?

7. How far did the frontier of Russia move at its greatest extent: (*a*) eastwards in 1920; (*b*) westwards in 1945?

Fig. 125.   Eastern
                    Europe

From this Task, you can obtain some idea of the bewildering changes that have taken place. A country can change position completely by over 100 miles, as Poland has done, or frontiers can change backwards and forwards over 300 miles as in the case of Russia. A nation gains and loses territory within a few years, as in Rumania. A country that ruled a great Empire is now only one of several small states, as in the case of Hungary. All this happened in forty years of the 20th century.

Plain, Valley and Peninsula

Now let us examine Figs. 125 and 126. On Fig. 125 you see the boundaries of the states, the chief hills and rivers, and the chief cities. The rivers are named on Fig. 125, the mountains on Fig. 126. Capital cities are underlined in Fig. 125. Here are some facts for you to learn from these maps.

Task 142.

1. Name the capitals of each of the seven states.
2. Which country has a frontier on the Carpathians?
3. Through which countries does the Danube flow?
4. Which is the chief river of Poland?
5. Which country is composed of three parts:
   (*a*) mountains in the east;
   (*b*) plateau in the west;
   (*c*) lowland in the centre?

Task 143.

1. Which of the seven countries is without a coastline?
2. Which countries are almost entirely lowland?
3. Which country is separated from its coast by high mountains? What are they called?
4. Which country has the least amount of lowland?

Task 144. There are two great trans-continental routes across this region, both shown in Fig. 126. One is along the northern plain. One is along the Danube valley. Name the chief cities along each route. Through which country are the two linked?

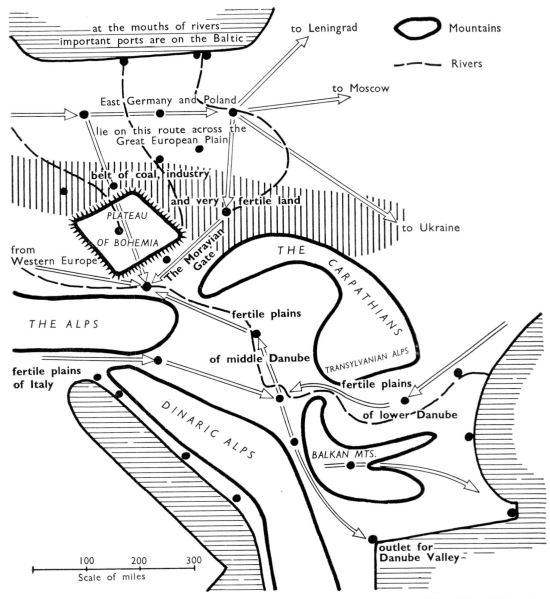

at the mouths of rivers
important ports are on the Baltic

to Leningrad

Mountains

Rivers

East Germany and Poland

to Moscow

lie on this route across the
Great European Plain

belt of coal, industry

and very fertile land

to Ukraine

PLATEAU
OF BOHEMIA

from
Western Europe

The Moravian Gate

THE
CARPATHIANS

THE ALPS

fertile plains

of middle Danube

TRANSYLVANIAN ALPS

fertile plains
of Italy

fertile plains

of lower Danube

DINARIC ALPS

BALKAN MTS.

outlet for
Danube Valley

100   200   300
Scale of miles

Fig. 126.   *The main*
routes of Eastern
Europe

Lands of Bitter Winters

Because these countries lie on the edge of the great Russian land mass, and some distance from the Atlantic, they have long and very cold winters. Rivers freeze for six to eight weeks or more every winter, snow lies on the ground throughout January and February and biting east winds from Russia make life unpleasant. Occasionally an Atlantic depression moves along the Baltic, or a Mediterranean depression moves northwards. These bring snow rather than rain.

On the other hand, summers are hot and showery and are excellent for the farmer. In the Danube valley, and Balkan Peninsula, some months have average temperatures over 70°F. and thus maize will succeed. The region is one of great possibilities for the farmer.

The Poor Relations of Europe

What sort of people inhabit the great border zone we have been describing? To begin with let us notice how many there are there. The figures are for 1963.

The Northern Group

	Population	Area
Poland	30 millions	120,000 sq. m.
Czechoslovakia	14 millions	50,000 sq. m.
Hungary	10 millions	36,000 sq. m.

The Southern Group

Rumania	19 millions	92,000 sq. m.
Yugoslavia	19 millions	100,000 sq. m.
Bulgaria	8 millions	45,000 sq. m.
Albania	1 million	11,000 sq. m.

This gives a total of 101 million people, and when this total is divided by the total number of square miles of territory, it produces a density of two hundred and fifteen per square mile, which is relatively high.

Task 145. Add the populations and the areas of the Northern Group. Then work out the number per square mile for this group. Do the same for the Southern Group. How do the two groups compare with the average density? What conclusions do you draw from this?

These people, numbering nearly one hundred millions, are very mixed in race and language. From the earliest times, tribes and peoples moved in along the Northern Plains and the Danube valley fighting one another, expelling one another, accepting one another till all became mixed up together.

Some of the late-comers found little room in which to settle, and were forced to stay in the east. Others were thrust back again, *e.g.* the Turks, pushed into the Danube valley in the sixteenth and seventeenth centuries, were finally stopped at Vienna, in the seventeenth century, and then were slowly pushed back into Asia, by the twentieth century. In every case peoples have left behind some evidence of themselves in the form of racial types, languages, religious beliefs and habits of thought.

The Effects of Conquest

The unfortunate history of these regions has had a profound effect on life and habits. Conquerors usually parcelled out their conquests in large estates. So large estates have been the rule here up to the present time. The peasants on the estates had to provide the owners with what they needed, and beyond that they showed little interest.

Improvement of soils and farming methods were of no interest except in a few enlightened cases. Thus farming methods became quite out of date and inefficient, and the peasants very poor and their living conditions often very bad.

Typical scene in Eastern Europe in 19th century

Because these peoples were organised into land-owners on the one hand, and poor peasants on the other, they did not produce a trading middle-class which is so necessary in every well organised nation. They became soldiers, not traders. Thus there grew up, in East Central European towns, large colonies of Jews who were the shopkeepers and traders over great areas. Germans were the technicians and managed any business requiring scientific or engineering ability. Jews and Germans formed middle and professional classes, and were very strong in the towns. In the Southern Group, Greeks appeared as well, and along the Adriatic Sea the traders were Italians. Thus the mixtures of peoples became greater than ever. When, after 1918, frontiers were drawn *according to the wishes of the inhabitants*, those wishes were so conflicting that it was impossible to draw really satisfactory frontiers. This is one reason for the tragic practice of to-day where frontiers are fixed, and peoples are moved across them to fit the new political arrangements.

Plough in Eastern Europe in 20th Century

Task 146. Look at Fig. 125 and follow the frontiers of the states shown there. How often is a large river used as a frontier? How often is the Danube a frontier? Why do you think large rivers are not used as frontiers, when mountain ranges are often used?

A Lack of Industry

The great industrial developments in Western Europe, in the nineteenth century, left East Central Europe almost untouched. Turks and Russians paid little attention to industrial developments and in any case there was little coal to be had. Because of this, several things followed:

1. They had few large cities in which their people could find work.
2. The people were thus forced to stay on the land. Even to-day over 70% of the people of these states live and work in the country.
3. Because the land was inefficiently worked, it could not support all these people. Thus many emigrated and still there were too many. There is still great poverty amongst the peasants.
4. Because they have little wealth from the sale of manufactures abroad, the nations have not the money to help improve the farms, and to build better roads and railways.

Foreign Help Needed

These lands turned to Europe for financial help. At first, Britain, France and Italy helped. In the

Fig. 127.   *Harvesting rye in Poland*
CAMERA PRESS

1930's more and more control came to be exercised by Nazi Germany. Her traders, industrialists and technicians poured into all these countries, and her manufactures became more and more used. The whole region was becoming a satellite of Germany.

After World War II, Russia replaced Germany and all activities are now geared to hers. There are many developments in industry and farming with Russian aid and machines. The collective farm, so well established in Russia, is not always successful here, where so many peasants are now owners. They dislike bitterly the idea of merging their farms into a collective one. In 1960 nearly 80% of Polish farms, and 60% of Hungarian farms, were still in private hands.

Task 147.   Fig. 127 shows rye being harvested on a Polish farm:
(*a*) Are the methods old fashioned?
(*b*) Are the fields small?
(*c*) Do you think a peasant farmer could afford these machines? State what kind of farm you think this is.

Fig. 128. A modern Polish village

POLISH CULTURAL
INSTITUTE

Task 148. Look at Fig. 128. This shows a modern Polish village, but it is typical of the new villages all over East Central Europe. Each house stands in a small-holding.

(*a*) How do the houses compare with British farm cottages?

(*b*) Note the number of women with the cattle. Each is a smallholder's wife moving their own cows. Would this scene be normal in Britain? What does it tell you about the rôle of women in farm work?

The Countries To-day

1. *The Northern Group*

This consists of Poland, Czechoslovakia and Hungary.

They show more industrial development than the southern group, Poland and Czechoslovakia leading very markedly. This is due to: (*i*) good coalfields; (*ii*) German and Austrian technicians and managers having created organised industrial regions when they were in control.

So Czechoslovakia has a good industrial area in Bohemia, and Poland has one in Silesia. You can see them on Fig. 126.

CZECHOSLOVAKIA

Czech industry has always been famous, and even in the 19th Century its engineering products, armaments, pottery, glass and leather, were to be found all over the world. The main centres are Prague, Pilsen and Brno (*Brun*). Woollens are manufactured in the hill towns round the edge of Bohemia, where so many sheep are reared. Steel has long been an important product of Teschen and the Prague area. The Skoda armaments, the locomotive works, the new car industry and engineering depend on this steel.

Czechoslovakia has no sea coast, but the Elbe and Oder are both able to take 500-ton barges. The Elbe leads to the West German port of Hamburg and the North Sea. The Oder leads to the Polish port of Szczecin on the Baltic Sea. There is also the port of Bratislava, on the Danube, down which 500-ton and 1,000-ton barges move to the Black Sea.

A canal from the Oder to the Danube has been built by the Czechs and the Poles in the 1950's and these two rivers are now connected.

If you look at Figs. 125 and 126 you will see that Czechoslovakia has three distinct parts:

(*a*) the plateau of Bohemia;
(*b*) the valley of Moravia;
(*c*) the Carpathian mountain ranges.

The first two are inhabited by Czechs, and are industrialised, with good farming practice. The third region is Slovakia, the land of the Slovaks. These people are more backward and are chiefly peasants; but industry is spreading into their towns. Bratislava is the chief town. A great steel town is planned to be built before 1956 in Eastern Slovakia.

Prague is the capital of Czechoslovakia with a population of just under 1 million. It is a modern city with many fine streets, and with large industrial suburbs. In Fig. 129 you see a business street, with a statue of King Wenceslas, who was its king nine hundred years ago, when Bohemia was independent.

Fig. 129. *Prague*

Task 149. Notice the dress of the people in Fig. 129 and compare it with the dress in Fig. 141. Which country looks to be the more prosperous?

POLAND

Poland is almost entirely plain. Like the plains of Germany to the west, ice-sheets created large infertile districts by dumping gravel, sand, and boulders in ridges and sheets, As a result, the north, called the Masurian Lake Region, is very poor land, with much pine forest, heath, and lake.

The best farm lands are in the centre (Poznan, Lodz and Warsaw), and in the south (Silesia and Cracow). Everywhere is a monotonous scene of flat fields, pinewoods, marshes, drained and undrained, and sandy ridges.

Task 150. Look again at Fig. 127. What features of the description of Polish scenery, given above, can be seen in the picture?

Rye is the chief bread crop. It produces a very dark brown loaf, and is called *Black Bread.* It is the bread eaten by the poorer classes of all eastern and central Europe. Rye grows on poor soils, and ripens quickly in lands where winters are long and summers short. Wheat, sugar-beet, and potatoes are the other big crops. There is

Fig. 130. Poland, a
new steel tube rolling
mill

flax in Silesia. There are many cattle and pigs, and Poland is beginning to export animal products. Britain takes some. Machinery and fertilisers are now in great demand by the farmers.

Industry is chiefly in Silesia, where it was developed by the Germans and taken over by the Poles, partly in 1918, and totally in 1945. There is good coal and local zinc and iron, but a great new iron deposit at Nova Huta is now in full production, and a town of 100,000 has grown up there.

Fig. 130 is a view in a new tube rolling mill. It is typical of Poland, to-day. The plant has been made at Katowice and was being set up for production of steel tubes in 1960. Notice the enormous scale of the plant.

The Oder is a great waterway for trade, and the Vistula is being connected to it by canal.

Lodz has been a great textile centre since Russian days. Much timber is floated down the Vistula from the Carpathians, and Bydgoszcz (*Bid-gosh*) is an important timber centre. Wroclau (*Breslau* until 1945) is a great business city and market for the rich Silesian farmlands.

Poland, alone of the seven countries we are studying, has three large modern ports. Danzig, at the mouth of the Vistula, is her natural outlet, but the city was largely German before 1945 and so was made a free city. The Poles in the 1920's built Gdynia, probably the best and most modern port in Europe. Then, in 1945, they secured Szczecin from the Germans. All three ports are in use to-day. There is ship-building at Gdynia, Szczecin and Gdansk (Danzig).

Warsaw, the Polish capital, has a population of over 1 million. It is well situated in the centre of the country, on its main navigable river. It controls all routes into Russia from the west. It has many textile factories and machinery industries.

Task 151. What evidence is there in Fig. 130 that the picture was taken in winter, and that winter is a very cold season?

Task 152. Cracow was once the capital of Poland, and it is a very beautiful and historic city. Look at Figs. 125 and 126 and then write down some of the advantages which Cracow possesses as a town.

HUNGARY

Like Poland, Hungary is almost entirely plains but, unlike Poland, they are very fertile plains so that Hungary is a great farming country. It is a lowland, like Lombardy, enclosed in the loops of folded ranges and crossed by the river Danube. One of the big tributaries of the Danube is the Tisza. This is regarded by the Hungarians as the Poles regard the Vistula, and the Germans regard the Rhine—as their national river. All rivers in Hungary flow in broad marshy valleys which flood a great deal in heavy rains. It is noticeable how towns and villages avoid the rivers, and stand back from them.

The Hungarian plain is treeless like the Russian steppes. Its winters are very severe so that rivers and land freeze up from December to February. Its late summers are very dry, which probably explains why there are so few trees. Up to 1820 or so, this plain supported great herds of horses, cattle, sheep and goats. The typical Hungarian was a shepherd and horseman, or gentleman landowner. Since 1820 all

the best parts have been cultivated for cereals, especially wheat. Maize which ripens in the hot summers is also grown. Hungary has always a surplus of both cereals to sell abroad.

Fig. 131. *On the plains of Hungary*

BARNABY

Fig. 131 is a view on the great plains (or *Alfold*). You see the enormous expanses of cropland and the comfortable home. In the rear, not very clearly to be seen, is a village.

Task 153. Why are the houses so white? What is the crop in the foreground? How can you tell that a river is running across the plain on the far horizon?

In the North, where the land begins to rise to the Carpathians and there are many south-facing slopes to catch the sun, vineyards are found and one wine, *Imperial Tokay*, is world famous.

Task 154. Hungary produces the finest flour in Europe, but it is unknown in Britain. She also has ducks, geese and pig products for export in great quantities, but very few reach Britain.

Why is trade with Britain so small, when we need all these things, and why does Germany take so much of them? (*N.B. It has nothing to do with the Iron Curtain*).

Industry in Hungary

As an industrial country Hungary has less

advantages than Czechoslovakia or Poland. She has one small but good coalfield at Pecs (*Petch*) and small amounts of iron and bauxite, the clay from which aluminium is extracted. There is a small oil-field in the south-west near the frontier of Yugoslavia. All this is not much compared with the resources of Bohemia and Silesia and the great seaports of Poland. The inland position of Hungary is a great drawback for, except along the Danube, there is no way of moving materials cheaply in and out.

Nevertheless, there are great steel mills in the Budapest area, built with Russian aid. Her aluminium is being developed, and there are textiles (especially wool), tobacco and shoe industries in Budapest. In addition, there are industries depending on her farm products, *e.g.* flour-milling, brewing, sugar-refining, meat-preserving. These are in all the larger towns.

Task 155.

(a) If Hungarian products are sent *up* the Danube, how far can they go by river? (see Chapter 3). How would they reach Britain or Scandinavia?

(b) If they go *down* the Danube, how will they reach Russia, Spain and the Middle East? Which country is best placed for receiving the goods?

Budapest

This is the capital, with a population of nearly 2 millions, and the only very large town in Hungary.

g. 132. The rliament Buildings, udapest

RNABYS

If you look at Fig. 125 you will see that it lies on the Danube, near where the river emerges from gorges caused by its cutting through a ridge which crosses the plains of Hungary. Its position is a natural meeting place for routes across Hungary. It contains most of the industrial developments in the country. It is a strikingly handsome city as seen from the river. Fig. 132 shows the Parliament Buildings, built when Hungary, along with Austria, ruled a great empire. Note the great barges which carry so much Hungarian trade.

2. The Southern Group

These lands are Yugoslavia, Rumania and Bulgaria, with the small, unimportant country of Albania.

The general term *Balkans* was formerly used to describe the region, but *Balkan Peninsula* is better.

Task 156. A peninsula has water on three sides, at least. What are the three seas on the sides of the Balkan Peninsula?

In these countries, development has been much delayed by their poverty and lack of good communications. The blight of Turkish rule lay on them for centuries and was only removed finally in 1913. Nowhere were the evils of *landlordism* better seen than here.

The Peoples

Since people are based on valleys, the tangle of valleys has produced a tangle of peoples. This is brought out in Fig. 133. It is a diagram-map and shows the main valleys which cut into the highland masses. In each of these valleys a small national group has established itself and has spread over the highland from the valley. You can see the Bulgarians, Macedonians, Serbs and Bosnians (who are a branch of the Serbs), have all originated in particular valleys. The Rumanians grew up on the plain of the lower Danube. The Slovenes and Croats inhabited the plains of the Middle Danube and the valleys of the Sava and Drava tributaries. Dalmatians and Alban-

Fig. 133. *The peoples of the Balkans*

ians grew up on the Adriatic coasts, mixed up with many Italians.

Task 157. Look at Fig. 133.

(*a*) In what valleys did the Bulgarians, Serbs and Macedonians arise? (See an atlas map).

(*b*) Which people spread into Transylvania?

(*c*) Which people were best placed for controlling all routes in the peninsula?

RUMANIA

Fig. 125 shows the following regions making up this country:

(*a*) the wide fertile plains along the lower Danube and around the eastern edge of the Carpathians;

(*b*) the highlands of Transylvania;

(*c*) some of the edge of the Hungarian plains.

Farming is similar to that in Hungary. On the plains it is based on wheat and maize in great quantities, and many orchards of apples, pears, plums and peaches. The valleys of Transylvania show similar types of

*Fig. 134. Modern
plywood factory*
CAMERA PRESS

farming, but also there are many cattle reared. Often
rearing of cattle and sheep is connected with timber-
cutting in the Carpathians. The farms lie in forest
clearings. Much timber is floated down the rivers to
Galati on the Danube, where big timber industries are
found. In Fig. 134 is a modern plywood factory using
this timber.

Rumania has much wheat and maize for export.
It goes chiefly to Soviet Russia and the other countries
of the Balkans. Sulina is the port, on the mouth of
the Danube, which handles this trade.

Petroleum is the backbone of the prosperity of the
country. There is an oilfield north of Bucharest whose
production is reaching twelve million tons per year,
more than is needed by Rumania herself. Some is
exported, and to help this, a pipe line from Ploesti on
the oilfield to Constanza on the Black Sea, has been
constructed.

Task 158. How would Rumanian oil reach:
(*i*) the U.S.S.R.; (*ii*) Yugoslavia; (*iii*) Bulgaria; (*iv*)
Albania?

Task 159. Use your atlas, and draw a large map
of the mouths of the Danube. On it show the ports of
Sulina, Braila and Galati, and the oil port of Constanza.

Fig. 135 is a scene in a valley of Transylvania.
It shows a cattle market in the foreground and a village
in the rear, beyond the river. Notice especially the

g. 135. *A Rumanian cattle-fair*

ITISH RUMANIAN
IENDSHIP ASSOCIATION

g. 136. *Rumanians sheep-skin coats*

ITISH RUMANIAN
IENDSHIP ASSOCIATION

various dresses of the people. Some are in modern western dress, but many wear the old traditional costumes, including the round-shaped men's hat peculiar to Rumania. The bitter winters all over the Balkans result in sheepskin coats being very common. In Fig. 136 you see two Rumanians wearing rather elaborate ones.

Task 160. What are the men wearing under the sheepskins in Fig. 136? In Fig. 135 you may see many men also wearing this garment. Garments such as sheepskin coats would be very expensive in Britain, almost too dear for anyone but the rich to buy. Why do ordinary peasants wear them here?

Bucharest ($1\frac{1}{4}$ millions) is the capital and only really large

Fig. 137. A R
Farm in the Marit
Valley, Bulgar
FOX PHOT

town in Rumania. It has a good central position on the plains and has some industries based chiefly on local farm products, *e.g.* brewing, flour-milling. There are also some metal and machine industries.

BULGARIA

This small country of very tough, hardy peasants, has good plains along the Danube and the lovely, fertile Maritza valley. The rest is bleak highland. It is a country of peasant farmers with the usual crops of south-east Europe. Many sheep and cattle move up and down the valleys from summer to winter, as in

Fig. 138. T.
Metallurgical Pla.
at Dimitro
CAMERA PRE

the other lands of south-east Europe. One crop deserves special mention. It is shown in Fig. 137. Roses are grown on a tremendous scale in the Maritza valley and crushed to produce the essence from which Attar of Roses is manufactured. These very expensive perfumes are an export of the country. This scene is on a large Government experimental station. Notice the weather station in the middle distance.

Fig. 138 is evidence of the attempts being made in Bulgaria to introduce industries. There is useful coal, and small quantities of metallic ores, but hydro-electric power is being developed in the Balkan Mountains and other highlands. The picture shows a new steel plant being erected. Coal and iron from the U.S.S.R. move in easily across the Black Sea through the port of Varna. The capital is Sofia (800,000), on the main route from Istanbul to Belgrade.

YUGOSLAVIA

This country differs from the others of East Central Europe in that, although a Communist state inside the Iron Curtain in 1945, it came out again a few years later, owing to differences of opinion with the U.S.S.R. on the application of Communistic principles. Thus it is a country which is neither in the Communist bloc nor in the Western family of nations.

A Federal State

It is also different in that it is a Federal State. This means that it is divided into a number of separate republics, all of which manage their own internal affairs such as taxation, roads and education, but are subject to a Federal government at Belgrade, which manages defence, coinage, postage, foreign affairs, etc., for the whole country. There are six of these republics, and they are shown in Fig. 139.

This federal arrangement has been found necessary because of the different histories of the different parts of the country. Only Serbia and Montenegro were independent in 1912. Macedonia was still under Turkish rule. The rest were governed by Austria. Bosnia had only been taken over by Austria in 1908.

Fig. 139. *The
Republics of
Yugoslavia*

—▪—▪— Boundary of Yugoslavia

———— Boundaries of the Six separate Republics
formed in 1946

Added from Italy 1945-54

Croatia and Slovenia had been Austrian for centuries.
Between the two Wars of 1914-18 and 1939-45, the
bickering and strife between the different parts were
continuous and almost wrecked the country. The
present federal solution has put an end to that.

Yugoslavia has great fertile plains in the north,
where life is similar to that in Hungary, and with
similar products. Her wheat, maize, fruits and animal
products move easily up the Danube to Germany and
Czechoslovakia. They do not move so easily to the
sea coast, because between the plains and the sea, is a
wide belt of high, difficult country, thinly peopled, and
short of good roads and railways. On the coast, beyond
these mountains, lies Dalmatia, a region of beautiful

Fig. 140. Kotor, Yugoslavia
FOX PHOTOS

gulfs and coastal towns, islands and mountains, which has become one of Europe's great holiday centres. Fig. 140 is a view of Kotor. You see the long gulf winding in from the sea between the mountain ranges, which look barren and uninviting. The small town, on its equally small plain, has many Italian features in its buildings, *e.g.* the church towers and the tiled roofs, but also there are eastern features, *e.g.* the Orthodox Church domes. Notice the ancient fortifications. It is a typical Dalmatian town.

Rijeka (*Fiume*) is a port in the north, and is connected by railways to Belgrade.

South from Belgrade runs the Morava valley, the home of the Serbs. This connects easily to the Vardar valley leading to Salonica. This is the highway to the Mediterranean from the great plains of the middle Danube. The Vardar valley is the home of the Macedonians.

Fig. 141 is a view in the main square of the Bosnian town of Sarajevo, its capital. Here one sees something of the poverty of the highland regions. The background looks stony and forbidding, the town lacks good buildings, the people do not seem well dressed. Notice

the minaret of a mosque, and
the old man in Turkish dress.
It is evidence of the strength of
Mohammedanism here.

Task 161. Compare the
town of Sarajevo with Kotor
and give any facts you notice
which suggest that Kotor is in
a more prosperous area than is
Sarajevo.

Belgrade

This city is the natural route
centre of the whole Balkan
Peninsula (see Fig. 133). It is
built on the Danube where the
valleys of the Sava, Drava, Tisza
and Morava all lead to the main
river.

It is not either a very large
or an imposing city, for it has
653,000 people out of a total
for the country of 18½ millions,
and it was very much dam-
aged in World War One. Zag-
reb, the capital of Croatia, is
nearly as large, and is much more imposing, being full
of fine buildings erected by the Austrians.

Fig. 141.   *The Main
Square, Sarajevo*

FOX PHOTOS

Task 162. The following were the approximate
populations of the six republics in Yugoslavia in 1955.

Serbia (with Vojvodina)	8	millions	200 sq. mile
Croatia	4	millions	196 sq. mile
Slovenia	1½	millions	240 sq. mile
Bosnia (and Herzegovina)	3	millions	145 sq. mile
Macedonia	1½	millions	130 sq. mile
Montenegro	½	million	75 sq. mile

(a) Why should Serbia have so many more than the
other republics?
(b) Why is Montenegro so scantily peopled?
(c) Why have Bosnia and Macedonia more scattered
populations than Croatia or Slovenia?

CHAPTER 10

CO-OPERATION IN EUROPE

We have now studied in greater or less detail, all the countries of Europe outside the U.S.S.R. It is only too obvious that in this continent, the economic life of the nations is sharply divided into two different systems:

1. *East of the "Iron Curtain"*, all economic life is strictly controlled by governments acting on "Marxist" principles. (Named after Karl Marx, the thinker who first put forward these principles).

2. *West of the "Iron Curtain"*, the countries allow more freedom from rigid government control and permit a freer movement of money—personal gain from commerce and industry. This is called a "Capitalist Society". It calls itself Free Europe.

In the first group, there is great unity of planning and purpose. All work together to promote a common progress, under Russian leadership. In the second group there is far less unity, and the need for it has become more obvious to the governments of the member countries. Thus there have arisen, since 1945, various plans for co-operation between the countries of which the following are examples:—

The Council of Europe

Established in 1949 was the Council of Europe. It consists of Foreign Ministers or their Deputies and other representatives. It may discuss any matter concerning the welfare of the members but it may only make recommendations on them. It cannot discuss matters relating to defence. It meets at Strasbourg in Eastern France (see pages 44 and 45).

Task 163. Why is Strasbourg a good meeting place for peoples of Western Europe? Which countries' representatives have farthest to travel?

The Common Market

Then there have been several attempts to form a *Common Market* for Free Europe. This idea is to have as large a market as possible within which there shall be a free trade area, where there are no special tariff charges. This idea has crystallised into a *Six* consisting of Belgium, France, West Germany, Italy, Luxembourg, and the Netherlands, and a *Seven* which includes Austria, Denmark, Norway, Portugal, Sweden, Switzerland and Britain, as shown on Fig. 142. Britain was invited to become a member of the *Six*, but, as in so many cases, Britain has to bear in mind the interests of the British Commonwealth. There are many trade agreements between Britain and members of the Commonwealth which would, or might, clash with a tariff agreement of the *Six*. Therefore, Britain has approached entry into the *Six* with great caution and has been active in promoting the union of the *Seven*. The *Seven* are less tightly bound together than the *Six*. Britain's position is a complicated one and much discussion is going on.

The Common Market countries are not only bound together in trade and production which puts round themselves a wall of tariffs against all other countries, they also intend to standardise all manufacturing methods and transport, and gradually create some form of political unity. The Seven, or European Free Trade Association, are not going beyond the idea of lowering tariffs among themselves,

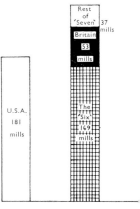

How populations the 'Six' and 'Seven compare with U.S.A and U.S.S.R

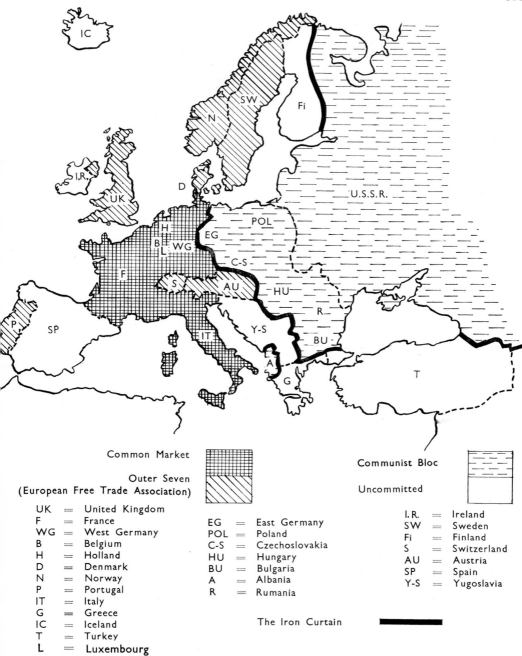

Common Market

Outer Seven
(European Free Trade Association)

Communist Bloc

Uncommitted

UK   =   United Kingdom
F   =   France
WG =   West Germany
B   =   Belgium
H   =   Holland
D   =   Denmark
N   =   Norway
P   =   Portugal
IT   =   Italy
G   =   Greece
IC   =   Iceland
T   =   Turkey
L   =   Luxembourg

EG   =   East Germany
POL =   Poland
C-S   =   Czechoslovakia
HU   =   Hungary
BU   =   Bulgaria
A   =   Albania
R   =   Rumania

I.R.   =   Ireland
SW   =   Sweden
Fi   =   Finland
S   =   Switzerland
AU   =   Austria
SP   =   Spain
Y-S   =   Yugoslavia

The Iron Curtain

ig. 142. *Trade Groups in Europe*

whilst still making separate tariff arrangements with outside countries. They want a loose system which will bring in all European lands outside the Iron Curtain.

However, there is no doubt about the general good of arrangements like the *Six* and the *Seven*, and Britain is doing all it can to harmonise their views with its Commonwealth commitments.

All these arrangements are an indication of the general European will to make a sound union in all matters which will strengthen Free Europe.

Task 164. Look at Fig. 142.

(*a*) Name the countries in Free Europe which are not committed to either the *Six* or the *Seven*.

(*b*) Why should Yugoslavia be one of these?

(*c*) How many Mediterranean countries are in either the *Six* or the *Seven*?

At the back of these discussions on the *Six* and the *Seven* is the European Coal and Steel Community. This was agreed in 1952, and is a plan based on working the coal, iron and steel industries of France, Holland, Belgium and West Germany as one unit.

The *High Authority* may fix maximum prices for steel, may control all price agreements, and promotes co-operation in mining methods and efficient production.

Thus we see how, in many ways, Europe is setting about solving its own problems. There are many other such ways, but old jealousies die hard. In Britain particularly, other calls prevent her from joining wholeheartedly in these proposals.

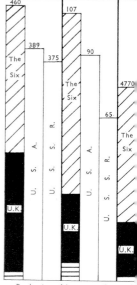

Production of Important Commoditi
Coal & Steel in million ton
Cars in thousands
=Rest of the 'Seven'

CHAPTER 11

ON THE WESTERN SIDE OF THE ATLANTIC

Our long survey of Europe is completed, and we now turn to the two large countries on the other side of the North Atlantic. They occupy, between them, over six million square miles of North America, more than two-thirds of all the continent. It is essential, then, that we begin by taking a brief look at this continent of North America.

Different kinds of Mountains

Look at Fig. 143. It shows that North America is built on much simpler lines than Europe, but it contains old, middle aged and young types of mountains.

(1) **The Western Mountain Ranges** correspond to those of southern Europe but they run in long north-to-south lines, whereas in Europe they run from east to west. The inside range, the Rockies, is the highest system with peaks over 14,000 feet, but there is another line of great ranges near the coast, which carries various names. Then there is a line of lower ranges along the shore, sometimes partly submerged as islands, sometimes forming peninsulas, and sometimes low ranges on land. Fig. 171 is a view in the Rockies.

Modern North America

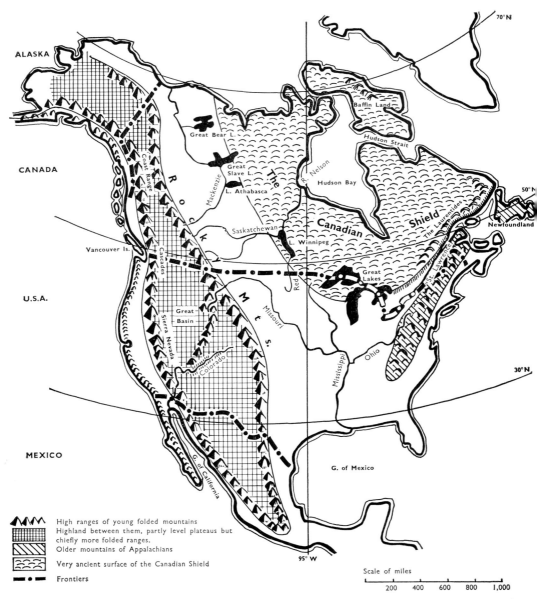

High ranges of young folded mountains
Highland between them, partly level plateaus but
chiefly more folded ranges.
Older mountains of Appalachians

Very ancient surface of the Canadian Shield

Frontiers

Fig. 143. The structure of North America

Task 165. Study Fig. 143.

(*a*) Name three ranges in the system running near the Pacific coast.

(*b*) In which country does the along shore range form: (*a*) islands; (*b*) a peninsula; (*c*) a mainland range?

(*c*) What lies between the Rockies and the ranges near the coast?

(2) **In the east are the Appalachians,** fairly old, worn down hill districts like the hills of central Europe and Britain. They are usually under 5,000 feet, but run in ridges parallel to the coast. Newfoundland is a detached part of the system.

(3) **The Canadian Shield** is one of the earth's oldest surfaces. Worn down from mountains over millions of years, it is now a low, very rough surface of hard rocks, with some ridges rising to 2,000 feet. Hudson Bay lies on the lowest parts, and is very shallow for its size. The edge is marked by a line of lakes, great and small. It is like the land occupied by the countries of Sweden and Finland in Europe. Fig. 155 is a view of the Shield and its surface.

Task 166.

(*a*) Name some of the lakes along the edge of the Canadian Shield.

(*b*) The highest parts of the Shield are in the Laurentides and Baffin Land. Find these on Fig. 143. The lowest parts are in Hudson Bay. Why do you think it is called a *Shield*?

Task 167. The rocks and age of the Appalachians are like those of the English Pennines. Measure in an atlas the length of the Appalachians, and compare it with the length of the Pennines.

Huge Plains

Between the mountain regions of east and west, lie enormous lowlands, remarkably level, and very fertile. They are crossed by equally enormous rivers. Fig. 143 shows these rivers to be in three great systems.

Task 168.

Which river system is contained entirely within the U.S.A.?

Which is the system in southern Canada? To where does it flow?

Which is the system of northern Canada? Into which Ocean does it flow?

Measure the length of the Missouri and that part of the Mississippi which continues it to the sea. If this were one river, it would be the longest in the world. (You can add 500 miles to your answer to allow for bends).

Task 169. If all these plains are so fertile, why should there be so very few people in the Mackenzie valley?

North American Climates

In Chapter 1 we made a brief survey of the climates found in the lands around the North Atlantic, and in Fig. 3 we showed the main types of climate found in North America and Europe. Look now at the climates of North America on Fig. 3, and read again the account in the chapter. The following facts are most important and must be clearly understood:

1. Westerly winds are the prevailing winds over most of Canada and the U.S.A.

2. These winds are in two streams: (*a*) from off the Pacific; (*b*) from off the Gulf of Mexico and the Atlantic.

3. Cold Polar winds are very prominent over Canada in summer, and over Canada and the U.S.A. in winter.

4. The mixing of these two air streams sets up many depressions and fronts which bring rain to most parts of the two countries.

5. The interior of the continent is extremely cold in winter, and this makes the air there very heavy. It is difficult for winds from the sea to enter because of this heavy air, so rainfall is small in winter, and what does fall is in the form of snow.

Westerly gales in the North Atlantic

Western Coasts of N. America. Forests, moors and snowfields

Task 170. After reading Chapter 1 on climate in North America, and studying Fig. 3, answer the following questions:

(*a*) In which parts do the Pacific westerlies give rain: (*i*) all through the year; (*ii*) only in winter?

(*b*) Which parts receive rains all the year from Gulf and Atlantic Westerlies?

(*c*) Which parts receive their rains chiefly in summer? Why is this?

(*d*) Which parts of the U.S.A. have a very dry climate?

The Great Regions of Canada and the U.S.A.

When we take into account the different climates of this great land mass, and also the main facts about its relief, we find that Nature has created certain large regions in the continent. We saw such regions in Asia when studying *The Asiatic World*, and in the Southern Continents in *The Southern Lands*.

In Fig. 144 are shown the regions as they exist in Canada and the U.S.A.

1. *The Oceanic Regions of the North-West*

Here the rains occur in every month, winters are mild, summers not very hot, because there is always so much cloud. There are very heavy relief rains against the mountain ranges. These ranges prevent the rains from moving inland, so that the oceanic region is a narrow one along the coast. Forests of enormous conifers like the Douglas Fir, Sitka Spruce, and Red Cedar, cover all the slopes and islands; and in the valleys, especially in the southern parts, deciduous trees like those in Britain are found. The northern part is like Norway, the centre like England, and the part in the U.S.A. like France.

2. *California*

The climate of winter rains and summer drought which we call *Mediterranean* occurs here. Depressions and fronts move south in the winter, but are further north in the summer. Winters are warm and summers very hot, for it is only 30° to 40° from the equator.

There is a good deal of woodland on the slopes of the hills, but the lowlands are often so short of rain as to need irrigation. It is a region like Portugal.

3. *The Eastern Region*

Atlantic air streams meeting polar air streams bring a great deal of rain to a wide area of eastern North America, all the way from the Gulf of Mexico to the Great Lakes. The rains are remarkably steady in amount throughout the year. The north has cold winters with much frost, but the winters in the south are quite warm. All the region has warm summers, but those of the south are very hot, with months of over 80° for average temperatures. The region was once covered in forests like those of Western Europe but, as in that continent, much of the forest has disappeared to make way for towns, factories and farms. The region is similar to central and northern China and Japan.

4. *The Interior Grasslands*

In the middle of the continent winters are very severe and the freezing of rivers and lakes lasts for many weeks. Summers are very hot, however, and it is then that the moist Atlantic and Gulf air streams are drawn in, to give summer rains. Enormous grasslands occur, with very few trees, but they grow poorer towards the Rocky Mountains. The Prairies are the better grasslands, the High Plains are the poorer ones. This region is like the Steppes of Europe and Asia.

5. *The Dry South-West*

On the borders of Mexico, and extending northwards between the high ranges, is the dry region of the U.S.A. Frontal rains from both Atlantic and Pacific are seldom able to pass over the mountain ranges, whilst to the south, near to Mexico, frontal rains do not occur. The dry Trades begin in these latitudes. (*The Southern Lands*, Chapter 7).

Winters are severe, for much of the area is plateau and mountain. Summers are very hot and dusty. Sage bush, creosote bush, cacti, tough grasses, thorny bushes, are the main types of plant cover. *Alkali* desert forms over big areas.

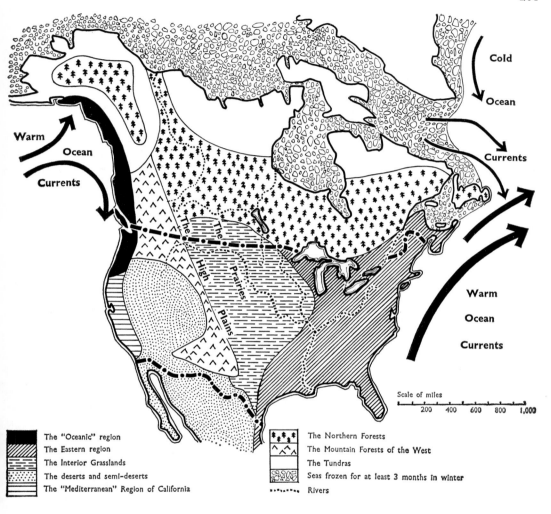

Fig. 144. *The natural regions of N. America*

The "Oceanic" region
The Eastern region
The Interior Grasslands
The deserts and semi-deserts
The "Mediterranean" Region of California

The Northern Forests
The Mountain Forests of the West
The Tundras
Seas frozen for at least 3 months in winter
Rivers

Cold Ocean Currents

Warm Ocean Currents

Warm Ocean Currents

Scale of miles
200   400   600   800   1,000

This region compares with Mongolia and Soviet Central Asia.

6. *The Mountain Forests of the West*

The higher slopes of the western mountains receive enough rain and snow, even in the dry belt, to support a woodland growth of pines and juniper. In some cases the woods are thick enough to make lumbering possible. This is especially so in Canada and the parts of the U.S.A. near to it.

7. *The Northern Forests and Tundras*

North of 50°N. the winters of North America grow very long and severe, and the summers become very short. We have seen this sort of country in Scandinavia and the U.S.S.R. Enormous extents of coniferous forest cover most of the southern portions, and this changes gradually into Tundra as one goes north, and the growing season becomes shorter and shorter.

The Canadian forest stretches for 3,000 miles from east to west, and 700 miles from north to south. It has only a few species of firs and pines, with birch trees and alder. Only these will survive in the poor soils, small rains, and fierce winter blizzards. Trees are very tall and straight. Many fur-bearing animals are found, *e.g.* bear, wolf, fox, beaver, mink.

Endless forests of the north

Tundra occurs where the ground becomes permanently frozen below the surface. The short summer thaws only the surface for a few inches. Stunted trees, like birch, grow with mosses, grasses and flowering plants. The season is only about six weeks long. For most of the year there are frozen wastes. This is the home of the Eskimo.

Task 171.

(a) Why should the sub soil in the tundra be frozen permanently? (See *The Asiatic World*, Chapter 10.)

(b) How does that explain why so much swampy land is found there in summer?

Task 172. Look at Fig. 144 and notice there the waters frozen in winter. How do you explain the fact that though these frozen waters are covering the mouth of the St. Lawrence on the east coast, on the west coast there is no freezing at all in the Pacific Ocean?

Task 173. For this task you will need an outline map of the world. In this chapter, and in Fig. 144, you have studied the major regions in North America, and corresponding regions in the continents of Europe or Asia have been given. Mark on your world map, with symbols similar to those in Fig. 144, the regions of America and the corresponding regions in Eurasia. Study your map and see if you can see a pattern in the way these different regions occur in the two land masses.

Contrasts in North America   1. *Winter in Eastern Canada.*   2. *Summer in California.*

CHAPTER 12

CANADA—A VIGOROUS YOUNG NATION

We are all familiar enough with Canada as the name of a land to which so many Britons have emigrated, but it may come as a shock to most of us to find that Canada is the second largest country in the world. Only the U.S.S.R. is larger. Canada stretches from east to west for 3,000 miles. The northern islands are within 6° of the North Pole, yet the Lake Peninsula of Ontario is nearer to the equator than are the French and Italian Rivieras. Canada extends further from north to south than does all Europe, and it is nearly as large as Europe, including Russia in Europe.

Its World position

We are also rather deceived if we think of Canada as being opposite to the British Isles. Look at Fig. 145. This is a view of the world with which we must become better acquainted. From it you can see that Canada lies opposite the U.S.S.R. Canada is directly between the two Great Powers of the modern world, the U.S.S.R. and the U.S.A.

Task 174. Notice, on Fig. 145, the position of Ottawa, the capital of Canada. Suppose direct flights were possible from Ottawa to (*a*) Delhi; (*b*) Tokyo; (*c*) Ankara; (*d*) Moscow. Name the countries, islands and seas crossed by each flight. What prevents these direct flights?

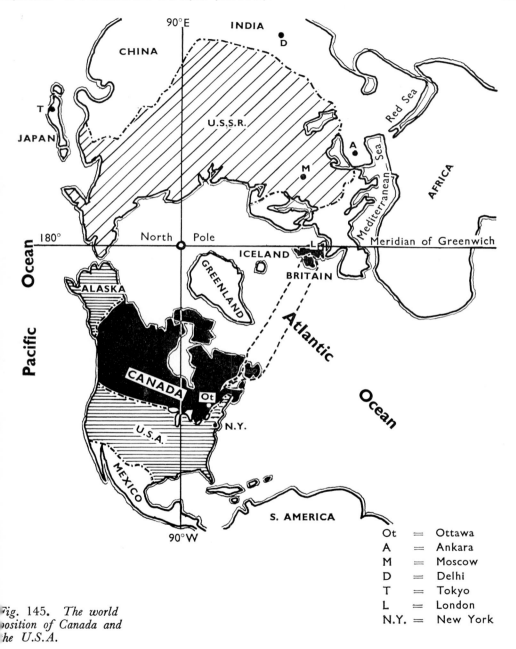

CHINA

INDIA

90°E

D

U.S.S.R.

T

JAPAN

A

Red Sea

Mediterranean Sea

AFRICA

M

180°

North Pole

Meridian of Greenwich

ICELAND

GREENLAND

BRITAIN

L

Pacific Ocean

ALASKA

Atlantic

CANADA

Ot

Ocean

U.S.A.

N.Y.

MEXICO

S. AMERICA

90°W

Ot	=	Ottawa
A	=	Ankara
M	=	Moscow
D	=	Delhi
T	=	Tokyo
L	=	London
N.Y.	=	New York

Fig. 145. The world
position of Canada and
the U.S.A.

How the people are distributed

Now let us examine Fig. 146. We should be familiar with much of it, for we recognise great areas of Tundra, Conifer Forest, and Western Mountains. These areas are hardly likely to contain many people and the map shows that this is so. Despite its great size, Canada has vast empty spaces and its population is only 18 millions. This gives a density of only 5 per square mile. So we have chosen a density of over 6 per square mile and shaded, in Fig. 146, the areas with such a density. It is a low one, yet not much of Canada reaches it. Notice that there are four separate areas of population.

1. *On the Atlantic Coasts*

Here live nearly two million Canadians in four provinces. (It is important to notice the Provinces of Canada, because each of the ten Provinces has its own government, and there is a Federal Government at Ottawa). There is Newfoundland, with its timber and fisheries, Nova Scotia, New Brunswick, and Prince Edward Island, where farming, sea fishing, and some lumbering are found. You will see them on Fig. 147.

2. *The St. Lawrence Valley*

A densely wooded series of Appalachian ridges separates the Atlantic coasts from the St. Lawrence valley. In this great valley, and in the Lake Peninsula, live $11\frac{1}{2}$ million Canadians, over 64% of all the population. Being between the Shield and the Appalachians, the valley is fertile and sheltered. All the main land and water routes of Canada pass through it. It is well farmed, and contains most of Canada's industry. It also contains the capital and the two largest cities in Canada, Montreal and Toronto. It is shared between the provinces of Ontario and Quebec.

3. *The Prairies*

800 to 1,000 miles of wilderness, chiefly coniferous forest, bare rock, and lakes, have to be crossed before we meet the next area of population. We then enter the great area of grasslands called the Prairies. Here

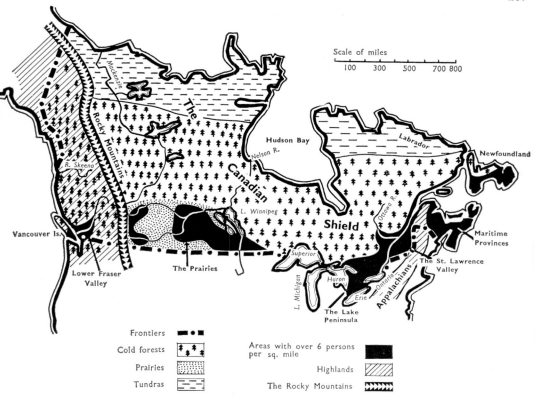

Scale of miles
100   300   500   700 800

Mackenzie
Rocky Mountains
R. Skeena
The Cold forests
Hudson Bay
Nelson R.
Canadian
L. Winnipeg
Shield
Labrador
Newfoundland
Ottawa R.
Vancouver Is.
Maritime Provinces
Lower Fraser Valley
The Prairies
Superior
L. Michigan
Huron
Erie
Ontario R.
The St. Lawrence Valley
Appalachians
The Lake Peninsula

Frontiers ■●■

Cold forests ‡‡‡

Prairies ░░░

Tundras ▭

Areas with over 6 persons per sq. mile ■

Highlands ▨

The Rocky Mountains ▶▶▶▶

Fig. 146. The natural regions of Canada

are to be found 3 million people, but the region is so large, that this only gives a density of about 10 per square mile. Here on these level, stoneless, almost treeless grasslands are great cereal farms, where huge machines in enormous fields produce much of the wheat we use in Britain. Coal and oil industries are of growing importance. Three provinces, Manitoba, Saskatchewan and Alberta, are found on the prairies, but each extends northwards into the forests.

4. *The Lower Fraser Region*

Once again wilderness faces us as we cross the Rockies, and enter British Columbia. Mountain ranges and plateaus follow one another, until we reach the Fraser valley (Fig. 146). Along the lower reaches of this river is the only reasonable amount of low land in the province and in it we find over 1½ million people. Half of them live in one city, Vancouver. This is a great port on the Pacific coast. The region is one of lumbering, salmon fishing, farming and mining.

Task 175. "Canada's people stretch from east to west like beads on a string, all within 300 miles of the U.S.A. frontier". Is this a good description? Can you give three reasons why you think so?

Task 176. To test what you have just studied:
(*a*) Which provinces use lines of latitude and longitude for boundaries?
(*b*) What parallel of latitude is used as part of the frontier between the U.S.A. and Canada?
(*c*) In which provinces is lumbering important?
(*d*) Why have Quebec and Ontario more people than the other provinces?
(*e*) What, roughly, is the population of Vancouver?
(*f*) Which are the smallest provinces?

Fig. 147. The Provinces of Canada

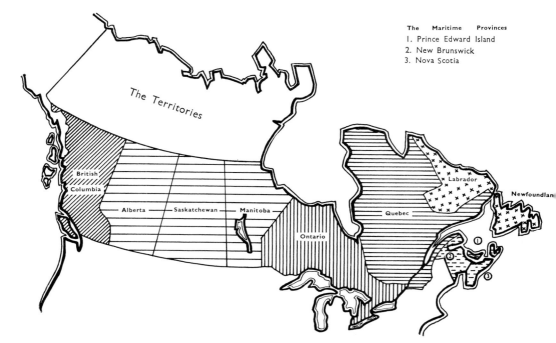

The   Maritime   Provinces
1. Prince Edward Island
2. New Brunswick
3. Nova Scotia

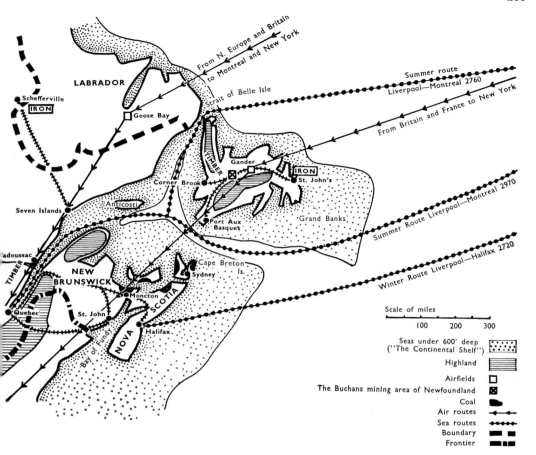

Fig. 148. The Atlantic entry to Canada

THE REGIONS OF CANADA

A. The Atlantic Coasts

We begin our survey of Canada's regions on the eastern side, on the Atlantic coasts. There is good reason for this. Here are the parts of Canada first sighted and settled by Europeans. The French entered the Maritime Provinces, and the British entered Newfoundland. Here also is the great estuary of the St. Lawrence river, the main seaway into Canada. By it, ships are now able to sail right into the Great Lakes. Then there are the two great international airports at Gander and Goose Bay, through which so many air routes enter Canada and the U.S.A. from the Atlantic.

Task 177. Look at Fig. 148.

(*a*) How many miles is it between Quebec and the point in the estuary opposite Port aux Basques? How long would a ship take to sail this distance at the rate of 300 miles in a day?

(*b*) Note the two summer sea routes from Liverpool to Montreal. Why is the one through Belle Isle Strait 240 miles shorter than the other? (Look at Fig. 145 where the routes are marked. A globe would be even better).

(*c*) Why is the winter route to Halifax used instead of one to Montreal? (See Figs. 6 and 144).

(*d*) What other port could be used in winter?

(*e*) Look at Fig. 145. Lay a ruler along the line London to New York, and another on the line Moscow to New York. Where do they cross Newfoundland and Labrador? Do the same for Ankara and New York. What conclusions do you draw?

A C.P. liner saili up the St. Lawren

Task 178. Look at a map of Canada. What other entry is there into Canada from the Atlantic besides the St. Lawrence? Why is it so little used?

The Maritime Provinces

As one sails into the estuary of the St. Lawrence, one passes between Appalachian ridges and valleys both to north and south. Those to the south form the Maritime Provinces, three small provinces, together equal in size to England and Wales. In the west, the densely forested ridges have few people. They live chiefly on the lowlands near the sea. They are mostly of British descent, but there are large groups of French Canadians as well, descendants of those French settlers who were here before the British took over in 1763.

The Maritime Provinces have a certain "British" look about them, owing to the mixture of woodland and cropland, meadows and country lanes, which have been brought into existence after 300 years of settlement.

The Harbour at
St. John's

The buildings are certainly different from those in Britain, for they are mostly of wood as one would expect in a land of much forest which is still lumbered. The summers are warmer than those of Britain and just as showery. They are ideal for British types of farming. Potatoes are an important crop in the north, and fruit in the south of Nova Scotia from which apples are exported.

Fishing is very important. On Fig. 148 you can see how much of the sea floor around the St. Lawrence estuary, is less than 600 feet deep. This is called the "Continental Shelf". Fish collect on these shelves in huge numbers. Every coastal settlement is a fishing village from which boats sail to the Grand Banks, and other areas. Cod, haddock and herring are the chief catches, with lobster and salmon inshore.

Cape Breton Island and the mainland near it possess valuable coal seams. Nova Scotia produces more coal than any other province. The mines run for miles under the sea. By using iron from Newfoundland, a large steel industry has grown up at Sydney.

The two chief towns are Halifax and St. John. Both are ports. Halifax has a very large harbour, which is ice-free in winter, so that it becomes the main winter port of Canada. St. John is on the Bay of Fundy, which has the highest tides in the world. Sometimes there is more than 60 feet between high and low tide.

Winters are severe in the Maritime Provinces. Long frosts are accompanied by much snow. The Labrador Current brings down so much icy water that the seas freeze all the coasts of the estuary. The warmer waters of the North Atlantic Drift keep the southern coasts ice-free.

Task 179

(a) Why should the government of Prince Edward Island employ a number of ice-breakers?

(b) At St. John (N.B.) a river enters the harbour over deep waterfalls. For a large part of the day, these falls disappear, and the water rushes *upriver* from them. Can you explain this?

Fishermen mending nets
Newfoundland

Newfoundland.   An Island of Fishermen

This island lies on the great continental shelf of eastern Canada, and is a little larger than Scotland. The shelf was formed by the sinking of the edge of the continent.   This sinking brought the sea up the lower parts of all the valleys, and so Newfoundland has hundreds of these drowned valleys, forming sea inlets which make good harbours.   From these harbours sail the fishing fleets to the Grand Banks.

This fishing can be both dangerous and uncomfortable.   The summer routes of shipping from Europe cross the middle of the Banks, and nets are cut and boats sometimes run down.   Then there is the dreaded fog which comes down on three days out of five in some months of the year.   The explanation of this fog was given in Chapter 1 (page 21).   It adds terribly to the hazards of fishing on the Banks.   Finally, in winter there is the raw coldness of the air, very near to freezing point, but full of moisture.   In Fig. 149 you can see fishermen drying cod at a small port in the island. "Cod is king" is a common saying in Newfoundland, but other fish mentioned in the paragraph on the Maritime Provinces, are also caught.   Great quantities of dried fish are exported to Mediterranean Europe, the West Indies, and South America.   Notice that everything is built of wood.   You also see the type of schooner used on the Banks.

Task 180

(a) Of what has the quay in the foreground been constructed?

(b) Fishing is done with lines of baited hooks, or with nets.   What method seems to be used in Fig. 149?

(c) Fishing is confined, in winter, to the south-west corner of the island. (Called the Avalon Peninsula).   Why is this?.

Sealing is a big industry, especially when ice-floes are about, and St. John's exports great quantities of seal oil.

The interior of Newfoundland has been called

Fig. 149. Drying cod at Wesleyville, Newfoundland
AEROFILMS

"a forest surrounded by fish". Few people live there. Nine-tenths of the Newfoundlanders still live along the south coast, with a half of them in Avalon. The cool, rainy summers followed by very cold, raw winters, do not encourage settlement, especially as soils are thin and the land rocky. This is a legacy from the Ice Age when ice sheets removed the soils. Nevertheless important developments are taking place in two directions.

(*i*)   A big mining area has opened up around Buchans (Fig. 148). Copper, lead, zinc and gold are mined.

(*ii*) There is a great paper industry at Corner Brook, and at Grand Falls near Gander. The forests are being cut for paper pulp, which is made into newsprint sent for use all over the Americas. As a result of this opening-up of the interior, a valuable farming colony is now established behind Corner Brook.

One single track railway runs across the middle of Newfoundland (see Fig. 148). All the developments so far have been on, or near to, this line. Other areas will develop when the railways are built there.

The capital, and only large town, is St. John's, in the Avalon Peninsula. Even so, it has only 88,000 people. It is the commercial centre of the island, makes fishing boats, and prepares for export all the products of the fishing industry. It is the nearest port of North America to Europe.

"The Land God gave to Cain"

This is the name given to the land called Labrador, which is administered by Newfoundland. It is a forbidding land. It is the eastern edge of the great Canadian Shield, with rough rocky surfaces, thin soils, and long icy winters. Much of it is tundra, and occupied by scattered Eskimo groups. Very little of the interior is properly known, but this state of affairs is coming to an end. In the far interior, on Knob Lake on the borders of Labrador and Quebec, a huge iron deposit was discovered in the early 1950's. It is now known to be one of the world's largest. U.S.A. and

Fig. 150. *Diggin for Iron Ore at Kno Lake, Labrad*

HIGH COMMISSIONER F
CANAD

Canadian money made development of the region possible, from a port on the St. Lawrence, at Sept Iles (Seven Islands). Railway and road were bull-dozed through the hundreds of miles of forest and tundra, and a town has grown up, just outside Labrador, named Schefferville (see Fig. 148). The ore comes down to Seven Islands, and then along the St. Lawrence to the great American steel belt on Lake Erie.

Fig. 150 is a view near Knob Lake. These barren wastes have become a hive of activity with modern machines and plant. Notice the train loading in the left rear. This is a midsummer view. Half the year it is a region with temperatures below freezing point.

Goose Bay, with its international airfield, is also helping to open up this forbidding territory.

THE REGIONS OF CANADA

B. *The St. Lawrence Valley and the Great Lakes*

Fig. 151. The St. Lawrence Valley and the Great Lakes

On entering the St. Lawrence valley, we follow the route which men have used ever since the French sea

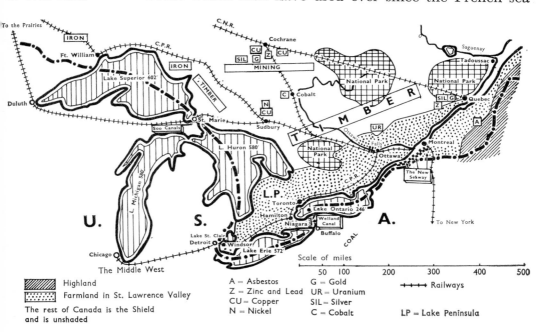

▨ Highland	A = Asbestos	G = Gold
▦ Farmland in St. Lawrence Valley	Z = Zinc and Lead	UR = Uranium
	CU = Copper	SIL = Silver
The rest of Canada is the Shield and is unshaded	N = Nickel	C = Cobalt

+++ Railways

LP = Lake Peninsula

captain, Cartier, entered the river 400 years ago and gave the country its name. We sail along the St. Lawrence. If we were on a great liner of over 20,000-tons, like the *Empress* ships of the Canadian Pacific Line, we should stop at Quebec, the old fortress town guarding the entrance to the valley (Fig. 156). Later we would probably sail 160 miles further up the river, to Montreal, the great city in the heart of the valley. Here ocean vessels used to stop, for the Lachine Rapids just above Montreal could not be navigated. The river itself is very wide, all the way to Lake Ontario, but numerous islands and rocky stretches spoil it for large ships. In 1959 the St. Lawrence Seaway was opened. This is a hundred miles of canals, locks, deep channels, and power stations constructed above Montreal. Now ships from the Atlantic sail into Lake Ontario (Fig. 152). In Fig. 153 you see a view of one of the locks on the new Seaway. The new channel runs alongside the river, which is wide and island-studded. Land traffic is heavy and the roads and railways which cross the Seaway are very numerous.

Task 181

(*a*) Whilst a ship is sailing through a lock, what happens to roadways and railways which cross at that point?

(*b*) How wide do you think the St. Lawrence is at this point?

(*c*) Why should it have been necessary to make a separate channel here for the Seaway?

(*d*) What lies on the opposite bank? (consult Fig. 157).

Fig. 152. The Seaway

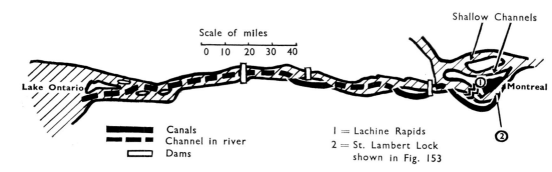

Scale of miles

0 10 20 30 40

Shallow Channels

Lake Ontario

Montreal

▬▬▬ Canals
▬ ▬ ▬ Channel in river
▭ Dams

1 = Lachine Rapids
2 = St. Lambert Lock
shown in Fig. 153

Fig. 153. The St.
Lambert Lock on the
St. Lawrence Seaway

OX PHOTOS

Through the Lakes

At the end of Lake Ontario a big snag occurs. Between this lake and Lake Erie, is a steep escarpment and a river, the Niagara, plunges over this scarp to unite the two lakes. Niagara Falls is world famous.

Task 182. Look at Fig. 151.

(a) What is the difference in height between Lakes Erie and Ontario? Ships have to be raised or lowered by this distance.

(b) What is the name of the canal that by-passes Niagara? If a lock is able to raise a ship by 30 feet only, how many will this canal need? Comment on the time taken to pass through it.

(c) What is the difference in height between Lake Erie and Lake Huron? Is this serious enough to need a canal? (Note the distance by water between them).

What waterways are used to connect them?

Once in Lake Huron, ships can sail direct to Chicago and Duluth in the U.S.A., and to Fort William in Canada, but notice that before they can enter Lake Superior another set of canals has to be used.

Task 183. What is the name of these canals? (There are two, one on the American side and one on the Canadian side. See Fig. 151). What height has a ship to be lifted here?

There, then, is the great Seaway, one of the finest systems of inland navigation in the world. From Port aux Basques, we have come nearly 2,000 miles. The loads carried are enormous. Nearly 50-million tons of freight went through the Seaway in 1959.

Task 184. A serious bottleneck has developed on the Seaway. Can you say where it is likely to be? Why?

Ft. William

Montrea

Task 185. Copy or trace Fig. 154 into your books. On it add the names of the lakes, their heights above sea level, the names of the canals and the Seaway.

Fig. 15

At the Centre of Things

The new Seaway is only one sign of the activity and movement along the St. Lawrence valley. Land routes reach out westwards to the prairies, south-westwards to the Middle West of the U.S.A., southwards to New York, and northwards over the Shield. It is the hub of Canadian life. It was the first part to be settled, and has always been the most important area in Canada.

Task 186. Look again at Fig. 151.

Describe the routes as shown on this map, between Montreal, and: (*a*) the prairies; (*b*) the Middle West.

It is not only the fact that it is the centre of move-ment in Canada that accounts for the valley being so well peopled. It is a large, broad valley with good farmland, and it has very warm summers, much warmer than those of Britain. Down in the Lake Peninsula, the latitude is that of Central France, so the summers there are warm enough to ripen peaches and grapes. British type fruits are found everywhere. There is much dairy farming, for the cities need milk daily. There is a high production of cheese, some of which is sent to Britain. One interesting crop is maple sugar. This is tapped from a deciduous tree, the maple, which is a native of Canada. The Maple Leaf has become the national emblem.

Industries on the Shield

The valley of the St. Lawrence cannot be understood properly, unless we consider also the vast extent of the Canadian Shield to the north of it. This Shield has great mining and lumbering industries that increase still further the wealth and importance of the valley. All the big cities and business centres lie in the valley, and the trade and production of the Shield are controlled from it.

Fig. 155. The Gatineau River, Quebec, and the power stations at Chelsea

HIGH COMMISSIONER FOR CANADA

First, there is the edge of the Shield against the valley. This is often steep, and the rivers have rapids, or even falls, where they enter the valley. Ottawa itself was built at the foot of one such falls. A great amount of hydro-electric power is generated along this edge and is used in the towns and factories of the valley. Then, on the Shield itself the rough surface creates many rapids and falls, and many of these are harnessed for power, for use in mining and lumbering industries.

Fig. 155 is a view on a Quebec river, showing two power stations. It is typical Shield country. There is the winding river in its rocky bed, with rapids in the middle distance, partly drowned by the lake behind the dam. The hard, rough, forest-covered Shield stretches endlessly away in the distance. It is important timber country.

Task 187

(a) Mention two places where the old, rocky river bed is now exposed.

(b) Why has the river been narrowed so much at both power stations?

'Ware Timber

The huge lumbering industry of eastern Canada is chiefly in the area of the Ottawa River, around Tadoussac and the Saguenay River, with a smaller region along the shores of Lake Superior and Lake Huron. In every case there is a waterway available to bring the timber to civilisation. Much of the great forest region is useless for timber because it is so isolated in this respect. You should compare this region with Siberia in *The Asiatic World*, Chapter 10, for conditions are very similar. Cutting has been going on for over 60 years, the first forests have disappeared from much of this part of the Shield, and sometimes the trees are part of a third growth. Replanting goes on all the time. When the trees are 35 to 40 years old they are cut down. They are young and small, and so unsuitable for timber, but they make excellent pulp from which paper is produced. The output of newsprint is quite fantastic. All the newspapers of both Americas, as well as many

Log jam on the Quebec River

of those of Europe, obtain their paper here.

Most of the big paper mills are in the valley. Ottawa is a very important centre.

Task 188

POSITION OF CANADA AS PRODUCER OF MINERALS 1963	
Nickel	1st
Platinum	1st
Asbestos	1st
Gold	2nd
Aluminium	2nd
Uranium	2nd
Zinc	3rd
Silver	3rd
Lead	4th
Copper	5th
Iron	5th

(*a*) What advantage is the long frozen winter to the lumberers?

(*b*) If you were the owner of a large stretch of forest in this region, and you cut trees down when 20 years old, how would you organise your territory so that there were always trees to cut?

(*c*) Compare this region with Sweden and Finland in Chapter 3. In what ways are the products different?

Minerals Galore

Away to the west of the Ottawa valley is a huge area of the Shield where mining overshadows everything else. It is not easy to get timber out from here, so the region was neglected till the building of the railway from Quebec to Winnipeg, during World War One. Before that, the building of the Canadian Pacific line from Montreal to Winnipeg, which was opened in the 1880's, had enabled the Sudbury district to begin mining operations. Find both these lines on Fig. 151. Copper, silver, lead, and zinc, as well as some gold, are the chief minerals. Good deposits of iron ore are found near Lake Superior. Enormous supplies of nickel and cobalt, the largest in the world, come from Sudbury and Cobalt. Two sources of uranium occur also, one near Ottawa, and the other near Lake Huron. Further supplies of silver, lead and zinc, with some gold are found near Quebec. Everywhere production grows, new mines appear, and Canada finds herself one of the world's chief producers of minerals.

Even in the small part of the Appalachians which extend to Canada, there are valuable mines for copper, zinc, lead, and asbestos. The country produces 70% of the world's asbestos.

The Cities

We have now seen four reasons for the importance of the St. Lawrence valley;

(*a*) It is a focus of land and water routes.

(*b*) It has very good farmland, and hot summers with plenty of rain.

(*c*) It is the business centre for the great lumbering and mining industries.

(*d*) It is the main entrance into Canada.

We can now add a fifth. Just across Lake Ontario and Lake Erie, is the largest coalfield in the world, and the largest industrial region in the U.S.A. Thus everything aids industry in the valley, and we should expect large and growing towns to be there.

Quebec

We have seen that Quebec is the entrance to Canada from the Atlantic. One of its interests, therefore, is

Fig. 156. *Quebec*

shipping. In Fig. 156 you can see the town and its port. The first town was built as a fortress, at a point where the St. Lawrence estuary suddenly narrowed and seventeenth century guns could command the river. The fortress was built on high ground, and this can be seen in Fig. 156, where the old walls can still be traced. You can see the high bluffs on which the old town stood, and the tributary river running into the St. Lawrence, which was a useful defence. To-day, the port lies all round the old fortress, and docks and warehouses spread along both rivers. In the background, along the tributary, are large paper and pulp mills and, between them and the docks, are shipbuilding yards. There are many engineering works. The main interest of Quebec, however, is government. It is the capital of the province, with its own Parliament and Civil Service. Only a small fraction of its people speak English. Quebec is the heart of French Canada.

Task 189. The population of Quebec in 1961 was 172,000. Look carefully at Fig. 156, and say what evidence there is in the picture, that the town is expanding.

Montreal

This is the largest city in Canada, and has a population of 1,191,000. It is situated where French-speaking Quebec meets English-speaking Ontario, and so is equally divided between the two languages. Montreal is the greatest inland port in the world if we count ships' tonnage using it. Ocean liners still stop here, but cargo vessels go on into the Lakes, and lake vessels come down river to it. Enormous quantities of prairie wheat arrive each autumn, to be transferred to ocean ships or to be left in storage.

It is the centre of all the Canadian railways, as is seen in Fig. 157. It was built on a large island, where the Ottawa and St. Lawrence come together. Until 1959, no ocean vessels could go beyond it, on account of the Lachine Rapids, so it became a great port. It has many industries especially cottons, woollens, clothing, and light engineering.

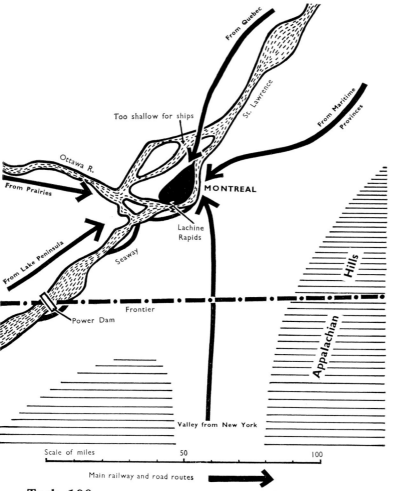

Fig. 157.   *The position of Montreal*

Task 190

(*a*) 2 million people live in and around Montreal. What proportion is that of all Canadians? (18 millions).

(*b*) Look at the portion of the Seaway on Fig. 157. Describe its course from Montreal to the edge of the map.

Ottawa

Ottawa is the Federal capital of all Canada.   A

great lumbering centre, it has many wood and metal industries. Most of its people, however, depend upon government services for their living. It is growing extremely quickly and nearly 300,000 live in and around it.

Toronto

This is a great city and port on Lake Ontario. Here one finds one's self in the middle of the great manufacturing belt of Canada, using coal from the U.S.A. and hydro-electric power both from the Shield and the power station at Niagara Falls. Many industries from the U.S.A. have entered Canada in this area. Motor cars, farm machinery, steel for bridges and buildings, chemical industries, glass and textiles are all found in the Lake Peninsula, especially at Toronto, Hamilton, and Windsor, opposite Detroit. Toronto is the business centre for all these, and for many of the metal industries on the Shield to the north. It is also the capital of Ontario, the largest and richest of Canadian provinces.

Fig. 158 is a view of the city from the lake. In the

Fig. 158. Toronto

AEROFILMS

Fig. 159. Steelwork at Hamilton, Ontario
HIGH COMMISSIONER FOR
CANADA

foreground is the harbour, much of it built on land reclaimed from the lake. In the rear the city stretches for miles, with the business centre easily identified by the skyscrapers. In and around Toronto are nearly as many people as in Montreal and its suburbs.

Task 191. Why do you think that the foreground of the picture has been built up out of the lake?

Task 192. Fig. 159 is a view of a steelworks in Hamilton. Look at Fig. 151. Why is hydro-electric power plentiful in Hamilton? Where is (*a*) coal, and (*b*) iron ore likely to be obtained? Comment on the houses of the workers as shown here.

The Frozen Winter

All over the St. Lawrence valley winters are troublesome. Not only does the land freeze for many weeks, but the river freezes from November to March, and the estuary is not open till April. The Lakes are too dangerous for navigation from early December till March. The depressions moving along the coast bring very heavy snowfalls over the frozen land, and snow-ploughs are always busy. This hampers trade, for ships can only berth in the Maritime Provinces, and they are a considerable distance from the valley. New York in the U.S.A. does a lot of trade for Canada in winter.

THE REGIONS OF CANADA

C. *Central Canada*

After leaving the St. Lawrence valley, we make our way westwards across the Shield for 1,200 miles, through forests of conifers and scenes like those in Fig. 156. A day and a half after our train leaves the valley, the landscape changes. The old, hard, barren rocks on the Shield, the numerous lakes, rapids and waterfalls, give way to a huge expanse of level plain, almost treeless, and covered with cultivated fields. It is a fertile land, with almost stoneless soils. It is called *The Prairies*. Here, organised in three Provinces, which also include large areas of the great forests to the north, is another of the concentrations of people in Canada.

Task 193. Look at Fig. 160.

(a) Name the three provinces in order from east to west.
(b) Roughly, what fraction of each province is prairie?
(c) What is the width of the prairies from Winnipeg to the Rocky Mountains?
(d) Between what latitudes do the Prairie Provinces lie? What do they use for boundaries in most cases?

The Gateway to the Prairies

Almost as soon as we enter the prairies from the east, we find ourselves in Winnipeg. All routes from east and west seem to meet in this city of 265,000 people. Fig. 160 shows this clearly. Not only is it the gateway from the east into the prairies, but it is also the gateway of a much older route. When the French held the St. Lawrence valley, the British established a trading company on the shores of Hudson Bay, the Hudson Bay Company. The British moved inland along all the rivers, trading with the Indians and trapping. Following the Nelson into Lake Winnipeg, they sailed down that lake and found themselves in the prairies. On the Red River, where a tributary joined it, they built

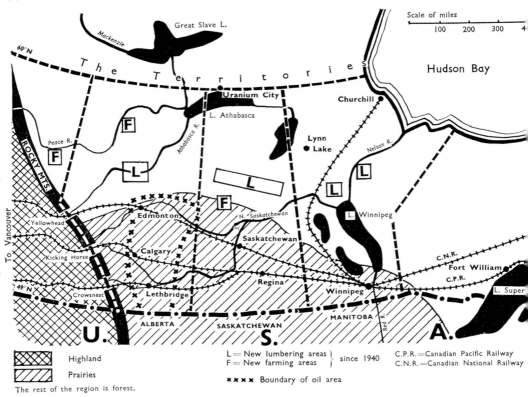

L = New lumbering areas } since 1940
F = New farming areas }

C.P.R. = Canadian Pacific Railway
C.N.R. = Canadian National Railway

Highland
Prairies
The rest of the region is forest.

× × × × Boundary of oil area

a fort and trading post, called Fort Garry, to trade with prairie Indians. From this fort, Winnipeg has grown.

Fig. 160. The positi of Winnipeg Central Cana

Task 194. Winnipeg is the front entrance to the prairies. Look at Fig. 160, and find three "back entrances" to the prairies in the west. These are passes in the Rockies. Name them and the three towns which lie below them.

Wheat is King

As soon as one looks around in Winnipeg, it is obvious that the city is concerned chiefly with wheat, its growth, harvest, and transport. A great part of the prairies is given over to wheat production. Farms are large, fields are enormous by British standards, and operations are carried out by big machines and few men. (See Chapter 13, Fig. 190 where similar conditions prevail in the U.S.A.). If you look at Fig. 161, you can see a typical scene near Regina, in the heart of the prairies. There are the level treeless plains, the large square fields, the farm buildings surrounded by trees planted as wind breaks, for winter blizzards are terrible on these plains. Notice the highway running straight for many miles across the land. Its centre is metalled, which shows it to be a great State highway. Prairie roads are usually unmetalled, and very rutted and muddy in wet weather. Stoneless plains make road metal difficult to find in any case.

Task 195. Compare the scene in Fig. 161, with that in Fig. 155. Make a list of the facts you notice, under the headings (*i*) the surfaces, (*ii*) the plant cover, (*iii*) the use made of the land by people.

Task 196. (*a*) Does the population density seem very great in Fig. 161? (*b*) Are there any signs of animal rearing? (*c*) Note carefully the land given up to the road. What does this suggest about the use of land in this region?

ig. 161. Prairie 'arm near Regina, askatchewan

IGH COMMISSIONER FOR ANADA

Growing the Wheat

Prairie wheat is "Spring Wheat". It is sown in April or May after the long winter freeze-up is over. Winters are most severe. Temperatures are below freezing point for four or five months, blizzards sweep the land, and outdoor work is impossible. The farmers repair machinery and visit neighbours. Snow is only light, because the air is too cold to hold much vapour, so there is no thick snow cover to protect the surface of the ground. Then, in April, the sun's heat begins to warm up the prairies, and the thaw sets in. Everything becomes damp and the fields soggy. Roads are quagmires. With the warm sun and moist ground, the wheat is quickly sown and grows rapidly. Then comes the hot summer, when day temperatures exceed 70° for over three months. At the same time ocean winds are drawn in to the heated plains, and showers are frequent. By August the fields are ripe for the harvest. The wheat has only been in the ground for three to four months, and sometimes less. Certain varieties will ripen in 80 days.

The Prairie in Sprin

Task 197.

(*a*) In which season was the picture in Fig. 161 taken? Give reasons.

(*b*) British wheat is sown in October and harvested in August. Compare this with the time taken in the prairies.

Moving North

If you look at Fig. 160 you will see three areas into which farmers have been moving for the last 20 years. Those on the Peace River are in the forests, but the area in Saskatchewan is in the Grove Belt, an area of mixed grassland and trees where the prairie changes into forest. All these new areas depend on quick ripening wheats like the 80-days type, for these can be grown in the shorter summers there. On Fig. 143 you saw that the soils of these regions were fertile and stoneless like those of the prairie. There is a wind in this region, which is a great boon to the farmers. It is called *the Chinook*. It blows down from the Rockies in the spring and is part of the first great currents of air to move into the continent from the Pacific, as the land mass heats up. As it moves down from the Rockies into the Prairies, it is very warm and dry, and causes a rapid thaw. The rapidity of this thaw adds some weeks to the growing season in the Peace River valley.

Transporting the Wheat

Little of the wheat grown in the prairies is intended for use in Canada. The majority of the crop goes abroad, especially to Europe. Britain's flour is made up mainly of Canadian wheat. The problem of carrying this wheat out to the Atlantic or Pacific coasts is a very big one. Not only are there great distances to cover, but there is a time factor as well. The freezing-up of the coasts and riverways begins in November. When the wheat is ready, a firm of hauliers who have bought the crop, bring their trucks to the field and harvest it. (Fig. 190). These trucks take the wheat to the nearest railway station where it is loaded into elevators, tall buildings with several floors. The wheat falls through from floor to floor as it is loaded on to the trains, and this process helps to clean it, and to sort it. Trains carry the crop to Winnipeg, the great collecting centre. Here it is sorted and cleaned again, graded and priced for the world export trade. Some is retained to be made into flour for local use, or to be sent to Montreal or Quebec by train. From Winnipeg the wheat goes various ways, but the bulk goes to Fort William, to be loaded on to ships. Carriage by train is too expensive for the grain, unless it is made first into flour. The much cheaper Lakes route, now called the Seaway, is essential if the trade is to go on. This route passes through Lake Superior, Lake Huron, the St. Claire river and lake, into Lake Erie. (Fig. 162). Two types of ship are now competing for this traffic. First there is the "whaleback" or Lakes steamer which is seen in Fig. 163 loading at Port Arthur. Whalebacks are very long, but take only a small depth of water. Living quarters and stores are all on deck level, and only the engines are below deck. The hull is one vast storage space

Elevators at a railway station

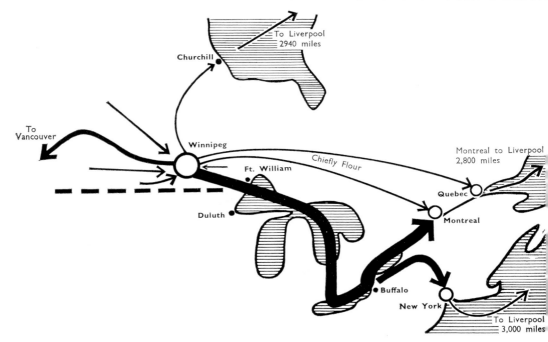

divided into compartments to prevent the grain from
moving about. They are loaded from the elevators,
as shown, by long pipes.

Fig. 162. *The
movement of Canadian
Wheat*

Now the Seaway is in being, there is a second type
of ship at Fort William. It is the ocean freighter which
has come probably from some port in Europe. It is
much larger than the whaleback, but cannot sail in
water less than 27 feet deep. This hampers it at the
lakeside ports, few of which have that depth. Then,
being more stoutly built because it has to weather
ocean storms, its cargo space is less than the whaleback's.

Task 198. In which parts of the ship shown in
Fig. 163, are (*i*) the engine; (*ii*) the officers' quarters?
Can you recognise the crew's quarters?

At Lake Erie, some of the wheat is diverted to New
York from the port of Buffalo. So much wheat comes
through, that the elevators at Montreal cannot handle
it all. Then we have to remember that Montreal closes

Fig. 163. A Whale-back loading wheat at Port Arthur

PICTORIAL PRESS

in November because of ice, and New York is always open. Traffic on the Lakes ceases in November, or December, and then the western route to Vancouver comes into action. Trains carry the wheat to this port which is always ice-free. Some of it goes to the East, but much comes to Europe via the Panama Canal.

There is a third route shown in Fig. 162, the one via Churchill on Hudson Bay. This is the shortest route to Liverpool, and the cheapest, but only a small percentage goes this way. The reason is that ice is active in Hudson Strait in October, so the export season lasts only five or six weeks.

Task 199.
(a) Why is the wheat for Vancouver forced to go by rail?
(b) How is the wheat carried to Churchill?

Task 200. On an outline map of the world, mark the Canadian prairies, Winnipeg, Vancouver, and Montreal. Show by arrows, the routes followed by the wheat to Britain.

Fig. 164. Prairie Farms and oil-drilling, Alberta

AEROFILMS

Industry in Central Canada

Up to a few years ago, the prairies were almost entirely farming land but, recently, there have been very important developments in Alberta. There is a large amount of coal under the prairies in this area, but it has not been exploited very much because there is so little demand in a region with few towns and industries. To send it to the St. Lawrence region would be far too expensive, for it would be rail travel for much of the way. Hence, apart from some mines in the Lethbridge area, there is no development. The coal is used by the railways, chiefly. Within the last ten years, another mineral, oil, has been found to exist in large quantities, chiefly within the region shown on Fig. 160. This is of great importance. There is a great deal of it, in both liquid and gas forms, and pipe lines have been made to carry it to Lake Superior, to Ontario, and to Vancouver. This means that all the Prairie Provinces and British Columbia have available large quantities of gas and oil.

Fig. 165. The endless forests of the Canadian Shield

HIGH COMMISSIONER FOR CANADA

Every week fresh wells are made. Look at Fig. 164. It is taken where the Grove Belt is beginning, and it should be compared with Fig. 161. One sees the same great fields under the plough, the same scattered farms, but there are many trees. In several places one sees the borings for oil which in most cases will become true oil wells.

Other developments are in the industries connected with the Shield. Lumbering is opening up just north of the Grove Belt, and mining is on the increase. Right up beyond the Prairie Provinces mines are developing. The aeroplane is playing a vital part. Look at Fig. 165 which shows once again the endless forests of the Shield, this time near Great Bear Lake, just visible on the horizon. The plane tells us that oil is being produced up here in the Arctic. There are enormous reserves.

Task 201. What evidence is there in Fig. 165 of man's activities? Why is the plane a flying-boat?

There is great variety of minerals. Copper and nickel at Lynn Lake, lead and zinc on Slave Lake, and

Fig 166. *A gold-mine at Yellowknife*

NATIONAL FILM BOARD OF
CANADA

gold at Yellowknife just north of it. Uranium City speaks for itself, and Canada is one of the greatest producers of this metal. Port Radium on Great Bear Lake is another source. Fig. 166 is a mine at Yellowknife, in the Arctic wastes of the Territories. Offices and living quarters are in the foreground, the mine is left centre, the crushing mill in the rear, and the oil fuel tanks are easy to identify. Notice how utterly barren is the landscape. There is no attempt to grow anything. Winter is eight months' long in such places.

Edmonton

The town benefitting most from all this is Edmonton, capital of Alberta. It has become the gateway to the North-west with railways, highways, air routes and riverways all going into the region. You will see this in Fig. 167. The Alcan Highway was a very clever feat of road engineering across most difficult country. It was built by the U.S.A. and Canadian Governments during the Second World War to carry troops and materials to Alaska, but it has helped greatly in opening up the north.

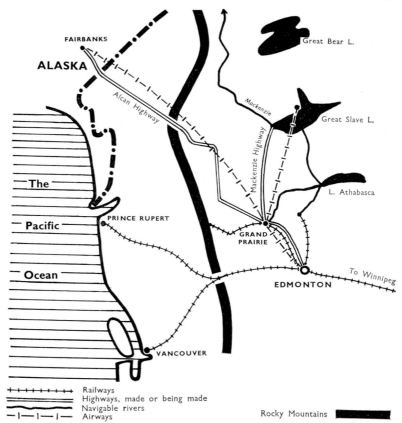

Fig. 167. Edmonton, the gateway to the North-west

FAIRBANKS

ALASKA

Great Bear L.

Alcan Highway

Mackenzie

Mackenzie Highway

Great Slave L.

The

L. Athabasca

Pacific

PRINCE RUPERT

GRAND PRAIRIE

Ocean

To Winnipeg

EDMONTON

VANCOUVER

+ + + + + + + + Railways
Highways, made or being made
Navigable rivers
—1—1—1— Airways

Rocky Mountains ▬▬▬

Task 202. In how many ways could you travel from Edmonton to (*i*) the Great Slave Lake; (*ii*) Lake Athabasca? Use Fig. 167.

Calgary

This town is the centre of a cattle-ranching industry on the prairies around it. In this corner of Alberta begins that great zone of cattlemen and cattle towns that extends right down the front of the Rockies into Texas. Rains are not good enough for crops. We shall see more of this later.

Scattered over the prairies, at wide intervals, are small towns where farmers do all their business. Most of these towns have between 5,000 and 10,000 inhabit-

Fig. 168. *The main
street of Portage La
Prairie*

E.N.A.

ants, and are usually on a railway. They are places where wheat is stored when brought from the fields. Fig. 168 is a view in one such town showing the main street.

Notice the great width of the street. As in Fig. 161, much land is given to the road. Land is plentiful here. Then notice how everyone seems to use a car. Farmers come great distances to do their business in these towns. Shops, cafés, hotels, garages and cinemas are to be found in all these towns, and all cater for the farmer.

Task 203. In addition to supplying the railways, the Alberta coalfield supplies big demands from the people who live on the prairies. Why should they use so much coal?

Task 204. In the Arctic regions, away from lumber camps and mines, and remote from roads or railways, trappers still catch silver fox, mink, beaver, etc., for their valuable skins, and hunt moose, caribou, and musk ox for meat. In Fig. 169 you see a modern trapper's house in the delta of the Mackenzie, as far

Fig. 169. A trapper's shack in the Mackenzie River Delta area

PAUL POPPER LTD.

north as one can go in Canada. It is a typical modern home, with electric light and power supplied by a small gas engine.

(a) Describe how the house has been constructed.
(b) How is it heated?
(c) Apart from electric light, what other signs of modern conveniences are there to be seen in the picture?
(d) How would goods from Edmonton reach this remote house?

The Native Races

It is convenient at this point, to say something of the native peoples who live in Canada, especially as they are in these central and northern parts. First, there are the Eskimoes. Only 11,000 are now to be found and they are disappearing as a race as a result of intermarriage with white people. They were a good example of fitting life to local conditions. You must have read many accounts of how they made light boats from skins and whalebone, and hunted in them for seals, walrus, and small whales. From these they obtained meat, skins for clothes and summer tents, fats and oil for fuel and light. Animal bones made spear heads, harpoons, knives and needles. Even the snow was used to build their winter home, the igloo. The Eskimo learned to live with the cold.

Early whaling ships, manned by white men, brought strange ailments which devastated the tribes. They killed or drove away the whales and cut down the numbers of walrus and seals. White hunters on land destroyed the musk-ox and caribou. Then came the traders who persuaded the Eskimoes to turn trappers and trade fox and other skins for food, clothes, weapons, and even fabricated huts. To-day the people dress more and more like white people, eat similar foods, and have white men's huts.

Half hearted attempts have been made to provide Mackenzie Eskimoes with reindeer. These tame caribou are from Asia (see *The Asiatic World*, pages 210-211). They came first to Alaska, but the Canadian experiment has not been a success. Most Eskimoes to-day are anything but comfortably off.

Indians live in the forests and prairies, and there are over 200,000 of them. Many of the forest Indians have become trappers, too, and there is some inter-marriage with the white people, but most of them live on Reservations, where they can preserve their own way of life. They can leave whenever they wish, and join in normal Canadian living. They are found in all walks of life in Canada.

THE REGIONS OF CANADA

D. Western Canada

British Columbia

There could hardly be a greater contrast between two regions than that between the Prairies and Western Canada. Whether the west-bound train leaves Calgary on the Canadian Pacific, or Edmonton on the Canadian National, it will follow a valley leading into the mountains, and this valley grows steadily deeper and narrower as the great ranges of the Rockies close in. Peaks tower over the track to a height of over 12,000

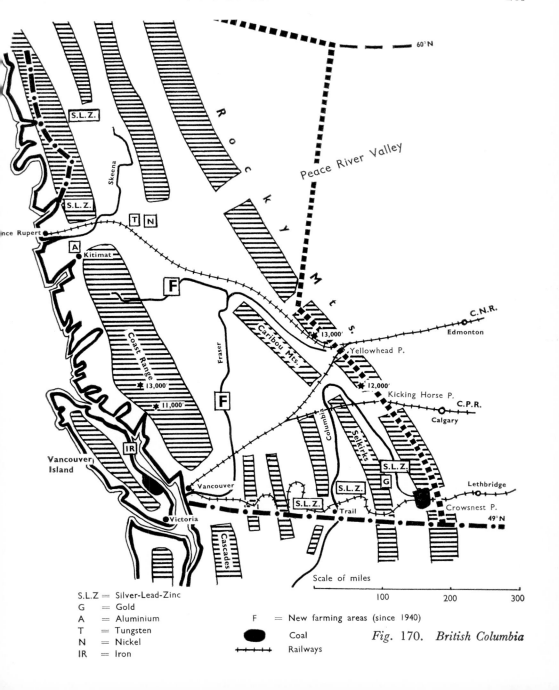

S.L.Z = Silver-Lead-Zinc
G   = Gold
A   = Aluminium
T   = Tungsten
N   = Nickel
IR = Iron

F   = New farming areas (since 1940)

Coal

Railways

Fig. 170. British Columbia

feet, as the pass is approached by which the range is crossed. One has then entered a region of young folded mountains, where range follows range, in long lines, with deep valleys between them. This continues right to the coast, whilst another range there gives rise to islands offshore. The railways tunnel through to the valley of the Fraser River, the chief river of Western Canada, and this leads to the sea opposite to Vancouver Island, where Vancouver is situated, the third largest city in Canada. It contains nearly half of the people in Western Canada.

Task 205. Examine Fig. 170.

(a) What is the name of the range towering above the coast? How do its peaks compare with those of the Rockies?

(b) Of what feature is Vancouver Island a part?

(c) What is the chief river of northern British Columbia?

(d) Which large river rises in Canada, then flows into the U.S.A.?

In Fig. 171 one has a view of the Rocky Mountains near the Kicking Horse Pass. The peaks rise to 10,000 feet. The valley floor here is 5,000 feet high, for we have

Fig. 171. The Rock Mountains, near t Kicking Horse Pa

AEROFILM

climbed 1,000 feet since leaving Calgary, one hundred miles away. Because of the height, only forests of conifers grow, but in the lower valleys are meadows and farms. The building is a famous holiday hotel, the Banff Springs. The gap made by the river is followed by the Trans-Canada Highway (the road you saw in Fig. 161), and the Canadian Pacific Railway. This picture makes clear how all movement in Western Canada is controlled by the ranges and valleys.

Task 206.

(*a*) Suggest three ways of spending your time in this district, if you were holidaying at the hotel in Fig. 171.

(*b*) Suggest two uses for the mountain slopes in the background.

The Empty North

There are not many people in British Columbia, and most of them are around the lower Fraser. Parts of the north are almost unknown. Without railways or roads, developments are impossible, for the rivers are too swift to be navigable. There are a few mining settlements, but these are near the coast, or near the railway.

A Land of Timber

Because Western Canada is mountainous, and lies right across the path of numerous depressions moving in from the Pacific, the rains on the coastal mountains are very heavy all through the year. The climate of the coasts is like that of Britain, with a rather warmer summer, and trees grow to an enormous size. Douglas firs, red cedars, hemlocks, and Sitka spruces cover the slopes of the Coast Range and Vancouver Island in dense forests of tall trees.

These forests provide the timber for one of Canada's greatest lumbering districts. Made-up timber of all kinds, especially for houses, and other buildings, is exported from here to all over the world. Paper is also made from the younger trees. In Fig. 172 one can see a tree being cut by the new power-saw driven by a motor. What a difference from the older method of hewing with axes, or saws operated by hand!

The picture shows a typical forest scene where most of the trees are only big enough for pulping.

Because of the steep slopes, many logs are carried down to the saw-mills on overhead cables, some are hauled on sledges drawn by diesels, some are carried on the railway. The rivers are too swift to use. Many of the big mills are on the lower Fraser, but there are many up the coast.

Task 207. How would timber from here reach (*i*) Britain, (*ii*) Montreal?

The heavy rains are confined to the coastal areas. Over the Coast Range rainfall diminishes very quickly, so forests become thin and poor and there is not much lumbering. New farming zones are springing up to supply lumberers and miners (see Fig. 170) but the rains are sometimes so small that irrigation has to be employed.

Fig. 172. Felling tree on Hollybu Ridge, near Vancouv
NATIONAL FILM BOARD
CANAL

Catching salmon the quick way

The coasts of British Columbia are deeply cut into by numerous fiords, like those of Norway. As in Norway, they are a great encouragement to fishermen. The chief fish is the salmon. Every year salmon swarm up the rivers to spawn, and the fiords and rivers are alive with them. Their instincts always lead them to the same river where they were spawned. After the eggs are laid on the river bed, the parent fish return to the ocean, and men set nets across the rivers and catch them. Fig. 173 shows a number of catchers in

ig. 173. Salmon
tchers at the mouth
the Fraser river

CTORIAL PRESS

the Fraser mouth, with fishermen overhauling their nets. You can see the floats from which the nets hang in the water.

Task 208. What is the reason for the wheel-like objects in the stern of the catchers?

The catchers are met by tugs which rush the catch to the canneries. The whole process of cutting up, cooking, and canning has been organised so expertly, that labelled tins are ready within an hour of catching. Canneries are found in many of the fiords, and round Vancouver.

Mining

British Columbia was, for much of its earliest period, simply a gold mining region. To-day, gold is not very important, but other minerals are. Silver, lead, and zinc are widespread, and several regions are large producers (see Fig. 170). Trail has one of the biggest plants in the world. Many fertilisers are also produced there. Tungsten and nickel are now being produced behind Prince Rupert. There is no doubt that there are many sources of minerals still untapped. The

*Fig. 174. The
aluminium plant at
Kitimat*

HIGH COMMISSIONER FOR
CANADA

Kitimat plant for making aluminium is one of the world's greatest plants, and is run by hydro-electric power. A river beyond the Coast Range was dammed to form a lake, a tunnel was run through the mountains to the coast where a great underground power-station produces enormous quantities of electricity. Local and imported bauxite are used. Western Canada is second only to Quebec in the amount of hydro-electricity produced.

Fig. 174 is a view of Kitimat showing the enormous size of the project. Much of the land on which it is built is artifically created, and you can see the work going on, on the right. The plant is 70 miles from open sea. Note the steep, forested background.

Task 209.

(a) What natural advantages has Western Canada for hydro-electric power?

(*b*) How does the Kitimat picture show that only sea communications are possible on this coast?

Coal is present in useful quantities on Vancouver Island, and in the Crowsnest Pass. These are sufficient for present needs. Iron ore is also mined on Vancouver Island and on the mainland opposite.

Farming

The lowlands of Western Canada, especially near the U.S.A. border, are excellent for farming. The lower Fraser has good dairy, fruit, and mixed farms as one would expect where the climate is like that of Cornwall or Devon. In the Columbia River valley, and its tributary valleys, it is drier and sunnier, so that fruit farms flourish. In the dry region, behind the Coast Range, there is some ranching of cattle.

Vancouver

This great city is on the most southerly of the fiords, and has a fine harbour. No other place in British Columbia can offer anything like the routes inland that are to be found here, so it has grown to be the terminus of all land routes. It is Canada's gateway to the Pacific, and has great exports of wheat, timber, salmon and minerals. It is the business centre for all British Columbia. It has 790,000 people.

Victoria

Situated on Vancouver Island, Victoria is the capital of British Columbia, but is much smaller than Vancouver. It is the most beautiful city in Canada, and is given over to government almost entirely.

Task 210. Prince Rupert, at the mouth of the Skeena, is still a very small port, with timber and fish industries. What is needed for Prince Rupert to grow large? (see Figs. 167 and 170, and page 243).

Task 211. Take an outline map of Canada, and on it show:

(*i*) the C.P.R. from Montreal to Vancouver;
(*ii*) the C.N.R. from Quebec to Vancouver.

On each line, mark the chief towns, and any important areas of production passed through.

CHAPTER 13

THE UNITED STATES OF AMERICA

—A GREAT WORLD POWER

We now come to the last of the North Atlantic Nations, and the most powerful, wealthy, and influential of them all. It is interesting to compare this great nation with its neighbour to the north, Canada. Both countries are very large, each is roughly three-and-a-half-million square miles, though the U.S.A. is rather smaller than Canada. Both stretch across the entire continent, from Atlantic to Pacific. Both have great mountain ranges in the west and plains in the middle. Both countries share the Great Lakes and the new Seaway. Between them lie some 3,000 miles of entirely undefended frontier. Their peoples have come principally from Europe. There is a great mixture of nationalities amongst them, but both countries speak the English language, and their civilisations owe much to British ideas.

Yet there are important differences. One of them is their positions in latitude. You have noticed already, that 49°N. is the boundary of the U.S.A. in the north, (*The Forty Ninth Parallel*, as it is called). The coast of the Gulf of Mexico is roughly along 30°N. Thus we can say that the U.S.A. lies between 30°N., and 50°N., whilst Canada lies roughly between 50°N., and

100 W

The

Empty

West

Fairly densely peopled (over 150/sq. mile)
Moderately peopled (over 20/sq. mile)
Thinly peopled

Frontiers

Scale of miles
100 200 300 400

Fig. 175. Where people live in the U.S.A.

70°N. This is a very important difference. Much of Canada is Arctic in its climate, but much of the United States is almost tropical in the heat of its summers. Then, except in the middle and north-east, the United States has mild winters, when plants will grow, but the winters of Canada are bitterly cold, except around Vancouver. Thus settlers were more attracted to the U.S.A. than to Canada, so that it is not surprising to note that whereas the population of Canada is only 18 millions, that of the United States is 188 millions.

Task 212. Look at Fig. 143 then answer the following questions:

(*a*) Why should the U.S.A. have far more people on the Pacific Coast Lands than has Canada?

(*b*) Which country has the greater area of Western Mountains?

(c) How does the amount of the Central Lowlands held by each country compare?

(d) More than half Canada is occupied by the Canadian Shield. What occupies more than half of the U.S.A.? Which country is the better off as a result?

Where the people live

Now look at Fig. 175 which shows where the people live in the U.S.A. First, it shows that only a few areas have a density of over 150 per square mile, and this is not a high density. In Britain, a density of 20 per square mile is regarded as almost empty country. So despite its wonderful temperatures, and its enormous fertile plains, the U.S.A. is not yet densely peopled. Second, the American people do not seem to find the western half very attractive, for it is almost empty, except on the Pacific coasts. Not many people have moved west of 100°W.

Task 213. Compare roughly the distribution of people in Canada with the distribution in the U.S.A.

Rainfall is important

It is obvious that other factors must be considered in deciding where it is good to live in the U.S.A. One very big factor is rainfall. In Fig. 176 you can see where the rainfall is good in the country. Rains come chiefly from depressions forming on the Pacific and Atlantic seaboards (see Chapter 1). The heat of summer draws the Atlantic air streams into the Central Plains, but high mountains prevent rains moving far inland from the Pacific. Thus, west of 100°W., the rains are poor, except on the Pacific coastlands, and the United States has a large western region in which crops can only be grown when irrigated and in which large areas are desert. The Americans call the line of 20 inches of annual rainfall the *Dead Line* because growing crops west of it can be disastrous unless irrigation is practised. Few Americans live west of the *Dead Line*.

Task 214. In Canada, all the prairies receive less than 20 inches of rain, and yet many crops grow

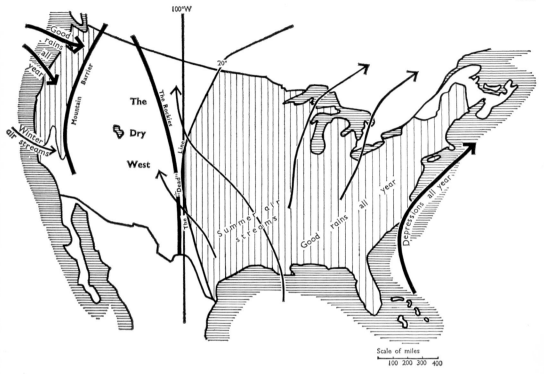

Fig. 176. *The rainfall of the U.S.A.*

there. Why should they grow well there, and yet require more than 20 inches of rain in the U.S.A.?

Task 215. Half of the United States is empty because it is too dry. Why is more than half of Canada empty?

The Regions of the U.S.A.

Before we begin our survey of the regions of the U.S.A., we ought to say a word about the States, themselves, which form the *United* States. When, in 1776, the United States was formed by throwing off the rule of Britain, there were in existence thirteen colonies which became the first thirteen states. They had always had a great measure of independence from each other and, in the new country, they were very anxious not to lose any of this. So each state retained

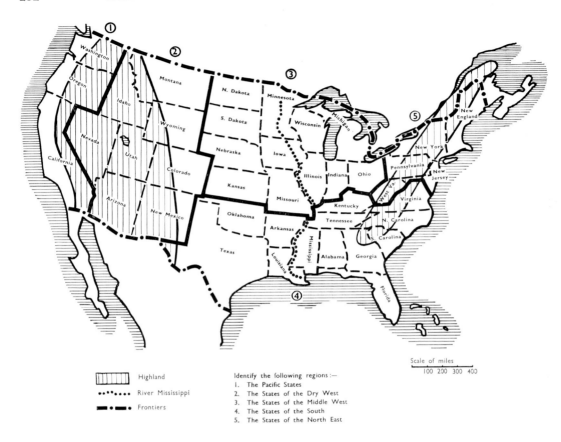

Highland

•••••••• River Mississippi

■•■•■• Frontiers

Identify the following regions :—
1. The Pacific States
2. The States of the Dry West
3. The States of the Middle West
4. The States of the South
5. The States of the North East

Scale of miles
100 200 300 400

Fig. 177. The States of the U.S.A., and the regions for study

a great many powers of government, and had its own Governor and Assembly. They created a Federal Government at Washington, which was built to be the capital. As new states were created each one received all these powers. Americans have always been very keen on preserving what they call their *State's Rights*, and view the Federal Government with a certain amount of suspicion, on occasions. To-day, there are 48 states inside the United States, and two more outside, Alaska, and Hawaii. Because they are so important, we have drawn our map of the Regions of the U.S.A. by following state boundaries. The result is seen in Fig. 177.

The flag of the U.S.A.

U.S.I.S.

Task 216. The flag of the U.S.A. is known as the Stars and Stripes. What do they represent? How many of each are there?

1. The Pacific States

There are three of these. They include the coastlands and part of the Western Mountains behind. Population in 1960 was 18 millions.

2. The States of the Dry West

This region includes most of the mountains and plateaus of the west, but also the High Plains east of the Rockies, where rains are too little for agriculture. There are eight states here, all thinly peopled. The total population in 1960 was only 6,800,000.

3. The States of the Middle West

This is a fertile, rich region with much industry. Chicago is the great metropolis. It contains twelve states and a population of 51 millions in 1960.

4. The States of the South

Here is a region of hot, moist plains of great fertility, the home of the cotton and tobacco crops, with many negro inhabitants. Industry increases rapidly. It is the region which broke away temporarily from the United States in 1861 and fought the Civil War. Thirteen states are shown, and in 1960 there were 48 million inhabitants.

5. The States of the North-east

Though by no means the most fertile part, the population was 54 millions in 1960, due to the enormous amount of industry and many large cities. Of the twelve states, eight are too small to name on Fig. 177. Of these Connecticut, Maine, Massachusetts, New Hampshire, Rhode Island and Vermont form New England; the other two are Delaware and Maryland.

Task 217. The greatest river system in America is the Mississippi and its feeders. The Missouri and the Ohio are the most important of these feeders. Take an atlas map of the U.S.A. and list the states which use these rivers as boundaries. What do most of the others use?

REGION 1. THE PACIFIC STATES

A. The North West

Southwards from Vancouver, we enter the U.S.A. and proceed along the side of Puget Sound. The Cascades rear their snow-capped tops on our left, and everything seems similar to what we saw in Canada. When, however, we pass Puget Sound, a broad valley opens out, running southwards for many miles. It lies between the Coastal Ranges and the Cascades. The Columbia flows across it. The Willamette flows along it from the south. This fertile valley is the heart of both the states of Washington and Oregon, who share it, Fig. 178. The *State of Washington* must not be confused with the *City of Washington*, the Federal Capital.

Rainfall is good all through the year, summers are very warm, winters are mild on the lowlands. It is a pleasant land for all farming of European types and landscapes show rich fields of wheat, flax, meadow grasses with many dairy cows, and numerous orchards of apples, plums, cherries and pears. In the towns are many canning factories for fruits and vegetables.

Life is similar to that in British Columbia

All this is very like life in Canada to the north. It is like it in many other ways, too. Lumbering is a very great industry. Just as in Canada, the mountain slopes are covered with dense forests of valuable timber trees, of which yellow pine and Oregon pine are much used. Saw-mills are found in many places, whilst in the towns, furniture and other trades in wood are established. Great quantities of timber are shipped from Portland and Seattle to the Far East and to eastern U.S.A. Salmon fishing is another big industry, as in western Canada, and canneries are frequent on the coasts.

Fig. 179 is a view of a great saw-mill near Seattle. Note the forested hills in the rear of the mill, and the suggestion of raininess and winds in the landscape.

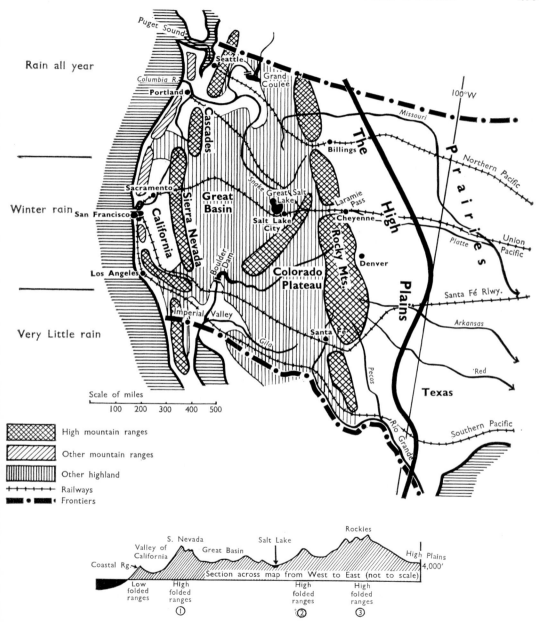

Fig. 178. *The Pacific States of the U.S.A.*

Fig. 179. Sawmill with logs in mill pond, near Seattle

Task 218. Will this mill be for timber products or paper? Why? You should find more than one reason in the picture.

East of the Cascades, rains are better than is usual on the plateaus. Wheat is grown on a very large scale in the Snake Valley (Fig. 178). There are many farms on irrigated land, and the Grand Coulee Dam on the Columbia, is an example not only of a huge barrage and lake used for irrigation, but of power for electricity production (Fig. 178).

Portland and Seattle are the principal cities. They are both large ports, for the Columbia-Willamette junction provides an excellent deep-water harbour at Portland. They have industries connected with timber, fish, and fruits, and shipbuilding is especially important in Portland. Seattle is the port for the trade with Alaska.

B. *California*

The Pacific coast of the U.S.A. has remarkably few good openings, for the lines of the mountains are parallel to the coast. Hence we have to sail for over 500 miles south from the mouth of the Columbia river before we come to another good opening, the Golden Gate, leading to the city and harbour of San Francisco. Here we find one of the world's great harbours, of enormous extent, which leads into the rich and fertile Valley of California.

A Mediterranean Climate

In travelling south to California, a change takes place in the climate. West winds and their depressions no longer bring rain in all months. They are not so common in summer which is a very dry season. On the other hand, summers are very hot, and winters are very mild, for the angle of the sun is high here. (Most of the valley is less than 40° from the equator). Sacramento, the capital of the state, is typical. Its lowest monthly temperature is 45° and, for four months in summer, its average temperature is never below 70°. In those four months it receives hardly any rain at all.

Fruits Everywhere

Life in the valley is rich and varied and population increases at a most remarkable rate. It has now over 15 million inhabitants, and only New York State has more. It all began with the discovery of gold in the Sierra Nevada in 1849. The first American settlers were gold miners (*Forty Niners*). For nearly two hundred years before that, Spaniards had lived there, in small numbers, ranching cattle. Both these occupations are still to be found, but they are over-shadowed by others. Fruit-growing, preserving, drying and canning are the great interests of the valley. Enormous farms produce oranges, lemons, grapes, figs, prunes, and all British-type fruits. Equally enormous spaces produce early vegetables. Everything is highly organised with efficient transport by road and rail, machines for planting and even harvesting in some

Fig. 180. *Orchar and vineyards ne Lindsay, Californ* U.S.I

cases. Many factories preserve the fruits and vegetables by canning. The fierce summer sun is ideal for drying fruits, *e.g.* raisins. Frozen products are now a big feature. Production reaches incredible heights, and exports go all over the world. There are also sales of wine and olive oil, chiefly to other parts of the U.S.A. Many Asiatics are found on the farms as pickers, and some are owners of farms.

Fig. 180 is a view in the south. The snow-capped Sierra Nevada range is in the background. Orchards and vineyards cover all the lower slopes in the picture. The region was semi-desert till the U.S. Bureau of Reclamation provided irrigation canals.

Task 219. How can you tell from the picture that the region is a semi-desert area?

The most irrigated State

Rainfall in the valley is highest in the north, as one would expect and, in northern California, great forests of redwoods are lumbered on the hill slopes. As one moves south, the rains diminish and the south is semi-desert or true desert. The Coastal Ranges shade the valley from the rain winds, but the Sierra Nevada receive heavy rains and snows. Rivers run into the valley carrying much water which is collected and then distributed by canals. Over 120 large irrigation schemes are found, and many millions of acres are watered. So much electricity is generated at the barrages, that over three-quarters of the energy used in California is electrical.

Irrigation has extended outside the valley, into the Imperial Valley near the lower Colorado. Nearly 100,000 people live here, entirely dependent on irrigation, growing vegetables, fruits, and sugar-beet.

Oilfields and Films, Los Angeles

Next to Texas, California is the largest oil-producing state in America. Most of the oilfields occur on the coast round Los Angeles, though there is one large field in the valley. Some of the wells actually draw from the sea bed.

In Fig. 181 you can see what such an oilfield is like.

ig. 181. An oilfield California

s.i.s.

Derricks rise up in hundreds, disfiguring the landscape. Each derrick means a well. This is the only large oil-producing area on the Pacific Ocean, and so it exports to South America and the East. It has brought enormous wealth to Los Angeles in the twentieth century.

Task 220. What are the cylindrical objects grouped around the derricks in Fig. 181? To where will the oil proceed from this field of derricks?

Fig. 182. *The Metr Goldwyn-May studios, Hollywoo Californ* U.S.I

Another enormous industry which has collected around Los Angeles is the Film Industry. The main geographic reason for its being here is the rare quality of the light in this dry, clear region. Another is the variety of landscape within fairly close distances: sea, mountains, desert, grassy plains, woodland and large modern cities. Fig. 182 illustrates what a huge industry it can be, and how much work it creates. The photograph is of the studios of one company (M.G.M.). Hollywood has many such companies.

Task 221. What would you say are being constructed in the block in the centre background?

Los Angeles with a population of 2,479,000, in 1960, is one of the four largest cities in North America. Aircraft, motors, steel and fish-canning are other industries found there.

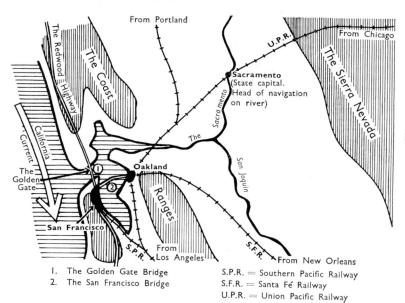

Fig. 183. The situation of Oakland and San Francisco

1. The Golden Gate Bridge
2. The San Francisco Bridge

S.P.R. = Southern Pacific Railway
S.F.R. = Santa Fé Railway
U.P.R. = Union Pacific Railway

San Francisco

This is the other large city of California, with 740,000 inhabitants, in 1960. It is the oldest city and a great port. All sea traffic into and out of the valley uses it. In Fig. 183 you see its position on the west side of the bay. It was built by Spaniards coming in from the sea, and all its connections in early days were by sea. To-day it is really on the wrong side of the bay, and Oakland grew up as the terminus of the land routes from the east. A wonderful feat of engineering built the eight-miles-long bridge linking San Francisco to the other side in the late 1930's. Shortly after, another bridge spanned the Golden Gate, carrying the National Highway connecting Canada with Mexico. The city has large shipyards, both civil and naval; makes motor cars, farm machinery and steel, and has salmon-canning and other food industries. One draw-

Fig. 184. San
Francisco, and the
San Francisco-
Oakland Bay Bridge
AEROFILMS

back to the port is the frequency of fogs. They are due to the presence of a cold current, which moves down the coast southwards. It brings cool air with it, and this chills the warmer air over the land causing it to condense vapour as fog. Fortunately these fogs do not affect inland places.

Task 222. Can you explain why, at San Francisco, the July temperature is only 58°, whereas at Sacramento, it is 74°?

Fig. 184 is a very impressive view of San Francisco, showing the great bridge across to Oakland. Compare the bridge with the great liner near it in dock. The flat island is artificial and was created to house an exhibition.

REGION 2. THE DRY WEST

This enormous region begins at the Sierra Nevada, which is a definite barrier to the rain winds from the Pacific. It then extends for 1,000 miles to the east to where the *Dead Line* of rainfall occurs. Thus it includes two regions:

(*a*) The Western Mountains. (*b*) The High Plains.

Find both these regions on Fig. 178.

A. *The Western Mountains*

Fig. 185. (A) High Folded Ranges (B) Tablelands and Canyons

This region is much wider than in Canada, and whilst there are plenty of high folded ranges, there are also large areas of tablelands and plateaus where, often, the rocks lie unfolded, and so create their own kinds of scenery. In Fig. 185 you see examples of each type.

A. In Great Basin   Rocks Folded

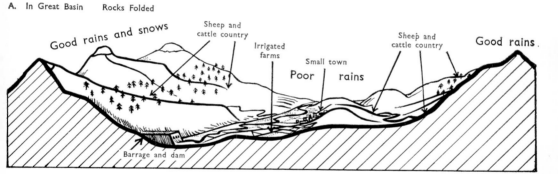

B. On Colorado Plateau   Rocks unfolded

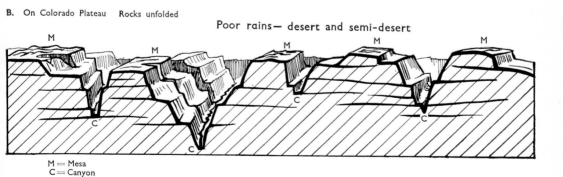

M = Mesa
C = Canyon

Task 223

(a) Name the rivers draining the northern and southern parts of the region.

(b) Most of the Great Basin has *inland drainage*. What does this mean?

(c) Why should the Great Salt Lake be salt?

(d) What is the distance between the crest of the Sierra Nevada and the crest of the Rockies, along a line through Salt Lake City? Compare this with the distance from Lands End to John O'Groats in Britain (700 miles).

Ranching and Irrigated Farming

In Fig. 185A one sees the high ranges, often snow-covered, where streams rise and flow down on to the much drier lower lands. A belt of conifer woods, with grassy slopes, lies below the snow line and, in summer, when they are free of snow and gay with grass and flowers, sheep and cattle are reared. In winter the animals go down to the main ranch in the valley, for winters in the Western Mountains are very severe. The ranches are usually based on one or more streams, which supply water for the animals. Occasionally a river has been controlled by a dam and is used for irrigation and hydro-electric power. In that case a valley will have irrigated farms. The crops on an irrigated farm are very varied, but they all grow fodder grasses for the ranches to buy. Salt Lake City is a great city founded by the Mormon settlers in the 1840's. It is in the middle of a large irrigated region.

Indians as well as white people herd animals. The Navajos of the Great Basin are famous sheep-herders, and from the wool of their flocks make coloured rugs and blankets which sell well to white people.

In the second type of country (Fig. 185B), the chief features are flat tablelands called *mesas* from the Spanish word for a table, and deep narrow valleys called *canyons*. The rivers have eaten down slowly through the rocks, the hard rocks standing out in steep faces, and the soft ones wearing away into terraces. Most of the canyons

Fig. 186. Union Pacific's "Challenger Streamliner" on its journey from Chicago to Los Angeles

E.N.A.

are dry, except in violent rain storms, but their floors provide the only worth-while pasture for beasts. Mesas are often very dry and burned up, but summer pasture can sometimes be found there.

The Colorado is the chief river here and, for much of its course, it flows in deep canyons. The Grand Canyon is over a mile deep. It is at the end of this Grand Canyon that the Boulder Dam was made, an enormous structure from which water is sent as far as the Mexican border to be used for irrigation.

Fig. 186 is a scene in the dry south-west of the U.S.A. showing a train proceeding to California. Notice that, as is usual in the West, the railway is single track.

Task 224. What features of the Dry West are shown on this picture?

Fig. 187. Copper ore being dug from a "copper-hill" in Arizona

U.S.I.S.

Mining Country

When we studied British Columbia we saw that the western mountains were rich in minerals, especially coal, copper, silver, lead, zinc, and gold. In the U.S.A. the same minerals are mined. Gold brought many *gold rushes* here last century, towns arose and declined, mines were opened and abandoned all within a few years. *Ghost Towns* are still to be seen, with empty buildings falling to pieces. Gold is not important now, but copper, lead, and zinc are of enormous importance for the U.S.A. and the world. Fig. 187 is a mine-working in Arizona. Terraces are cut out to remove the rock. Notice the mesa in the right background, and the desert cover on the slopes. Note the intense brightness of the desert sunshine.

Task 225. What is the advantage of mining in terraces?

Coal is available in many areas but, apart from the railways and mines, there is not much need for it. In any case, there is so much available in the east, that all the needs of the U.S.A. can be supplied from there.

Task 226. From what you have read up to this point, compare the products of the Western Mountains in Canada and in the U.S.A.

B. The High Plains

From the Western Mountains we can cross the Rockies by one of several passes followed by roads and railways. The famous one is the South Pass near Laramie, across which runs the Union Pacific Railway, the first railway to connect east and west in the U.S.A. Once across the Rockies with their 12,000 or 14,000 feet peaks, we enter enormous plains which, beginning here, stretch for 800 miles to the Mississippi. At first they are over 4,000 feet high and Denver, the chief city, is actually over 5,000 feet. This is higher than any mountain in Britain. This explains the name, the High Plains, or Great Plains as they are often called.

Task 227. Look at Fig. 178.
(a) Name, in order from the north, the rivers which cross the High Plains.
(b) Which valley was followed by the early travellers and the U.P. Railway?
(c) Into which river do most of these rivers eventually run?

These plains are high and very bracing, but winters are very severe, with terrible blizzards sweeping down from the Arctic. In summer equally hot conditions prevail, with hot winds sweeping up from the tropics. Rain falls chiefly in summer and is not only small, but very uncertain. Droughts are frequent and do great damage.

Eastwards the plains descend very gradually to the Mississippi and, at the same time, the rains increase. Below 3,000 feet, the Prairies begin.

Task 228. Look at Fig. 176. From where will the High Plains obtain their rains? How is it possible for both Arctic and tropical winds to penetrate so easily into the heart of the U.S.A.?

The great rivers form shallow valleys across the plains, but these are the only places where trees are to be found, especially the large cotton-woods, deciduous trees which are native to the central plains of America. The rest is hard dry soil, covered with various types of bunch grass and other rough grazing. In winter the grazing turns to hay on the stalk. This is the land of the old *Cattle Kings*, and the romantic *Wild West*.

Cowboys and Indians

Before 1860, these plains were in the hands of hunting Indian tribes like the Sioux and the Comanches who depended almost entirely on the buffalo for their existence. White people were either traders, who dealt with the tribes, or members of waggon trains passing through to the Far West as quickly as they could. Then came the buffalo-hunters who destroyed the great herds, and so robbed the Indians of their food. The Indians slowly left the plains to make way for the ranchers, who brought huge herds of cattle to replace the buffalo. These roamed semi-wild; there were no fences and no careful breeding. Every year a great round-up sorted out each rancher's animals for sale, and great trail-herds crossed the plains to the nearest railway, where a cattle town received them for the rail trucks. Railways were few, but people were fewer, and the cowboys were almost the only inhabitants.

Dust Bowls

After 1880, crop farmers or nesters began to appear, especially in the river valleys where water was more secure. Now these people had moved out west of the Dead Line, the limit of safe farming, and as more of the land was ploughed, disaster struck. The savage winds which sweep the Plains, carried off the surface soil, even dumping some in the Atlantic, but most of it was dumped on other states, from Dakota to Texas. Ruin was widespread. Nature had hit back.

To-day both rancher and crop farmer have changed their methods. Cattle still go east by rail to the cities

Fig. 188. On the way to summer pasture, a herd fords a river

NATIONAL FILM BOARD

and their stockyards, but none travel far to a railway. Great fenced fields contain them on the ranch, they are carefully bred, grasses are improved and fodder crops grown. The crop men farm in strips of different crops, *along* the slopes, and not *down* them. Trees are planted as wind breaks, and a very hardy wheat, *Turkey Red*, has been introduced from south Russia. It is better suited to hard dry soils than are American types. Nevertheless, the cattleman is still the dominant figure.

Fig. 188 is a modern scene on the High Plains in the north. Cattle are being driven to summer pastures in the hills. The bare open range is well shown. The river is very low after the winter period of small snowfalls. The scene in this area has not changed in eighty years. The only large town is Denver. It is the business centre of a large mining district in the Rockies behind. It is a great meat-canning centre, and is the capital of Colorado.

Western Texas, though not strictly on the High Plains, is part of the great ranching region. It was the first state to ranch cattle, breeding its famous longhorns, descended from Spanish cattle roaming wild in Texas.

Task 229. Name the ranching states in order from the north.

REGIONS 3, 4 AND 5
THE REGIONS EAST OF THE DEAD LINE

We have now completed our survey of the western and thinly peopled regions of the U.S.A. and must turn our attention to those regions lying east of the Dead Line of rainfall, regions which contain the bulk of the people. The map, Fig. 177, shows three great regions in this half of the country:

  Region 3 *The Middle West*
    „ *4* *The South*
    „ *5* *The North East*

Of these, the first two occupy the enormous fertile plains of the basin of the Mississippi and the Atlantic coast. In the entire world, there are few regions of fertility so great as these. The production of farm crops is quite staggering. One-half of all the world's maize, one-third of its cotton, and one-eighth of its wheat come from here. The region is not one of simple farming for local needs. It practises commercial farming, where one or two crops are grown on a big scale for sale to factories or cities all over the U.S.A. Quality of product is very important. There is much research into strains. Methods of production and transport are always being improved. The region is organised in enormous belts which specialize in one or two crops. These belts are shown in Fig. 189. They are arranged according to latitude, so temperature is an obvious reason for the different belts. Before we study the three great regions in detail, it is well to take these great crop belts and survey them as a whole.

Task 230. Examine Fig. 189.

(*a*) By reference to your atlas, or the sketch maps in this chapter, name the three tributaries of the Mississippi on the western side, and the two on the eastern side.

(*b*) Ten large towns are shown by initials. Look up their names, and the State in which each one lies (Fig. 177). Arrange your answer as shown on page 271.

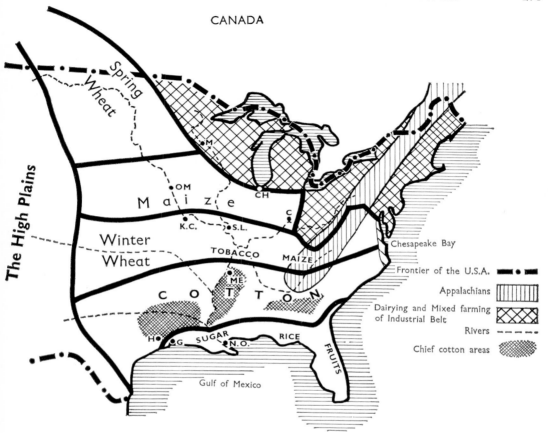

CANADA

Spring Wheat

The High Plains

Maize

OM

M

CH

K.C. S.L.

C

Winter Wheat

TOBACCO

MAIZE

Chesapeake Bay

C O T T O N

ME

H G SUGAR N.O. RICE

FRUITS

Gulf of Mexico

Frontier of the U.S.A. ▬·▬·▬
Appalachians ‖‖‖‖
Dairying and Mixed farming
of Industrial Belt ⬚⬚⬚
Rivers – – – –
Chief cotton areas ▨▨

Fig. 189. The Great Crop Belts of the U.S.A.

	Town	State		Town	State
M			C		
OM			ME		
CH			H		
SL			G		
KC			NO		

The Spring Wheat Belt

This is the belt we studied on the Canadian Prairies. The great grasslands spread southwards into the U.S.A., but the frozen winter is not quite so long, and the summers are a little warmer. The growing season

Fig. 190.   *Harvesting*
Wheat

E.N.A.

extends to about 140 days.   One sees the same enormous expanses of level, stoneless plains, the same large fields and the same machines.   Fig. 190 is a view of harvesting.

In Fig. 191 is a diagram of the climate of a town, St. Paul, which is not quite in the wheat belt, but which has the climate of that belt.   If you examine this diagram, you will be able to gather the following facts:

(*a*) the land is frozen from November to the beginning of April;

(*b*) April is the sowing time, August is the harvest time:

(*c*) temperatures average more than 60°F. for three-and-a-half months, and over 70°F. for two months.

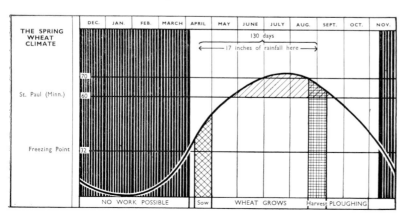

Fig. 191.   *The*
climate of St. Paul
(Minn.)
—the Wheat Belt

This shows that the belt has a very warm summer:
(*d*) during the time the wheat is in the ground, 17
inches of rain fall. This is a good rainfall for wheat.
Too much can ruin it.

Task 231. Here are figures for the growing season
at Winnipeg, in Canada.

	April	May	June	July	Aug.	Sept.
Temperatures	39°F.	51°F.	62°F.	66°F.	63°F.	53°F.
Rainfall	$1\frac{1}{2}''$	$2''$	$3\frac{1}{2}''$	$3''$	$2\frac{1}{4}''$	$2''$

Compare the Canadian town with the U.S.A. town
as regards:
(*a*) the number of months above 70°;
(*b*) the number of months above 60°;
(*c*) the amount of rain during the growing season.

Why should St. Paul be warmer and wetter than
Winnipeg in summer?

The Maize or Corn Belt

About the latitude of Chicago the summers begin
to be rather too hot for wheat, and summer rains are
quite heavy. In the same latitude in winter, temperatures remain below freezing point for two or three
months. The main crop now becomes maize or *Indian
Corn.* Omaha, in Fig. 192, has a typical climate.

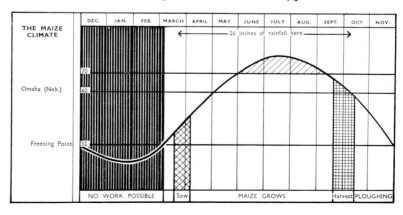

Fig. 192. *The climate
of Omaha (Neb.)
—The Maize Belt*

Maize grows quickly to a height of over 12 feet, so it needs good summer rains. It only ripens in September or October, so high temperatures are needed in summer. They must be over 70°F. for the crop to ripen.

All these conditions are met at Omaha. The frozen winter breaks up the soil and kills pests, but it does not interfere with the growing season.

The heads of the maize are called *cobs*. A cob will hold hundreds of grains. These are excellent for fattening cattle, pigs and poultry for the meat factories. One-half of the pigs and one-third of the cattle in the U.S.A. are in this belt. Even the High Plains cattle are brought here to be fattened. Fig. 193 is a scene in the maize belt. The field is very big by British standards, but not by those of the Middle West. The crop grows taller than the man, bottom left corner. The level fertile plain is clearly indicated. The picture was taken in Iowa, the heart of the Belt. The cob is well shown in Fig. 194. The amount of grain per plant can be appreciated from this picture.

Fig. 193. *The Mai*
cr
U.S.

Once maize begins to be grown, it is a continuous crop all the way through the South. It is a staple food of many negroes, and popular with white people. It is in the Maize Belt, however, that it is most important.

Winter Wheat and Tobacco

South of St. Louis winter temperatures are above

Fig. 194. *A full ear corn*
s.I.s.

freezing point and for twelve months of the year are useful to the farmer. In the same area summers become very hot. Now winter wheat appears. Sown in October, it grows through the winter and is harvested in May or early June, before the intense heat of late summer scorches it. So in Missouri, Kansas, Kentucky, and Oklahoma, are more large wheat fields where the professional harvesting teams begin work in May, and follow through till August, travelling north all the time. Tobacco is another world famous crop in this belt, especially in the eastern parts: Tennessee, Carolina and Virginia. The U.S.A. is easily the world's largest producer and grower of tobacco.

The Cotton Belt

On we go southwards and, all the time, the heat increases and the rains grow heavier We also notice that the numbers of coloured people are increasing and soon the great fields of cotton become the chief feature of the landscape. Winters are now so mild that many crops are grown in that season. Summers are tropical. This is the climate, shown in Fig. 195, of the town of Montgomery, Alabama.

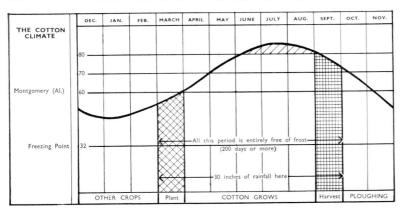

Fig. 195. The clima
of Montgomery (Al
—The Cotton Be

The cotton plant is a bush, planted in March. It needs rainfalls which are good, but not very heavy, and temperatures of over 80°F. for ripening. In Montgomery, there are 30 inches of rain whilst the cotton grows and two-and-a-half months with temperatures over 80°F. Almost the entire time the cotton is in the ground the average temperature is over 60°F., which is better than the best in Britain. Not a trace of frost must occur in all these seven months.

The cotton plant produces a white flower which dies. Then a large seed box grows. This is the *boll.* In it the seeds grow, surrounded by cotton fibres in the form of a *cotton wool.* When the boll bursts, at the time of ripening, the seeds scatter, borne on the wind by this cotton wool. So it is most important that the cotton is collected quickly after the boll bursts. Until recently, negroes supplied much cheap labour for this task, but now there are large but expensive machines to do the collecting on the very wealthy farms. After collection, the cotton is *ginned*, when the seeds are separated from it. It is then baled, ready for transport to the factories of the U.S.A. and foreign lands.

Fig. 196 is a scene on a smaller farm owned by a negro. Many negroes and white people own these smaller farms, though there are many large plantations as well. The owner is taking cotton to be ginned. His home lies partly behind the waggon. Other farms

lie to the left. Notice the cotton bushes with bolls bursting all around. The waggon is drawn by mules, the universal beast of burden until one can afford a lorry. In the rear is one of the many forests which grow on the poorer soils of the South, and which supply the materials for the buildings on the farms.

Task 232.
(a) In what month was the view in Fig. 196 taken?
(b) How will the two young sons be useful to the farmer?
(c) Why do the schools in the Cotton Belt have long holidays in September?

The Boll-Weevil
This is a maggot that eats away the bolls and destroys the cotton. It appeared after 1900, and flourished in wetter areas. Nothing could rid the farms of it and the best cotton lands, in Carolina and Georgia, began to decline in production. It was found that the boll-weevil did not like drier regions, so cotton has moved more and more into Texas, until to-day it grows over half the crops (Fig. 189). Some of the best varieties of cotton are now produced on irrigated farms in Arizona and California where the boll-weevil cannot survive.

The Coastal Swamplands
Along the coasts of the Gulf of Mexico, in Florida,

and along the Atlantic coasts nearby, is a belt of low-lying land, very hot and wet, and with many swamps. These regions are too hot or too wet for either cotton or maize, but are very suitable for the wet tropical crops like rice and sugar-cane. They are planted and harvested by machines, with few men, unlike the way these crops are produced in the tropics. *Carolina Rice* is sold to Britain.

Fig. 197. Orang groves in Floria

EWING GALLOWAY N.

Florida is a low peninsula, with great heat, heavy rains and hardly a vestige of winter. Dense forests, with swamps, called *Everglades*, cover most of it, and little has been done to open up the interior. The coasts are different. On the Atlantic coast are holiday towns like Miami, and on both coasts are great areas of citrus fruit farms, especially grape fruit and oranges. The produce goes all over the U.S.A.

In Fig. 197 one sees a great area of orange groves in Florida. The natural forest is to be seen in the background. Notice how light and sandy is the soil. All these developments are close to the sea.

Task 233. Compare the scene in Fig. 197 with that in Fig. 180. Make a list of points that you think important.

On the Atlantic coast of Florida we find Cape Kennedy, where space flights are launched. It is on a long sand spit, running along the shore, which is typical of Florida's Atlantic Coast.

CHAPTER 14

THE EASTERN REGIONS OF THE U.S.A.

3. The Middle West and the Great Lakes

This region is bounded by the Appalachians on the east, the High Plains on the west and the Ohio on the south. It was opened up and settled after 1810, and the rich lowlands attracted many people from the poor soils of New England. The Indians were displaced westwards, the forests were cleared and farms established, all within one generation.

One of the factors aiding rapid settlement was the navigability of the rivers. Look at Fig. 198. The Mississippi, the *Father of Waters*, as the Indians called it, or *Old Man River* as the negroes called it, moves steadily southward across the Middle West, a broad waterway, navigable right up to Minneapolis. The Ohio leads across from the Appalachians, and is navigable up to Pittsburgh. The great Missouri takes vessels westwards up to Omaha, and beyond.

In early days, the settlers moved along these rivers, down the Ohio, and up the Mississippi to St. Louis, then along the Missouri. By these ways they moved fairly quickly, carried heavier loads, and were safer from Indian attack than if they had moved on land. Besides the settlers of mid-western lands, there were others moving further west along the trails to California and Santa Fé. These settlers left the rivers at Kansas City (then named Independence).

For all these people, St. Louis, at the junction of the Mississippi and the Missouri, was the trading centre, boat-building centre, and fitting-out centre for all things needed for the Far West. Later it built the steamers which still ply on the great rivers. The trappers of the empty west brought their furs to St. Louis. To-day it is a big city, with industries in boat-building and furs as well as others mentioned later.

Task 234. By how many routes can one sail to St. Louis? From what cities do these routes come?

The Rise of Chicago

Later came the railways, and traffic developed along the Great Lakes. Fig. 198 shows clearly that, at this stage, the centre of activity moved from St. Louis to Chicago, at the southern end of Lake Michigan. At this point the Lakes route met the rail route from New York and the Atlantic. From it, the railways radiated over the prairies carrying settlers to the wheat and maize lands there. So, from a small fort in 1830, Chicago has grown to a city of over $3\frac{1}{2}$ million inhabitants, with 34 main lines of railways running into it and having much trade as a port on the Lakes. It stands for all that is meant by *The Middle West*, rich farms, industries based on them, great steel industries, trading along the Lakes, rapid increases in population, and an abundance of energy and confidence in the future.

Task 235

(a) What are the distances from Chicago to (i) Omaha; (ii) Duluth; (iii) Pittsburgh?

(b) Notice the railways marked U.P.R., S.F.R., N.P.R. By reference back to Chapter 13, say what are their full names, and to which cities on the Pacific they run.

Meat Industries

The great crop-belts shown again on Fig. 198 have given rise to a great variety of industry in the towns of the Middle West. Minneapolis has become the milling and business centre of the wheat belt just as did Winnipeg in the Canadian prairies. To the east, round Lake

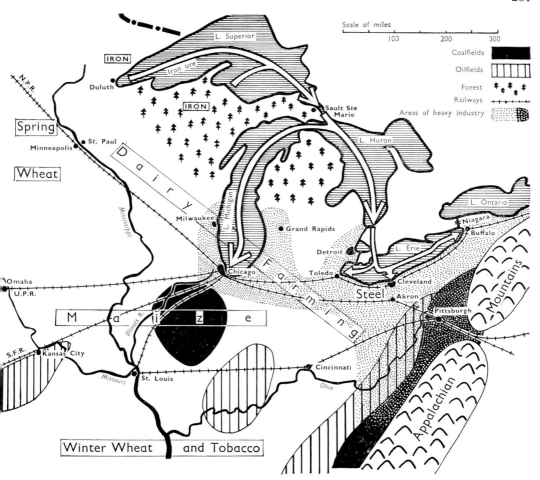

Fig. 198. The Middle West and Great Lakes

Michigan, occurs the only extension of the Canadian Shield into the U.S.A. and the poor soils are still forested. Paper industries are the result, but at Grand Rapids is the largest furniture-making industry in the U.S.A. Immediately south of Lake Michigan the farming is mainly for the supply of fresh milk, vegetables, cheese and butter to the many cities. The farms are smaller and there are more farmers than in the Wheat Belt.

In the Maize belt, however, with its huge numbers of animals, there are many different industries. Animals

Fig. 199. *Part of the*
Chicago Stockyards
PAUL POPPER LTD.

are fattened, then sent to the stockyards to be killed,
after which their meat is either frozen or canned, their
hides made into leather, and their bones into glue or
fertiliser. Maize and winter wheat are milled into
flour, vegetables are canned, and meat extracts (e.g.
Bovril) are manufactured. Cereals for the breakfast
table also are produced.

Thus we find all these industries in the towns, most
of which have arisen on river crossings, or on the lake
shores. Milwaukee, Chicago, St. Louis, Omaha,
Kansas City and Cincinnati are shown on Fig. 198.
In Fig. 199 is a scene in a Chicago stockyard showing
animals in pens to be fattened, and the great meat
factories behind. It is a common scene in the Maize
Belt towns. The Chicago yards can hold, at one time,
75,000 cattle, 300,000 pigs and 50,000 sheep. The
enormous size of the industry can be deduced from this.

Task 236.

(*a*) What is corn flour? Of what is the breakfast cereal
Corn Flakes, made? Why should it be an American
firm that produced them originally?

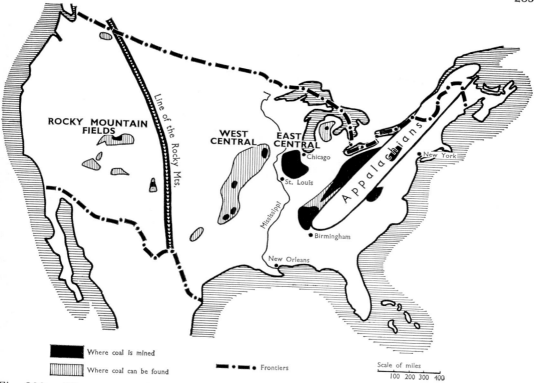

Where coal is mined

Where coal can be found

Frontiers

Scale of miles
100 200 300 400

Fig. 200. The Coalfields of the U.S.A.

(*b*) The international firm of Heinz began in Cincinnati, and it has its headquarters there. Why should such a firm be established there?

(*c*) Why should Kansas City be a great centre for wheat flour milling?

The Steel Industry

Along the south shores of Lakes Erie and Michigan lies the greatest concentration of steel industries in the world. The U.S.A. output of steel is colossal, easily the largest of any country. Most of it comes from this area. Three geographical factors have helped to locate it:

(*i*) enormous supplies of coal nearby;

(*ii*) enormous supplies of iron ore around Lake Superior;

(*iii*) the Great Lakes waterway to carry the ore cheaply to the coal.

Coal in the U.S.A.

The coalfields of the U.S.A. are so large and productive that they produce about one-fifth of all the coal in the world. By far the largest amounts come from the two fields shown on Fig. 198. These are the Appalachian and East Central fields. Fig. 200 is a map of the coalfields of the U.S.A. You can see that little is mined in the West Central and Rocky Mountain fields. So much is available east of the Mississippi that little is required elsewhere. Thus the Great Lakes region is very near to enormous coal supplies.

U.S. coal is easier to mine than British coal. It does not lie so deep and its seams are less disturbed. Thus machinery can be used on a far greater scale, and production per man is high. Fig. 201 is a scene in a coal mine. It is interesting to note the size of the machine hauling the trucks, the great size of the gallery,

Fig. 201. Hauling coal in a mine

AEROFILMS

and the thickness of the coal seam itself. All are on a bigger scale than those in British mines.

Task 237. How is the haulage machine driven? What do you think is the thickness of the coal seam?

The U.S.A. leads the world in the production of iron, as well as coal, and the fraction produced is about one-third. The most important areas are shown on Fig. 198 around Lake Superior. Here are low ranges of almost nothing but iron ore of high iron content. Vast workings of the type seen in Fig. 187 are removing it in huge terraces. It goes down to the lake where the long compartment-boats carry it to Chicago and Milwaukee on Lake Michigan, and Detroit, Toledo, Cleveland, and Buffalo, as well as several smaller towns, on Lake Erie. Here the ore meets the coal from the nearby coalfields.

In Fig. 202 is a view of the American Locks at Sault Ste. Marie showing a number of these large compartment-boats entering or leaving the locks.

Task 238.
(*a*) Which lakes are connected by the canal and locks at Sault Ste. Marie?
(*b*) How many boats can be seen in this view? Each carries about 10,000 tons of ore. How much ore is round the lock at this particular moment? Does this suggest a busy trade?
(*c*) Why has summer time to be such a very busy time here?
(*d*) Why are all the boats using the right-hand locks?

Almost every kind of steel goods is made in the towns on the Lakes. Detroit is the greatest motor-car making town in the world. To go with this, rubber is needed, and Akron is the greatest rubber-making town in the world. Other towns make steamers, ships' plates, rail stock, bridges, etc. Farm implements are another great industry, especially at Chicago and Milwaukee. The largest steel town of them all is Pittsburgh, on the coalfield. It lies where Fort Pitt stood at the point

Fig. 202. The
American Locks at
Sault Ste. Marie

Fig. 203. A Steel
Plant at Pittsburgh

FAIRCHILD AERIAL SURVEYS

where the trails across the Appalachians entered the
Ohio valley. In Fig. 203 you see a giant steel mill.
Like so many of the mills, it is in one of the valleys
running out to Pittsburgh from the Appalachians.
You notice the use of water transport, the very large
trucks on the railways, and the area of sidings.

Task 239. How many blast furnaces are there?
How can you recognise them?

In, and around, this steel area there are very many
other industries. Rubber has already been mentioned.
There are also chemicals, glass, aluminium, and every
kind of machine manufacture. A major portion of
the industry of the U.S.A., this huge industrial nation,
is found around the Great Lakes, as shown on Fig. 198.
In addition to the factors listed on page 283 there is
another one which helps to create this large industrial
region. It is the region most easily reached from the
great ports and dense populations on the Atlantic coast.
The railways, shown on Fig. 198 coming into Pittsburgh and Buffalo from the east, are following the two
easiest routes across the Appalachians from New York
and Washington.

Fig. 204. *The bridges across the Chicago River, Chicago*
U.S.I.S.

Chicago

One cannot leave the Middle West without some reference to the great city which is at its heart, and which controls so much of its activities. Already we have seen that it is an enormous rail centre and a Lake port; that it has large *maize belt* industries and the steel industry. Because it is so important a rail centre, it has extensive industries making rail equipment. The new Seaway has added to the importance of this city, now ships can sail right up to it from the Atlantic. It has grown to be America's second largest city, and is still growing. The view in Fig. 204 is taken near the centre, with a view of Lake Michigan in the background. There are many remarkable and imposing buildings, and fine broad highways with busy traffic. The canal connects Lake Michigan with the Illinois river which runs into the Mississippi (Fig. 198). Using this canal, large barges can sail from the Lakes to New Orleans.

Task 240. This picture of Chicago shows many very modern features of city living which are not found in many British cities, as yet. Can you name any?

4. *THE SOUTH*

South of the Ohio, we enter the region known as *The South* or *Dixie* as it is often called. The Ohio river was the northern boundary of the slave-owning states. On the Atlantic side, a line called The Mason-Dixon line marked the same boundary. The name *Dixie* came from this.

From the opening-up of the southern lowlands in the 17th Century right down to 1865, there were large estates owned by wealthy white men, and operated by large numbers of negro slaves. These slaves were, on the whole, well treated, but it was a bad system. It was morally wrong, and it was wasteful of land. The combination of heat, moisture and rich soils of the South should have produced much more from the soils and supported many more people than it did. As it was, great clearings were made in the forests which covered all the South. Cotton, sugar and tobacco were grown, without rotation of crops, and so the soils grew poor. New clearings had to be made, and the others reverted to waste.

The Civil War of 1861-65 put an end to this system. It freed the slaves and left the white people impoverished.

The South became a backward region without industries. Industries were created almost entirely in the North.

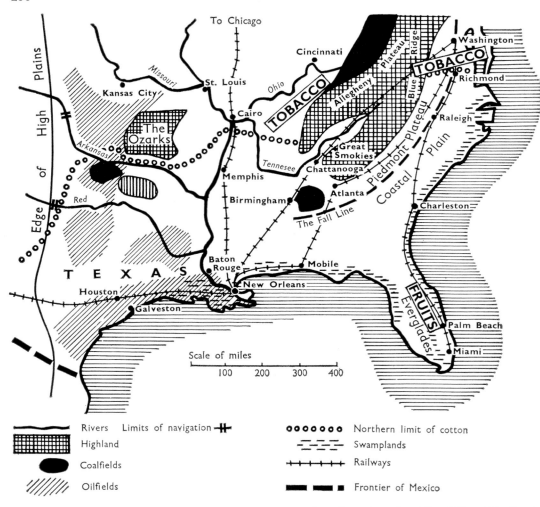

Fig. 205.   The South

Since 1920, all that has changed. The South of to-day has many great and growing industries, more prosperous farming and increasing wealth.

The Great Rivers

First of all, the South is a land of huge rivers flowing slowly across enormous lowlands. The Mississippi river is the heart of the South. Steamers and barge-trains sail along it and its tributaries to the limits of the region. One-hundred-million tons of shipping sail along it every year.

Task 241. Examine Fig. 205, which is a map of the South.

Measure the distances along the rivers from New Orleans to: (*i*) Kansas City; (*ii*) Cincinnati; (*iii*) Chattanooga; (*iv*) the limit of navigation on the Red River.

The scene in Fig. 206 is taken on the Mississippi, 900 miles from New Orleans, before the Missouri or Ohio rivers have joined it. Even so far from the sea, it is a very large river. There are many sandbanks, and navigation on it is a very skilled task. Barges and steamers draw only a foot or two of water. They are wide and flat-bottomed. The view shows a barge-train being *pushed*, not pulled, by a steamer.

Task 242. The barge-train is proceeding down-stream to New Orleans.

(*a*) What would you expect the barges to be carrying from the Middle West?

(*b*) Are they carrying much on deck?

(*c*) Will they be able to carry much below decks? Why?

Flood Plains

A close look at Fig. 206 will give you the impression

Fig. 206. A barge train on the Mississippi at Hannibal

.s.i.s.

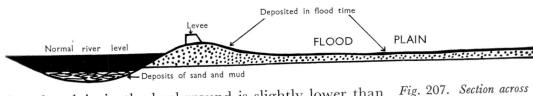

Fig. 207. *Section across a flood plain*

that the plain in the background is slightly lower than the river itself. Also, the river seems muddy, and we have already said that sandbanks are frequent. These are all features of a river meandering across a wide and level plain. The subject was dealt with in *The Foundations*, Chapter 3, but on the Mississippi the features are on a gigantic scale.

Fig. 207 explains the differences in levels. Slow-running rivers drop much sediment on to their beds and so build themselves higher beds. Flooding is frequent, and much sediment is dropped on the flood plain over which the waters run. Most sediment is dropped at the point where the river leaves its bed. This creates higher banks, and the river gradually grows above its flood plain. Men then try to contain it with embankments of their own making. These are called *levées* (from the French). All the rivers of the southern plains have these *levées*. If they collapse, enormous damage can be done to the flood plains. In Fig. 206 the *levées* will be hidden by the trees on the far bank. The rise in the foreground is a hill.

Other features which occur all over the Mississippi flood plains are shown in Fig. 208. There are great areas of swampy land. When drained they can be used to give rich crops of cotton and maize. Otherwise they remain useless cane brake. There are numerous *cut-offs* which the river has abandoned, and which can become a source of malaria. Rivers meander miles to gain only a short distance. This is a nuisance to shipping.

Roads, railways and towns avoid the flood plains, and keep on safer ground.

Task 243.

(a) Why are the two places chosen for towns in Fig. 208 so suitable?

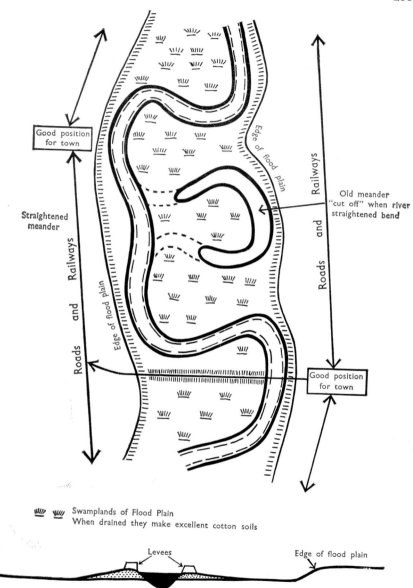

Fig. 208. *A typical stretch of the lower Mississippi, and a section at the same place*

(*b*) How does the figure show that the river is at a big disadvantage for transport compared with roads or railways?

The Tennessee Valley

The Tennessee rises in the Appalachians and flows for over 700 miles to join the Ohio (see Figs. 205 or 209). It has many feeders, in its Appalachian valley course, which flood suddenly when downpours occur on the mountains. So the Tennessee was notorious for frequent and disastrous floods, for destruction of hillside soils, and for creating malarial swamps on the valley floor with the material washed from the hills. The U.S. Government took it in hand in 1933. They converted it into a series of twenty-eight huge lakes, *The Great Lakes of the South*, each behind an enormous dam. To-day the river does not *flow*, but falls gently from lake to lake at each dam. The largest lake is 185 miles long. All floods and movement of water are rigidly controlled at the dams, which are all under a master control at Chattanooga. Serious flood damage is now unknown, the whole waterway is navigated by very large barges, electric power is created at the dams and is plentiful and cheap. Farms and villages are all using electric power and tools. Industry is settling there, *e.g.* aluminium and fertilisers. The Tennessee is tamed.

Task 244. For a fuller account of this river see *The Foundations*, Chapter 5, and then give a list of the improvements to the Tennessee which impress you the most.

Industry in the South

The South has several big advantages for industry:
1. there are large and good coalfields round the western and southern margins of the Appalachians;
2. there are good iron supplies on the eastern and southern margins;
3. there is water-power where the rivers leave the Appalachians;
4. there are enormous local supplies of cotton;
5. there are extensive forests of Southern Pine on the

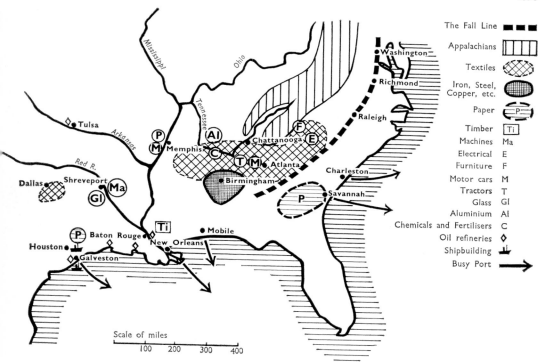

Fig. 209. Industry in the South

more infertile sandy parts of the South. This is a fast-growing, valuable timber tree;

6. there are enormous supplies of oil west of the Mississippi.

Textiles

The main manufacture is of cotton goods. The cotton mills are found in a belt around the edge of the Appalachians, from North Carolina to the Mississippi (Fig. 209). Woollens, rayon, nylon, and other synthetic fibres are used, too. Atlanta and Chattanooga are the main centres. Seventy-five per cent. of all the textiles in the U.S.A. are manufactured here. Fig. 210 shows a scene in a weaving mill in North Carolina. Everything is extremely up to date. Electric power is used.

Task 245. Which of the six advantages, listed above, apply to the textile industry?

The Piedmont Plateau

On the east, the Appalachian ridges fall to a low and rather rough surface of old hard rocks, across which streams run in deep valleys, with frequent rapids and small falls. This is the Piedmont Plateau (*pied-mont* is French for foot-hill, and the English word *foothills* has a similar meaning). This plateau ends at the Fall Line. (See Figs. 205 and 209). This is an old coastline, and the low cliffs of the old shore now cause rapids and falls on the rivers. East of the Fall Line, the sea bed has emerged as a low plain of rich soils, with a swamp belt near the sea. Out at sea, the water is shallow, and many sand banks and bars have formed. Fig. 211 shows all these belts in section. It was on the rich plain that cotton estates arose, and the swamps sheltered fugitive slaves. At the Fall Line, the main towns grew up, for here ships had to stop. They were

Fig. 210.   A weaving room in a Carolina cotton mill

AEROFILMS

Fig. 211.   The Atlantic Plains of the South, in section

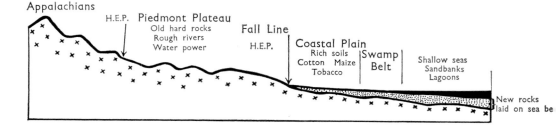

Appalachians

H.E.P. Piedmont Plateau
        Old hard rocks
        Rough rivers   Fall Line
        Water power   H.E.P.   Coastal Plain
                                    Rich soils   Swamp   Shallow seas
                                    Cotton Maize Belt   Sandbanks
                                    Tobacco   Lagoons

New rocks
laid on sea be

at *the head of navigation.* Raleigh and Richmond, with their tobacco factories and warehouses, are on this Line, but modern industry is on the Piedmont Plateau.

Iron and Steel

The second industrial region east of the Mississippi is around Birmingham, in Alabama. Coal, iron, and limestone are all found in great amounts within a radius of eight miles. Thus, steel industries have grown up. Pipes, tanks, railroad cars, motor-cars, tractors, are well known products. Copper-tubing and aluminium-ware are other industries. The old cotton port of Mobile has taken on a new look, with the need for modern port facilities to deal with the trade of the Birmingham area. Memphis, a great cotton-shipping and business centre on the Mississippi, also makes mechanical pickers for the fields.

Paper and Furniture

The forest industries are especially important in Louisiana and Alabama, as well as in Georgia. Furniture of high grade is made in North Carolina, and paper round Savannah.

Oil in the U.S.A.

West of the Mississippi, *oil is king.* Enormous deposits are found in Texas, Oklahoma and Kansas, and Louisiana has now joined the list. So much is available that output is restricted to present needs. Pipe lines run all over the centre and east of the U.S.A. to take oil to the refineries. Refining is a costly and complicated process, demanding much plant and labour. Notice that it concentrates along the Gulf coast, for export; in Kansas, for local use; in the cities of the Middle West, for use in industry; and in the Atlantic coastal cities, for all purposes. Texas has already been noted as a big cattle state, and the chief cotton state. Now we see it as the chief oil state. It is the State of the *Three Kings*: Cattle, Cotton, and Oil.

Other industries are appearing in Texas. At Dallas is a very big industry in clothing; at Houston, the State capital and business centre of oil and cotton, is a large paper industry, and ships are built there. At

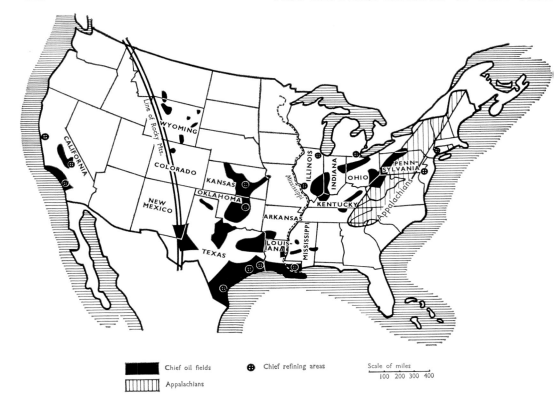

Chief oil fields

Chief refining areas

Appalachians

Scale of miles
100 200 300 400

Galveston, a Gulf port built on a sandy island offshore, is more ship-building. Shreveport, in Louisiana, has a big glass industry.

Fig. 212.   Oilfields in the U.S.A.

Task 246. The States of Illinois, and Texas have each a population of between 10 and 10½ millions. Make a comparison between these states to show why each has so many people.

Task 247. Oil pipe lines carry crude oil from central Oklahoma to Chicago and to Toledo at the western end of Lake Erie, for refining. Another pipe line runs from near New Orleans to Toledo. Use Fig. 212 which shows the U.S. oilfields, and measure the distance covered by each of these pipe lines.

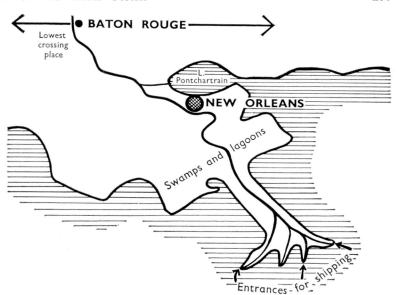

Fig. 213. The Mississippi Delta

Task 248. Again using Fig. 212, count how many states in the U.S.A. contain supplies of crude oil.

New Orleans

Just as Chicago and St. Louis stood out as the centres of routes in the upper Mississippi valley, so New Orleans stands out in the lower valley. It is a sea port, yet it is 100 miles up the river from the sea. The delta of the great river is enormous and building out quickly. The material which the Mississippi carries down to the sea from the centre of U.S.A. is phenomenal, and no sea currents can remove it. Each branch pushes out to sea a long arm of sand and mud, like an under-sea tip. Fig. 213 shows this.

New Orleans was built on a swamp which gives it many serious drainage problems. It has also flood problems, for the water of one-third or more of the U.S.A. comes to the sea here. Lake Pontchartrain, however, is used to take the bulk of the floods, and so save the *levées* in New Orleans. In Fig. 214 one sees the flat delta, the winding river and the great extent of the city. It was built by the French, as its name

suggests, and many of its people still speak a French dialect.

Task 249. New Orleans trades a great deal with South and Central America, exporting the goods and crops of the Mississippi basin. Name some of the exports and some likely imports.

Fig. 214. New Orleans, looking towards the Mississippi Delta
AEROFILMS

5. The North East

On page 253 we said that this was the most densely peopled part of America. It contains one-third of the people of the U.S.A. It was the first part to be settled, and has had nearly 300 years of civilisation and development. Of the twelve states and the District of Columbia, which are included in this region, nine states were numbered in the original thirteen which broke away from British rule in 1776. Though occupying only six per cent. of the area of the United States, it is the wealthiest and most industrial of all its regions.

Task 250. Examine Fig. 215.

(*a*) Name the five chief rivers that flow into the Atlantic across the plains.

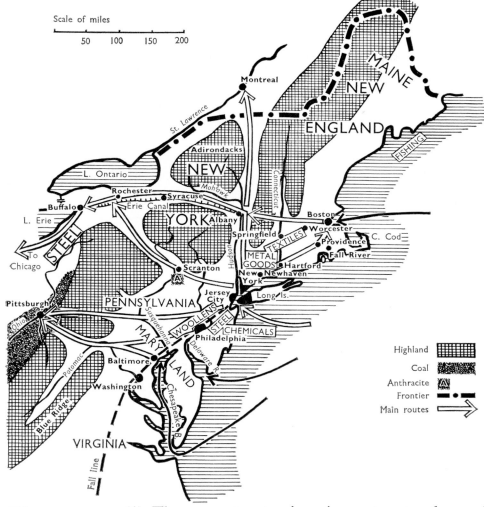

Fig. 215.
The North East
(U.S.A.)

(b) Three great estuaries give entry to the region. Which are they?

(c) Which river system gives the best route across the Appalachians?

(d) How far is it from (i) Washington to Boston; (ii) New York to Montreal?

Compare with London to Liverpool, 200 miles, and London to Edinburgh, 370 miles.

Fig. 216. A farm in Massachusetts
AEROFILMS

Farming is not easy

The North East consists of Appalachian ridges and valleys and the coastal plains between them and the Atlantic. These plains are not so fertile as those in the South, for the fertile sea bed did not emerge from the sea north of Chesapeake Bay. Notice how the Fall Line, in Fig. 215, disappears by the time New York is reached. North of New York the old coast is now slightly under the sea. These plains were covered by ice in the Ice Age. This has left boulder clays, sandy ridges and stony soils. New England is the worst off in this respect. To make the land fertile much harder work is needed than in the South. Winters, too, became very severe north of Chesapeake Bay. Very cold winds blow from the continent, especially when a depression lies along the coast. At the same time, these depressions bring rain and much of this falls as snow. There are heavy winter snowfalls. North of New York there are many weeks of freezing temperatures.

On the other hand, summers are long and warm. The autumn or *Fall* is a delightful season. Farmers can operate successfully then. All their farming is directed towards supplying fresh foods, milk and flowers to the great towns which are all over the North East. Dairying, *truck farming* (market gardening), poultry-farming, nurseries, vegetable farms, etc., are the usual types. In Fig. 216 is a farm in New England, the least favoured part for soils. The buildings look solid and prosperous, and the scene is very like many in southern Britain, with trees and meadow grass. There is an old established air about it. It shows a very pleasant summer view.

Task 251

(*a*) Fig. 216 shows a dairy farm. What use could the large building in the rear be to the farmer?

(*b*) How would you describe the soils of the slope in the foreground?

(*c*) Does anything tell you that it is not a view in Britain?

Industry

When industry was established in the late 18th Century, the North East was the only part of the U.S.A. that had many people in it. The only source of power at that time was falling water, driving a water wheel. The region had plenty of water-power on its rather rough surface, similar to that of the Piedmont Plateau of the South, so industry flourished, especially in New England and the Fall Line towns. The manufacture of cottons and woollens was established early, and great skill in spinning and weaving was acquired. Equally skilful was the metal working of Connecticut, and Springfield became famous for guns.

Steam-power came in the 19th century and so coal became of great importance. Now, there is no coal in the North East except for the valuable anthracite field at Scranton. Coal from Pittsburgh has to undergo the long haul across the Appalachians. Even after the railways came, that was expensive.

Nevertheless, industry stayed in the North East because it had three great advantages:

(*i*) it was on the coast, with many good ports, so all materials could be brought in easily;

(*ii*) there was a very large local market in the dense population of the coastal plains;

(*iii*) there was the great skill of the workers.

So industry stayed, and coal was hauled to it. Every railway crossing the Appalachians continues to send streams of coal-trains over to the east. It is fortunate that there are so many usable gaps by which the railways can cross.

Task 252. Using Fig. 215, say how coal from Pittsburgh can reach the following towns, noting which river valleys help: (*i*) Boston; (*ii*) New York; (*iii*) Baltimore.

The manufacture of cottons is concentrated in New England, in such towns as Providence and Fall River. Woollens became important using imported wool from Australia and Argentina. Rayon, nylon, and other synthetic fibres are now used also. From Philadelphia to Boston, textiles are to be found in every town.

This area has been heavily hit by the rise of textile industries in the South. It now produces only twenty-five per cent. of the United States textiles, but it produces the highest grades.

In Connecticut metal industries flourish. The old industry in guns and ploughs has expanded into an enormous output of expensive, highly finished goods

Fig. 217. In
machine tool factory a
Springfiel
U.S.I.S

such as machine tools, typewriters, scientific instruments, electric motors and machines of all kinds. Neither coal nor iron is found locally, so the products are those using not too much of any metal. Springfield and Hartford are the chief centres. Waterbury makes watches. The Baltimore district makes locomotives and rolling stock for railways. The ease of import of raw materials has resulted in a large chemical industry between Philadelphia and New York.

Fig. 217 is a scene in a factory, in Springfield, which makes machine tools. These are the tools on whose accuracy everything made in factories depends. Notice how elaborate is the equipment, and what a skilled type the workmen appear to be. Often several generations have worked in the same trade.

The Hudson Valley

Of all the rivers running into the Atlantic in the North East, the Hudson is by far the most important. It leads inland for 300 miles, and is navigable for ocean steamers up to Albany. Its wide valley breaks right across the Appalachians into Canada, and its feeder, the Mohawk, has a similar valley leading to the Great Lakes (see Fig. 215). The great size of the river is seen in Fig. 218. It shows its lower course, with the great

Fig. 218. The Hudson River Valley

U.S.I.S.

lava cliffs of the Palisades, in the foreground. Notice the railway and road on the far bank. The most important railway in America is the one running from New York to Chicago along this valley. It forms the great highway to the middle of America from the Atlantic. New York owes its outstanding importance to being at the mouth of this river.

All along the valleys of the Hudson and Mohawk are industrial towns making locomotives, electrical goods, textiles, office equipment and machinery. Albany is the most important. It is a big river port, a centre of routes and a milling and oil town. The Erie Canal gives a water route to the city of Buffalo, so that barges sail from Lake Erie to Albany, and thence to New York.

Task 253. Look at Fig. 215 and describe the routes meeting at Albany.

Maine

Even in this crowded region there is a great area of what is practically wilderness. The Appalachians and the bulk of the State of Maine are very like New Brunswick across the border. Extensive forests exist and have become a resort for those who like a wilderness holiday. It is not surprising that Maine has less than 30 people per square mile. Wild life includes moose and bears. Fishing is a very popular pastime. Nearer the coast, farming is of the hardier kind, chiefly for hay, potatoes and cattle. Maine is famous for its potatoes. On the coast are numerous fishing ports, with fleets going to the Grand Banks. Here, too, the holiday-maker is catered for, especially those who like boats.

The Great Cities

On the Atlantic coast of the North East, there lie four great ports, entry points for all coming to the U.S.A. from Europe. They are Boston, Philadelphia, Baltimore, and New York.

Boston is the nearest port to Europe (Fig. 215). It distributes goods inland through Albany. It is the commercial centre of New England, and a large fishing port with a population in 1963 of nearly 700,000.

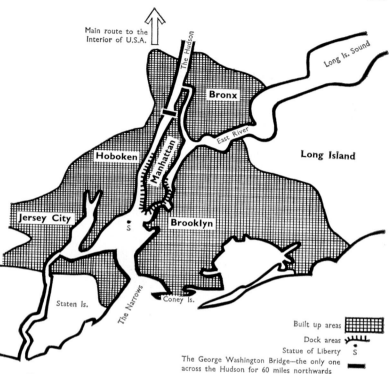

Fig. 219. *New York*

Labels on map: Main route to the Interior of U.S.A.; The Hudson; Long Is. Sound; Bronx; East River; Long Island; Hoboken; Manhattan; Jersey City; S; Brooklyn; Staten Is.; The Narrows; Coney Is.; Built up areas; Dock areas; Statue of Liberty S; The George Washington Bridge—the only one across the Hudson for 60 miles northwards

Philadelphia is on a fine estuary, that of the Delaware. It is a big centre of industry, and is the port for the Delaware basin. This includes the anthracite field round Scranton, and coal is an important export from Philadelphia. Its population of 2 millions has changed little in many years.

Baltimore, on Chesapeake Bay, is the nearest port to Pittsburgh. It had the first railway across the Appalachians to connect with the great coalfield. It is a great exporter of coal to Europe. Its population of nearly one million grows but slowly.

Overshadowing them all is New York, with over ten million people living in and around it. This enormous seaport and business centre does over half of the trade of the U.S.A. It is by far the most important entry into the United States from Europe. Its position at the mouth of the Hudson has already been

Fig. 220. New York,
the Lower Manhattan
Skyline
AEROFILMS

mentioned. It was built on Manhattan Island (Fig. 219). This remains the business centre and contains most of the docks. Space is very limited and extremely valuable whilst every firm requires offices there. Thus the skyscraper is the solution. A striking view of some of them is seen in Fig. 220. The view is from the East River (see Fig. 219).

Task 254.

(*a*) From which district was the photograph taken? (see Fig. 219).

(*b*) Where are Porto Rico and Santo Domingo, the places named on warehouses on the dock? What would you expect to be imported from there?

Task 255.

(*a*) In the last 60 miles of the Hudson river, only one bridge crosses it, shown in Fig. 219, and that is only for passengers and motor vehicles. How is this going to effect the movement of, say, coal from Pittsburgh to New England? (Look at Fig. 215).

Fig. 221. Washington
U.S.I.S.

(*b*) Thousands of ferries and barges are always at work in New York harbour. Why are so many needed?

Washington

This city of 764,000 people is the Federal capital of the United States. It was specially built, on the Potomac, for this purpose. It is outside all the states in its own District of Columbia.

It is a carefully planned city, as can be seen in Fig. 221. It is given over almost entirely to government buildings. In the centre is the Capitol, the Houses of Parliament of the U.S.A. The business section is in the right rear, towards the Potomac.

Task 256. In what direction is the camera pointing in Fig. 221? (see Fig. 215). What state lies across the river?

Alaska

In 1958 Alaska was admitted to the United States as the 49th State. Previously it had been a *Territory* administered by the Federal Government. Purchased

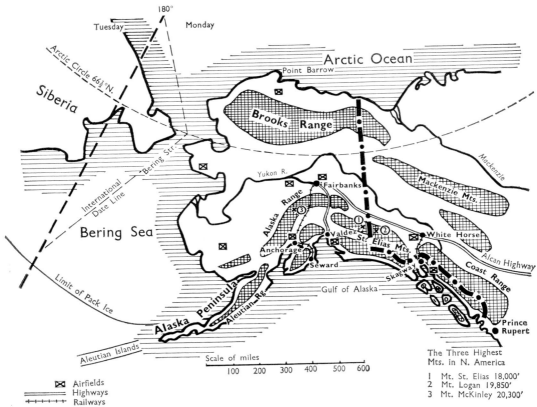

Airfields
Highways
Railways

Scale of miles
100   200   300   400   500   600

The Three Highest
Mts. in N. America

1 Mt. St. Elias 18,000'
2 Mt. Logan 19,850'
3 Mt. McKinley 20,300'

Fig. 222.   Alaska

from the Russians in 1867, it has proved a very valuable investment.

Alaska lies roughly between 60° and 70°N. Half of it is in, or near to, the Arctic Circle. Tundra and coniferous forest cover most of it. Great mountain ranges run across it with wide river valleys between. The Yukon is the chief of these rivers. Look at Fig. 222. The highest ranges occur near to the coast, where the St. Elias Mountains are the highest single range in North America. Pacific westerlies pile up rain and snow against these ranges, with the result that snowfields and glaciers cover the higher parts. The glaciers make their way down the valleys, and sometimes enter the sea before they melt. Such is the case in Fig. 223.

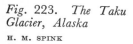

Fig. 223. The Taku Glacier, Alaska

H. M. SPINK

This picture shows the inhospitable nature of the Pacific Coast of Alaska. Conifers grow wherever there is soil for them to do so, numerous fiords run inland as on the coast of British Columbia, further south. Those with glaciers entering them are not much use, but others give shelter and anchorages for entering the country. All the main entries are from fiords. Seward, Anchorage, Valdez and Skagway are the most important. The seas are stormy, but at least they are always ice-free.

Beyond the ranges it is a different story. Rains and snowfalls are smaller, the winter freeze-up is both long and severe, winters last for nine months, and seas and rivers freeze for six. Only 95 days exist between the last killing frost of spring and the first of the following winter. In Fig. 224, a view of the Alcan Highway near the Canadian border, is some typical valley scenery. The small and rather scattered conifers show the change-over to tundra that is taking place. Inhabitants are very few. The total population of Alaska is only 248,000 in an area of over 586,000 square miles. Such views as this are typical of southern Alaska. North of the Yukon, there are only tundra, some Eskimo reindeer-keepers and a few military posts.

Fig. 224. *The Alcan Highway*
CANADIAN GOVERNMENT TRAVEL BUREAU

Task 257.

(*a*) What is the Alcan Highway? It has already been mentioned in Chapter 12.

(*b*) The road is a gravel road, as are all roads in Alaska. Why is road metal no use in such a climate?

(*c*) Why are the entries into Alaska all on the south coast, requiring difficult mountain crossings, and not on the west coast where the Yukon valley gives a broad valley inland?

Alaskan Wealth

What has such a country to offer to men? First, there is the wealth in the sea. The salmon fisheries are greater than those of Canada, and bring in enormous profits. Then there is a fair amount of gold production. This is chiefly around Fairbanks where the dredging method is used. Gold is found in beds of gravels of very great age. These are permanently frozen, because the summer thaw is unable to overcome the winter freeze-up. Powerful jets of steam are directed on to them. These thaw the soils and wash out the gold.

Lumbering is important on the Pacific coasts, as in Canada. Lumbering in the Yukon area is chiefly for Alaskan needs. All buildings are of wood. There is no metal available.

Farming is extending in the Fairbanks area. In the 95-day season, the sun is shining for 20 to 24 hours each day, so that, even if the angle is low, the heat accumulates to give remarkably high temperatures. Vegetables are the main crop. All the rest of their food and general needs are imported from the U.S.A. through the port of Seattle.

Alaska has a very active and busy season of about three months, when all work out of doors is done, and this is followed by a long nine-months' winter when only indoor work can be done.

Fairbanks is the chief town. It is small by normal standards (population 10,050) but it is the route and business centre of the State. The town has a large and busy airport. A highway reaches it from the U.S.A. overland through Edmonton, and a railway reaches it through the mountains from the south coast. Juneau, on the coast, is the capital.

Fig. 225. Seattle Airport which handles most of the air traffic with Alaska.

E.N.A.

Airfields are common in Alaska (Fig. 222) and every tiny settlement has its airstrip. The aeroplane is used almost like a taxi. In such a thinly peopled land other forms of transport are very costly.

Dog teams are still a necessity in most areas.

Task 258. Measure the length of the railway from Seward to Fairbanks, as shown on Fig. 222. Try to list some of the difficulties of operating this line.

Task 259. On Fig. 222 is shown the meridian of 180°. On the Siberian side, the day is given as Tuesday, whilst on the Alaskan side it is Monday. How do you explain this?

Task 260. Fig. 225 is a view of Seattle airport, from which a great number of planes fly to Alaska. It is typical of airports all over the U.S.A. and Canada. Air travel is used much more than in Britain.

(*a*) Why should the U.S.A. and Canada have more use for airways than has Britain?

(*b*) Study Fig. 225 and make a list of what is needed in a large modern airport.

Suggested aids for teacher and pupil using this book

The following is a selection only of the enormous choice of films and film strips available through Educational Foundation for Visual Aids, 33, Queen Anne Street, W.1., either to hire or purchase.

Aids:	S.F.B.W.	Silent Film, Black and White.	Sd.F.	Sound Film.
	S.F.C.	Silent Film, Colour.	Sd.F.	Sound Film.
	F.S.B.W.	Film Strip, Black and White.		
	F.S.C.	Film Strip, Colour.		

Producers:	C.G.	(Common Ground).
	G.B.	(Gaumont British).
	V.I.S.	(Visual Information Service).
	N.F.B.C.	(National Film Board of Canada). Distributed by Unicorn Head.
	B.I.F.	(British Instructional Films).
	E.P.	(Educational Publications).

(A) General

Landscape of Glacial Erosion. F.S.B.W. 11 years upwards. C.G. 1953.

Glaciers and their work. S.F.B.W. 13 mins. 12-15 years. E.F.V.A. 1957.

Story of Rivers. F.S.C. 11-13 years. G.B.

Mountain Building. F.S.B.W. 11-13 years V.I.S.

Weather. Sd.F.B.W. 11 mins. 13-15 years. G.B. 1949.

British Air Routes. 1. Atlantic. F.S.B.W. 11-15 years. C.G. 1952-3.

British Air Routes. 2. Europe. F.S.B.W. 11-15 years. C.G. 1949.

(B) Products

Tree to Paper (Norway). F.S.B.W. 11-15 years. Hulton 1957.

Tree to Paper (Canada). S.F.B.W. 10 mins. 11-15 years. B.I.F. 1948.

The Story of Wheat. F.S.B.W. 11-15 years. N.F.B.C. Unicorn Head 1948.

Timber from Forest to House. F.S.B.W. 9-13 years. N.F.B.C. Unicorn Head 1947.

Tobacco from U.S.A. F.S.B.W. 11-15 years. E.F.V.A. 1952.

Sweet Sap (Maple Sugar). F.S.B.W. 11-15 years. N.F.B.C. 1947.

Minerals from Western Mountains. F.S.B.W. 13-17 years. N.F.B.C. 1955.

Iron and Steel supplies of world. S.F.B.W. 10 mins. 11-15 years. G.B. 1949.

Miners of Americas (Canada, U.S.A. Guiana). F.S.B.W. 9-15 years. C.G. 1957.

(C) Regional

Mediterranean Lands. F.S.B.W. 9-13 years. V.I.S.

Farmers in Europe (Switzerland, Holland, France). F.S.B.W. 9-15 years. C.G. 1952.

The Rhine. F.S.B.W. 11-15 years. C.G. 1952.

The Rhine. Sd.F.C. 12 mins. 11-15 years. Boulton-Hawker 1957.

Land behind the Dykes. Sd.F.B.W. 20 mins. 11-15 years. G.B. 1950.

1. West Germany. F.S.B.W. 11-15 years. Unicorn Head 1954.

2. East Germany. F.S.B.W. 11-15 years. Unicorn Head 1954.

Yugoslavia, Land of Contrasts. F.S.C. 11-15 years. Hulton 1957.

Iberian Peninsula. Sd.F.B.W. 11 mins. 11-15 years. G.B. 1950.

Alpine Farm. S.F.B.W. 10 mins. 9-15 years. B.I.F. 1946.

Switzerland. F.S.B.W. 11-15 years. C.G. 1956.

Lombardy. S.F.C. 15 mins. 11-15 years. Boulton-Hawker 1948.

Tuscan Countryside. Sd.F.B.W. 12 mins. 11-15 years. Boulton-Hawker 1954.

Factories, Mines, Waterways (Western Europe). F.S.B.W. 11 years and over. G.B. 1949.

The Danube Basin. F.S.B.W. 11-15 years. C.G. 1955.

The Rhone Basin. F.S.B.W. 11-15 years. C.G. 1953.

Food for Paris Markets. Sd.F.B.W. 20 mins. 11-16 years. G.B. 1954.

Everyday life in Italy. F.S.C. 11 years and over. E.P. 1959.

(D) Regional

The Lumber States (N. America). Sd.F.B.W. 21 min. 11 years and over. G.B.

Cattle and the Corn Belt. Sd.F.B.W. 19 mins. 11-16 years. G.B.

Canada. Sd.F.B.W. 14 mins. 11-16 years. Gateway 1958.

Journey across Canada. F.S.C. 11 years and over. C.G. 1959.

Winter in Canada. Sd.F.B.W. 18 mins. 9-13 years. N.F.B.C. 1953.

Maritime Provinces of Canada. Sd.F.B.W. 11 mins. G.B. 1950.

Newfoundland. F.S.B.W. 11-15 years. N.F.B.C.

Prairie Provinces. Sd.F.B.W. 11 mins. 11-15 years. G.B. 1949.

Fur Country. Sd.F.C. 22 mins. 11-15 years. N.F.B.C.

Canada's New North. F.S.C. 11 years and over. C.G. 1958.

An Industrial Lake Port (Buffalo). Sd.F.B.W. 20 mins. 11-15 years. F.S.B.W. 11-15 years. G.B. 1948.

Living in a Metropolis (New York). Sd.F.B.W. 20 mins. 11 years and over. F.S.B.W. G.B. 1949.

U.S.A. South Eastern States. Sd.F.B.W. 10 mins. 11-15 years. G.B. 1950.

U.S.A. South Western States. Sd.F.B.W. 10 mins. 11-15 years. G.B. 1950.

Water for dry land (Western U.S.A.). Sd.F.B.W. 20 mins. 11-15 years. G.B. 1950.

Tennessee Valley Authority. F.S.B.W. 13 years and over. C.G. 1949.

BOOKS AND PAMPHLETS USEFUL FOR REFERENCE

How People Live. Norway. *Dr. W. R. Mead.* E.S.A. Pub. Dir. 1960. (First of a Series, 1960).

The Changing Face of the World. *Hebe Spaull.* Rockcliff, Salisbury Sq., London. 1955.

This is Yugoslavia. *Hebe Spaull.* Rockcliff. Salisbury Sq., London. 1955.

Europe. *Pickles.* Dent.

Europe. *Stembridge.* Oxford.

People of the World. 1. Farming in Canadian Prairies. 2. Lumbering in Canada. Oxford.

U.S.A. Its Geography and Growth. *John Murray.*

Cargoes on the Great Lakes. *McPhedan.* Harrap.

56 page magazine on St. Lawrence Seaway (1959). Journal of Commerce.

Posters and illustrated booklets on France available on application to French Government Tourist office, 66, Haymarket, London S.W.1.

Farm Studies. Association of Agriculture, 53, Victoria Street, S.W.1.

  12. Apple farm in Annapolis (N.S.).

  13. Dairy farm in Quebec.

  14. Mixed farm in South Ontario.

  15. Grain farm on Portage Plains.

Who are the Americans? *W. D. Whitney.* Guild Books.

Practical Work Books. U.S.A. Nelson.

Text Book of Canada. Atlas of Canada. Canada House.

Leaflets:

Petroleum Information Bureau, 29, New Bond street, W.1.

1. Oil in the U.S.A. Free.

2. World's Oil Reserves. Issues.

Numerous film strips and illustrated pamphlets and books are available from such companies as Shell, Esso, British Railways, French Railways, etc.

INDEX

INDEX—*continued*

INDEX—*continued*

INDEX—*continued*